NIALL GOOCH, CAPE TOWN

CW00592060

REFLECTIONS
IN PRISON

03/01/03

REFLECTIONS
IN PRISON

EDITED BY MAC MAHARAJ

Published by Zebra and the Robben Island Museum

Zebra is a division of Struik Publishers
(an imprint of New Holland Publishing (South Africa) (Pty) Ltd)
PO Box 1144, Cape Town, 8000

This publication is No. 4 in the Robben Island Memories Series.
It is partly sponsored by the W.E. Kellogg Foundation.

First edition 2001

10 9 8 7 6 5 4 3

Publication © Zebra 2001
Text © Mac Maharaj 2001

Cover photograph © Brentan Geach

All rights reserved. No part of this publication may be reproduced,
stored in a retrieval system or transmitted, in any form or by any
means, electronic, mechanical, photocopying, recording or otherwise,
without the prior written permission of the copyright owners.

PUBLISHING MANAGER: Marlene Fryer
MANAGING EDITOR: Robert Plummer
COPY-EDITOR: Christa Büttner-Rohwer
COVER AND TEXT DESIGN: Beverley Dodd
TYPESETTING: Monique van den Berg

Reproduction by Hirt & Carter (Pty) Ltd
Printed and bound by CTP Book Printers

Trade edition ISBN 1-86872-354-2
Corporate edition ISBN 1-86872-374-7
Auction edition ISBN 1-86872-375-5

www.zebrapress.co.za

Log on to our photographic website www.imagesofafrica.co.za for an African experience

CONTENTS

For Zarina, Milou and Joey
and for all who gave so much
to liberate our beloved country.

FOREWORD

As I read these fascinating essays, I was struck so forcibly about the importance of memory, of history, for both the individual and the community.

A loss of memory is sometimes no more than a slight annoyance – such as when we have forgotten where we parked the car. But it can be more serious. What would happen if a renowned neurosurgeon who had perfected a particular surgical procedure and could carry it out almost in his sleep were to forget what the next step happened to be? Normally he would remember what to do, but now his mind has become blank. And what happens if I forget who I am or those to whom I am related? My identity is linked very intimately to my memory, and relationships would be impossible if memory went – that is why Alzheimer's disease is such a horribly distressing ailment. To what extent is the patient still the same person as she was before the disease assailed her if she cannot recall significant individuals and events of her past?

Without memory it would be virtually impossible to learn: we could not learn from experience, because experience is something remembered. I would forever have to start at the beginning, not realising that a hot stove invariably burns the hand placed upon it. What I know is what I remember, and that helps to make me who I am.

Nations are built through sharing experiences, memories, a history. That is why people have often tried to destroy their enemies by destroying their histories, their memories, that which gives them an identity. That is why new immigrants who want to become naturalised citizens of a new motherland are asked to appropriate significant portions of its history, its collective memory.

I pray that our people and especially our children will, by reading this collection of essays, remember the very high price that has been paid to achieve our freedom. It is so easy today to romanticise Robben Island as a tourist attraction and to forget the harsh conditions that many of our leaders experienced there. Who can forget the images in that photograph of Nelson Mandela, Walter Sisulu and others sitting in long rows carrying out a thoroughly pointless and soul-destroying task – breaking rocks into small pieces? The system was intent on breaking their spirits in this and other ways.

If we do forget, we will place a very low premium on our new and hard-won freedom. We might then fail to cherish it, nurture it and guard it as something utterly precious, bought at very great cost – not to be frittered away wantonly.

Many feared that those incarcerated on Robben Island might have gained reputations of greatness whilst in prison that set us all up for huge disillusionment when we later discovered that our heroes had feet of clay. Mercifully, that has not happened, and we have evidence in these essays demonstrating that these were quite extraordinary persons, who in those very dark and sombre days, even before the Soweto Uprising of 1976, revealed indomitable spirits, holding on to shreds of hope and optimism when there was little objective evidence to justify it all. The essays invoke so many intriguing questions, both large and small. How, for example, did the writers obtain so much detailed information about surveys and statistics?

These essays are worth reading too for those suffering from amnesia about how apartheid benefited some and caused untold and unnecessary suffering to the vast majority in our beautiful land.

Did George Santayana not declaim, 'Those who forget the past are doomed to repeat it'? We need to know our past, to acknowledge it, to atone for it where appropriate, and so to resolve never to let the awful parts of it happen again.

DESMOND TUTU

WHERE THOUGHT REMAINED UNPRISONED

These essays were written clandestinely in Robben Island prison in 1976, save one that was written and smuggled out of prison in 1978.[1] All the contributors were serving long prison sentences – four were serving terms of life imprisonment. Each was aware that writing these essays, smuggling them out of prison and publishing them were forbidden by the laws of the time.

The apartheid regime had unleashed a reign of terror against the anti-apartheid struggle in 1960. It had silenced almost all opposition voices in South Africa by 1965. Detention without trial, torture, deaths in detention, imprisonment, including a number of political executions, banishment to remote areas, bannings and house arrest had seen to that. Fear stalked the land.

The apartheid state, through its security police known as the Special Branch (SB), appeared omnipotent and omnipresent. It was the time of the informer and the secret agent. They were there to give evidence in court in awesome anonymity – the mysterious Mr Xs and Ys, the Q 17s and 18s of the court records. The turncoat, the informer and the secret agent strutted the stage. They were fêted, hailed as saviours, interviewed by the media and were busy publishing books about their exploits.

Privacy had been raped. Apartheid's grand design of thought control was rampant. The liberation organisations had been declared illegal and driven underground. Thought itself had been driven into the catacombs.

Insecurity and fear permeated the air. It was almost as if one could not trust one's own shadow. It was the same all over: in exile, in prison, within the country – maybe a little better in exile or in prison; worst of all within the country for those who survived.

In exile, Oliver Tambo, Moses Kotane, J.B. Marks, Yusuf Dadoo and Joe Slovo – scattered across Africa and Europe – strove to regroup. Their biggest nightmare: what if the centre could not hold? But then, where was the centre? And the painful realisation: they were the centre, divorced from their base! Even in exile, the movement had to withdraw behind a tight veil of secrecy imposed by the fact that the struggle had been declared illegal by the apartheid regime.

A WORLD APART

The threat of the informer and the spy was present in prison too. The prison authorities worked hand in glove with the SB. They tried to bend and break political prisoners. They selected hardened criminals who were serving time – murderers, rapists and fraudsters – and put them together with political prisoners. They tasked them to serve as provocateurs and informants, and to abuse and intimidate us. They pored over our incoming and outgoing letters, recorded our visits and planted listening devices in our cells.

Some of their efforts were pathetic. On Sunday morning, 3 January 1965, Laloo Chiba and I are herded into a small compartment of a closed prison truck at Leeuwkop Prison. We are bare-foot, dressed in khaki prison shorts and short-sleeved shirts. A third prisoner, Raymond Nyanda, joins us. He is wearing a prison jersey, a white canvas bunny jacket, prison socks and shoes. Soft spoken, shining skin and none of that harassed, unkempt look of the usual prisoner. Three other prisoners join us. We are put into leg irons and handcuffed in pairs. My ankle is locked to the ankle brace of the right leg of my partner; handcuffs attach my left wrist to his right wrist.

The compartment, separated from the driver's cab and the back of the truck, has seating space for four. It is intended for warders when they ride shotgun, accompanying prisoners packed into the back of the truck. The six of us have standing room only and take turns to rest on the seats. The contortions we have to get through to effect this shuffling around must have been the inspiration for the Rubik's cube. Our truck is escorted by a van containing warders. Also escorting us is a sedan car in which Brigadier Aucamp, the head of prison security, is travelling with his wife and daughter, presumably a family holiday reimbursed as escort duty allowance.

Our attempts to protest against our conditions are stifled. Each prisoner is locked in thought. Something doesn't fit. How is it that Raymond Nyanda has clean clothes, shoes, socks, a jersey and a canvas jacket? He breaks the silence, introduces himself; claims he is a political prisoner who was a reporter in Durban for the *Sunday Times*. His brother-in-law, he tells us, is Leslie Messina. Leslie, we know, is living in exile in Swaziland. He was the general secretary of the South African Congress of Trade Unions (SACTU). Already in my mind there lurks the idea that from prison we may be able to communicate with Leslie through Raymond. Some of the others begin to question him. It is becoming an interrogation. Suspicion churns through my mind. I must ward off an interrogation. We must not arouse Raymond's suspicions. We need to find ways of establishing whether he is a plant and what his mission is. The trip becomes nerve-racking. We are unable to talk freely, share experiences and bond as freedom fighters.

We reach Robben Island on 5 January. Laloo, Raymond, Andrew Masondo and I are taken to the 'segregation' section of the prison.[2] This is where our leaders are being kept in single cells after the Rivonia Trial. We are about 40 prisoners in this section. Smoking is a punishable offence in prison, but we begin to notice that Raymond, though he does not smoke, has access to tobacco. He courts the friendship of one of our comrades. He gives him a Parker ballpoint pen as a present. Our leadership is convinced that Raymond has been put among us to spy. We talk to him but treat him with reserve.

What tempts a man – a black man in apartheid South Africa – to sell his soul? We conclude that he is in prison for fraud and has probably been promised a shortened sentence and an easy life in prison. His prison card states that he is serving a six-year sentence for a political offence. A few months later we are working at the lime quarry with picks and shovels. The prison commander drives over and loudly calls for Raymond. Within earshot he says, 'Raymond, you have won your appeal and your sentence has been shortened. Come along, you are being released.' Exit Raymond Nyanda. Mission accomplished or mission failed? Months later we get hold of a smuggled copy of the *Financial Mail*. We find a snippet of news in it: Raymond Nyanda, financial adviser to a Soweto tycoon, has committed suicide.

We begin to organise ourselves in prison. We demand the right to study. We are granted the privilege to study by correspondence provided we can pay for the course. We do not have a single shelf, desk or chair in our cells. After a year we are granted a single bookshelf and counter without a chair or bench. Later we get benches.

Conditions in prison are harsh and the rules are stringent. Any abuse of our study privilege could lead to its withdrawal. Contraventions of prison regulations are punished harshly and summarily. The punishments: denial of meals, spare diet for up to 42 days, lashes and even additional prison sentences.

We organise ourselves by fair means or foul. We are denied all news of the outside world. We smuggle newspapers, journals and books. At one stage we get hold of a pocket radio. We are not allowed to smoke. We smuggle tobacco. We are not allowed to talk among ourselves. We defy this rule until the authorities are unable to enforce it. We are kept separate from the bulk of the political prisoners. We set up a clandestine committee charged with devising ways to communicate with them. Our cells are raided. We find ways to conceal our communications and our smuggled books. We make a false compartment in a bench. We turn a piece of rusted metal into a set of keys to open the prison locks, including the master lock.

Much of this is done in strict secrecy – not even our fellow prisoners are in the know. Everything clandestine that we do is carried out under the strictest discipline and on the basis of the need to know.

Our lifeline is news of the world outside prison: the welfare of our loved ones and friends, the struggle within the country, the activities of the movement in exile and the solidarity action of the world at large. We monitor minutely every snippet of information we can get hold of, mull over its significance. We make the world our own. We follow the developments and progress of humankind's struggle in every corner of the world.

Each of us buries his pain in the pain of our loved ones. We fume and fret about them, and we subsume their travails in the struggle to overthrow apartheid. We grit our teeth, steel ourselves and arm ourselves in every possible way to continue the struggle until freedom reigns. Surrender is unthinkable. Death or victory became our watchwords.

THE STORY BEHIND MANDELA'S AUTOBIOGRAPHY

My release date is creeping up on me. Towards the end of 1975 'Kathy' Kathrada broaches the idea that Mandela should write his autobiography. Mandela, Sisulu, Kathrada and I discuss the proposal. My release, which is due at the end of 1976, would give us an opportunity to smuggle the manuscript out of prison. It is an enormous challenge. Can we pull it off? First, there is the writing. Mandela will have to write purely from memory. Then there is the secrecy. He cannot indulge in the luxury of keeping his notes in his cell. Whatever he writes each night must be out of his hands the next morning. He has no access to reference works. Conditions require that when he sits to write at night he will not have access to what he has already written. And how shall we get the manuscript out safely?

We maintain the utmost secrecy in writing the autobiography because the authorities are likely to impose summary and collective punishment on the entire body of prisoners. We fear divisions among ourselves should this happen, both between the different political organisations, and possibly even among our own organisation's members, especially if the authorities were to withdraw our study privileges. We are mindful of the critical role of the privilege to study in enabling most of us to maintain our sanity in this harsh and brutal environment.

We plan to execute the project in a concentrated burst. We have to plan for the fact that, even though I shall only be due for release on 17 December 1976, the authorities might descend on me at any time, months before my release date, and whisk me away from Robben Island, thereby unwittingly preventing the smuggling of the manuscript.

We would have to transcribe the manuscript from Mandela's handwriting into a fine tiny handwriting on a daily basis. Mandela's original version would end up with Kathrada, who would be responsible for concealing it in prison.[3] The transcribed version, written in a form suitable for concealment and smuggling out of prison, became my responsibility. We drew Laloo Chiba into the team.

Mandela started writing in January 1976. He wrote an average of 10 to 15 pages a night. Within three months he had completed the task.[4] We had worked faster than we had planned. It was better to be early than to be caught by my premature removal from Robben Island.

We convinced ourselves that we had devised means of concealment that would escape detection. It was the first time we would be smuggling out such a large quantity of written material.

HOW REFLECTIONS CAME TO BE WRITTEN

I was restless. We had worked at such a pace that I could not see myself settling back to normal prison routine, simply waiting for my release. So I proposed another project involving the essays that belong to this collection. I approached my colleagues on a one-to-one basis.

I proposed a broad theme, 'Problems of the National Liberation Struggle in Southern Africa', and left it to each contributor to select a specific topic. We chose 'Southern Africa' to enable Andimba Toivo ya Toivo, the general secretary and founder member of the South West Africa People's Organisation (SWAPO), to participate. We made sure that the contributors were not drawn exclusively from the ANC camp. All the contributors I approached readily agreed to participate. We agreed that I would edit the collection after my release.

We gave ourselves three months, from April to June, to complete the task. I kept a tight rein on the completion date, urging and cajoling each contributor until all had finished writing.

Within South Africa, apartheid appeared secure. Our rulers kept ratcheting up the reign of terror. Those who dared to stand up, ended up in prison. The Sabotage Act of 1962 had been replaced by the Terrorism Act. The power to detain without trial now allowed for indefinite detention. Torture in detention had become routine. Official inquests explained away deaths in detention as suicide. The SB continually harassed the families of exiles and prisoners.

But one could read other signs in these events. Yes, terror reigned supreme, but the flame of resistance had not been extinguished.

The struggles in Namibia and Rhodesia were hotting up. Angola, Mozambique, Guinea-Bissau and the Cape Verde Islands were prised out of colonial rule in 1975. In South Africa, there were the 1973 strikes in Natal. The independence of Mozambique and Angola had inspired our youth and students.

But no one detected the rebellion simmering beneath the relative calm. The Soweto Uprising of 16 June 1976 rent the surface calm and sounded the death knell of apartheid.

This collection of essays was written on the very eve of the uprising. There is no hint in them of the uprising, which exploded even as were writing the last pages. This very fact, in my view, enhances rather than minimises their significance. Optimism after the event is easy to latch on to. Optimism before the uprising had to find justification in a fundamental analysis of the southern African reality – and it would be scrutinised more intensely before acceptance. As it turned out, the road from the Soweto Uprising to freedom was still going to be a long one.

Here then, we have a snapshot of the thinking of each contributor at the time. All the contributors save one, John Pokela, who went into exile after his release, and became the Chairman of the Pan-Africanist Congress, are still in our midst and active in the affairs of South Africa and Namibia. The essays give us an opportunity to look into the mindset of each contributor and see the distance each has travelled to the present.

It is for this reason that, when I retrieved the essays from safekeeping, I contacted the contributors and suggested publication even though almost 25 years had elapsed. At the same time I urged that in editing them I would also retain the language and formulations they used. I wanted no hindsight to creep in. Each essay should stand as a marker in the evolution of each one's thinking and approach.

The evolution of thought and ideas in individuals and society fascinates me. It is only the sycophant and hagiographer who believe that anyone walks the political stage with ideas and outlook fully formed, fully developed.

In this context, the transition of South Africa from apartheid autocracy to democracy holds the world in thrall. Just as we, in prison, made the struggle in every part of the world part of us, so too the world sees in South Africa's transition part of itself and its hopes.

As we settle down in a democratic order to reconstruct our society and build our nation, it is necessary that we rewrite the history of our country. Inevitably there will be those who, in this exercise, will add their own gloss. There will also be some who will falsify that history. And there will be events in that past that will need interpretation and reinterpretation. It is therefore imperative that those who lived part of that history should, in telling their stories, never falsify the facts. Without that authencity, interpretations would be fatally flawed.

This collection is offered as one small contribution to that storehouse.

The essays did not see the light of day when they should have. There are good explanations for this. Most of the contributors had insisted that I should publish only if their respective organisations' leaders authorised publication. As it happened, the leaders of some organisations did not come forward with the necessary permission. In one case the hesitancy was not fickle. He was concerned about the implications of such a publication for his organisation at that particular and sensitive juncture, and I understood. And so it came to pass that the essays gathered dust for 25 years.

A RELEVANCE TODAY?

The significance and the impact of the essays, had they been published at the time they were written, would have made them a landmark of defiance feeding the resurgent flames of revolt that were sweeping through South Africa in the wake of the Soweto Uprising. Their impact on anti-apartheid thinking would have been profound. It is easy, but futile, to dwell on the 'what ifs' of history. Ifs make sense only when they absorb the past and are rooted in the present with a view to enabling us to make choices about the course of action we should take to shape the future.

Are we then to view these essays as a collection of historical artefacts – as artefacts of the sort that archaeologists and palaeontologists scrape and polish and put together to read how people lived in a bygone age? Their only interest then would be to service scholars and historians who immerse themselves in finds that we ordinary mortals find difficult to get excited about.

Let us pose the question another way: has South Africa's advent to democracy on 27 April 1994 stripped the collection of its relevance to our country and the world of today?

Race has been a defining feature of South African society for centuries. More than seven years into a democratic order founded on a constitution that upholds equality, our society appears to be traumatised by the phenomenon of racism. There are those who seem to believe that the end of apartheid rule meant the end of racism. For some it is a non-issue; for others, racism should already have become a non-issue. Perhaps our society had to pass through the euphoria generated by the first democratic election to be able to grapple with the need to de-racialise our society.

The problem of race, ethnicity and multi-culturalism is one critical issue the twentieth century failed to resolve. It plagues rich and poor nations. It simmers and erupts in the United States, the European nations, the Latin American countries, Australia, Asia and Africa. No country, be it capitalist or socialist, developed or developing, has yet produced an enduring response.

That is why the debate and the solutions emerging in South Africa will continue to attract the interest and attention of all. The overwhelming majority of the world shares the vision of non-racism that drives us. We look to each other to find ways of realising that vision.

It is sobering to recognise that even the crafting of that vision in the crucible of the South African struggle was no easy task. The essay by John Pokela, who later became Chairman of the

Pan-Africanist Congress (PAC), shows a deep distrust of the term 'multi-racialism', and his espousal of 'non-racism' does not come to grips with the cultural-linguistic diversity of our country. If one bears in mind that for a while after the Sharpeville massacre in 1960 the PAC was seen as a leading liberation organisation, one realises that Pokela's views once had a resonance in South African society as well as in Africa. But the failure of the PAC to grow into a significant political party in democratic South Africa is a reflection on the adequacy of its vision. On the other hand, the rise of the Black Consciousness Movement (BCM) in the 1970s under the leadership of Steve Biko presented a different challenge to the vision of non-racism, because it explicitly posited the unity and commonality of Africans, Coloureds and Indians to the exclusion of whites. It is a measure of the seriousness of the challenge it posed that Nelson Mandela devoted an essay to an assessment of the BCM in which he patiently and clinically analyses its achievements in order to critique its standpoint. The fact that the overwhelming majority of the youth who were inspired by the outlook of the BCM at the time found a home in the African National Congress (ANC) points to the need for an understanding of a reactive assertiveness as a phase in the evolution of non-racism among those against whom white minority rule discriminated.

At the same time it would be a mistake to think that those who charted the vision of non-racism in South Africa (and they were mainly located in the ANC and its allied organisations) proceeded from the same set of assumptions or arrived at the same conclusions. Though Nelson Mandela and Walter Sisulu are driven by the strategic objective of building the broadest possible platform against apartheid as well as for the post-apartheid era, Mandela is clearly also occupied with the management of the process. The distinction warrants scrutiny because fallouts often occur over implementation strategies rather than over objectives. (Does this, perhaps, explain why Mandela was the first to discern the possibility of the moment to press home on the regime the need for negotiations as a means to resolve the South African conflict?)

White minority rule always sought to perpetuate its tenure by decreeing differentiated treatment of blacks. Using race categories it legislated and entrenched differential treatment for Africans, Coloureds and Indians. Later it refined these techniques even further and sought to use ethnicity to differentiate between Africans. Have developments diffused the 'time bomb' Sisulu worries about that was being primed by apartheid's stimulation of ethnicity based on exclusivism? In such an environment the anti-apartheid forces could be expected to experience tensions within and among race groups. Generally such tensions remained latent, submerged in the drive for unity in the liberation struggle.

In a certain sense the contributors can be seen as unwittingly debating among and against each other. A careful reading of their views on racism allows us to detect some of these tensions and discern the different assumptions from which they proceed. This applies particularly to the contributors who come from the same home, the Congress Alliance (Mandela, Sisulu, Mbeki, Kathrada and Nair). Contributions by women and white participants in the struggle are a missing element in this collection. Despite this unavoidable shortcoming, the collection enables us to see the strategic perspectives, tactical considerations, methodologies and the material and psychological conditions that shaped the contributors' thinking, and therefore have to be taken into account as we devise ways and means that will take our country to its desired goal. They bring a much-needed historical depth to the current debates.

Much has been done by the ANC-led government over the past seven years to create an environment and an institutional and legislative basis for addressing the inherited inequalities based on race. Thus, the agenda of deracialisation is pre-eminently a matter of 'work in progress'. But we must be careful not to pass off the matter as an item 'carried forward'.

The current debate and discussion has only just begun. There is enough of a track record to enable us to make assessments and stimulate debate about what we are achieving and what needs to be done. We have to ask whether there is a growing sense that we are moving forward and gathering ever-widening support, and whether there aren't some 'unintended consequences', to borrow a phrase used by President Mbeki in another context, and how we overcome these.

A majority tendency in support of non-racism has been manifest in the post-1994 era. At the same time there is a growing perception that the diverse cultures are not pulling in the same direction. The test of the existence of a majority tendency therefore raises the question of whether this is a sufficient condition for success in building a non-racial society.

The movement for the realisation of equality for women and the building of a non-sexist society yields a useful pointer. In most societies, including South Africa, women form the majority of the population. For much of the time the women's movement correctly concentrated on building a majority tendency among women for equality. Some in the movement realised that unless they drew men into the struggle for equality and non-sexism this goal may remain elusive.

South Africa has taken enormous strides in laying the foundations of a non-sexist society. This achievement should never be taken for granted. *Reflections in Prison*, which brings together some of the foremost thinker-activists of South Africa, demonstrates that as recently as 25 years ago the concept of a non-sexist society did not even feature in the discourse in any significant way! Furthermore, it was within the ANC and its broader constituency that this concept took root rapidly and enabled South Africa to leapfrog much of the world. How this came about is in itself worthy of scrutiny and debate so, that we understand the internal impulses and the external environment that made it possible for the ANC to become the vehicle for steering this change.

The challenge of unity in diversity (!ke e: /xarra //ke[5]), which is emblazoned on the coat of arms of democratic South Africa, is awesome. Issues of race, ethnicity, language and culture, as well as religion, bear an enormous emotional content. Stereotyping, fear, chauvinism and, above all, hatred animate these issues. Inevitably, major social changes bear within them all kinds of insecurities that have to be managed. The real test is that these insecurities should never be allowed to reach a point of distrust in the emerging social order and the forces that lead the process of change.

The principled positions, the strategic clarity, the consciousness that drove us to ensure that the just cause of the denied majority became a national cause in the interest of the entire nation, oppressed and oppressor, permeate these essays. As we debate and shoulder the tasks of building the nation, we need to carry forward the knowledge we have acquired and use it to help us chart the way forward.

One often experiences a sense of glibness when commentators and contemporary historians gloss over our past and simply explain the 'miracle' of South Africa's transition to democracy in terms of a way out of a stalemate in the struggle. Some of the essays in this collection show that there was a line of thought, articulated in the manifesto at the launch of Umkhonto weSizwe (MK) in December 1961, that recognised the calamitous consequences of a race war in South Africa and continuously sought to leave space for a negotiated resolution even as we escalated the armed struggle. A sound understanding of the South African 'miracle' can become a useful contribution to the world-wide search to resolve conflict in and between societies.

These are some of the issues that present-day South Africa and many other communities of the world are still grappling with. *Reflections in Prison* yields insights that are topical and should not be ignored as we forge ahead.

A final word: for my part, retrieving and ensuring this publication discharges me of a special obligation to the contributors. It was an enterprise I had foisted on them. They did their part. The unfinished business lay on my side. My thanks go to all who encouraged, cajoled and helped me complete this task.

MAC MAHARAJ
JOHANNESBURG
MARCH 2001

NELSON MANDELA

Nelson Rolihlahla Mandela was born on 18 July 1918 in Mvezo in the Transkei. He went to Johannesburg in 1941, where he met Walter Sisulu. The two of them, together with Oliver Tambo, Anton Lembede, Peter Mda and others, founded the African National Congress Youth League in 1944. They led the process that culminated in the ANC adopting the militant Programme of Action in 1949. Mandela was appointed National Volunteer-in-Chief (with Maulvi Cachalia as his deputy) of the Defiance Campaign, which was launched on 26 June 1952. In the court trial that followed, he and the other accused were given nine months' suspended sentences. Mandela was elected President of the Transvaal ANC in October 1952. In 1953 he was banned. The ban was renewed repeatedly. He was among the 150 leaders arrested in 1956 for treason. The trial continued until 29 March 1961, when they were acquitted. Mandela immediately went underground to organise and lead the national strike of 31 May 1961.

He was a founding member and Commander-in-Chief of Umkhonto weSizwe (MK). While underground, he slipped out of the country in 1962 to undergo military training and organise support for the armed struggle, and visited various African countries and the United Kingdom. Shortly after his return he was arrested near Howick, Natal, on 5 August 1962 and sentenced to five years' imprisonment for organising the 1961 strike and for leaving the country without a passport. While serving his sentence on Robben Island he was put on trial with those arrested at Rivonia.

The accused in the Rivonia Trial were Nelson Mandela, Walter Sisulu, Govan Mbeki, Ahmed Kathrada, Dennis Goldberg, Raymond Mhlaba, Andrew Mlangeni, Elias Motsoaledi (all of whom were sentenced to life imprisonment), Rusty Bernstein (acquitted and re-arrested) and James Kantor (who was discharged mid-trial).

In 1986 Mandela took the initiative from prison to engage the apartheid regime in a process that led to the negotiated resolution of the South African conflict. He was elected President of the ANC in 1991, and was elected President of the Republic of South Africa after the first democratic election, held on 27 April 1994. He also served as Chairman of the Southern African Development Community (SADC) and the Non-Aligned Movement. He retired after the 1999 election.

He has received numerous international awards (including the Nobel Peace Prize in 1993), decorations from at least 30 states, the freedom of more than 40 cities around the world and at least 50 honorary doctorates from universities worldwide. He is founder of the Nelson Mandela Children's Fund. After retiring as President, he established the Nelson Mandela Foundation. He is currently Chairman of the team facilitating a negotiated resolution of the conflict in Burundi.

His autobiography, *Long Walk to Freedom*, was published in 1994 by Little, Brown & Co., London.

NELSON MANDELA
BY KAGISO PAT MAUTLOA

PROFILE

Tempered steel. By 1976 Mandela had developed an immense capacity for self-control.

This did not come naturally to him; his self-control was consciously cultivated and nurtured. He explained it in this way: 'When one is faced with [provocative] situations you want to think clearly, and obviously you think more clearly if you are cool, you are steady, you are not rattled. Once you become rattled you can make serious mistakes.'[1]

There was a period in prison when I became 'ratty'. Any provocation by a warder would incite me to backchat. I began to accumulate prison charges for cutting remarks and intemperate language. Mandela called me aside. My reactions, he explained, were correct and we ought to challenge the warders. The warders were at fault and were being provocative. The problem was that an injudicious word by me was picked on by the authorities to charge me. Prison rules and regulations were stacked against the prisoner. Patiently he advised me to maintain my stance; but instead of erupting sponta-neously, I should pause, count to ten, measure my response, and choose my words. That way, he said, the anger would still charge my response, but I would be in control; my anger would not con-trol me. Rather simulate the anger needed to give effect to the response, he counselled. That way your response would cut to the quick while keeping your defences intact.

From that time, it was the warder who squirmed with frustration. Never again did a warder suc-ceed in pinning a charge against me. The advice stuck. My problem now is that I am often not sure when I am simulating anger!

How did Mandela achieve such extraordinary self-control? The secret, I believe, lies in his ability for introspection in the privacy of his self. The exercise of 'thinking clearly' involves many elements.

The first element involves analysing the issues and getting a firm grip of the critical elements, such that one has a clear guide to one's positions and line of march.

Mandela's greatest achievements stem from engaging with others by proceeding from *their* assumptions and carefully marshalling arguments to move them to his conclusions. His line of advance is developed on the other party's line of attack. In private, he never stops trying to under-stand the other side, be it the enemy, an adversary, an opponent or his own colleague.

The second element of his introspection is his critical look at himself. It is never easy to hold up a mirror to oneself. In the courtroom of one's conscience there are usually witnesses for the defence only.

Self-control is not self-denial. What it achieves is an unparalleled focus. Iron is iron but there is a world of difference between a blade shaped out of wrought iron and a stiletto blade fashioned from tempered steel.

Mandela's personality is steeped in a passion for life and concern for the people. He is above all a servant of the people.

CLEAR THE OBSTACLES AND CONFRONT THE ENEMY

NELSON MANDELA

In writing an essay of this nature one may be tempted to take us back to Van Riebeeck's days[2] and give a catalogue of all the injustices done to us with hardly anything to say on the burning questions that plague us today. We need to spell out the stumbling blocks on the way forward and offer suggestions for overcoming them. My main effort will lie in this direction.

The most urgent problem facing us is that of unity. To see the problem in perspective, we must first of all draw a clear line between the enemy and the oppressed people and at all times carefully compare the strengths and weaknesses of both sides. Failure to make this distinction has brought its own chain of problems and made some elements in the movement concentrate their fire on those who have always borne the brunt of the attacks from the enemy. Polemics are inevitable in a movement that is active. The more complicated the situation, the more bitter the controversies are likely to become. But there is a wide difference between constructive criticism that will pave the way to a consensus and mere invective that tends to harden the differences. The dividing line between the activities of plain government stooges and those elements in the liberation movement that delight in vilifying their fellow freedom fighters may be quite thin. In both cases the effect is to discredit the movement in the eyes of the people and to blur the demarcation lines between the enemy and us.

The immediate programme before us is to defeat the Nat regime and its apartheid policy.[3] In this regard we can count on our side a wide range of forces who are hostile to all forms of colour discrimination, who would give us their moral support and who are ready to harass the enemy if only through taunts and jeers from a distance. Others are prepared to fight oppression to the bitter end, even though they differ with us on the means to be used in fighting against it. All these are valuable allies and even potential freedom fighters. We should reason with them constantly and patiently, and invite them to advance as far as they can go. This is an important aspect of our work. But the force that will shatter the enemy and on which we should concentrate all our resources is the political organisations we ourselves have built and which have led the people in the struggle for a free South Africa for more than 80 years. Our main task is to link up and to confront the enemy with a mighty force that enjoys the undivided loyalty of the oppressed people as a whole.

Unity is not easily achieved when dealing with several organisations, some of which have a large membership and have dominated the political scene throughout their history, while others are comparatively small and fear to be swallowed up by the big ones. In this connection, the African National Congress (ANC) and the Pan-Africanist Congress (PAC) will play a key role, and a firm declaration committing these two organisations to a joint programme will represent a major breakthrough that will cut down more than 50 per cent of our problems. Unity between the ANC and the PAC has been blocked by differences over the Freedom Charter,[4] the role of communists and other national groups and allegations of extreme nationalism. It may well be that the Sino-Soviet dispute has crept in,[5] making it even more difficult to bridge the gap. The relations between the ANC and the non-racial Liberal Party were warm on the national level and lukewarm in some provinces. Again the main bone of contention was the reluctance of the Liberal Party to work with communists. But even in areas where relations were not zealous, contact was always maintained and ideas regularly exchanged.

At the same time the Non-European Unity Movement (NEUM), a small but vocal organisation concentrated mainly in the Cape, makes venomous attacks on the Congress Alliance (that is, the ANC, the South African Indian Congress (SAIC), the Coloured People's Congress (CPC), the white Congress of Democrats (COD) and the South African Congress of Trade Unions (SACTU)) and labels all these as bourgeois nationalist reformist organisations that collaborate with the enemy. There is no other group that is as bitter in its condemnation of the Congress movement as the NEUM. Trotskyites are active in its ranks and the Congress movement seems to be discredited in their eyes by the mere fact that it admits communists as members. The NEUM has never been able to answer the widespread charge that there is no other organisation in the liberation movement in South Africa that has created so much disunity and confusion among the oppressed people as the NEUM. For this reason any suggested programme of unity which includes the NEUM immediately rouses strong opposition from all sides.

An examination of the policy documents of the NEUM, the utterances of its membership and the whole record of the organisation bear out this charge, and the general hostility towards them is understandable. Speaking for myself, my thoughts and actions are influenced by the knowledge that the ANC is in the forefront of the struggle, that its Freedom Charter is the most radical policy document ever adopted by a political organisation in South Africa, and that it is the organisation that will deliver the final blow against the enemy. But I also believe that a united liberation movement will ensure us speedy victory. In this connection there is no danger in making the unity programme broad enough to include anyone in the liberation movement. If any particular organisation does not want to join us we will fight without it. If it does join us it will be bound by the conditions laid down as a basis for unity.

With the exception of the white members of the COD and the SACP who are kept in Pretoria jail and women prisoners who are kept in the Barberton and Kroonstad prisons, all the organisations mentioned above are represented on Robben Island.[6] In addition we have as our intimate comrades members of the South West Africa Peoples Organisation (SWAPO), iron men who remain undaunted and whose hostility towards and struggle against apartheid in this prison have never flagged. We have also recently been joined by a few members of the South African Students Organisation (SASO) and the Black People's Convention (BPC), all of whom are fine and dedicated people.

A new organisation that has recently joined the progressive forces is the Black Women's Federation, whose aim it is to rally African, Coloured and Indian women around the issue of human rights and equal opportunities. It is active in various parts of the country. It promises to become a powerful force capable of giving dynamic leadership to the women of South Africa.

Here in prison, policy differences do not prevent us from presenting a united front against the enemy. This experience can be generalised and applied to our political work outside jail. The two situations differ fundamentally in one respect: here we are primarily concerned with the general improvement of jail conditions and with resisting any particular measure we consider unjust. But the general fight against racial oppression immediately raises the important question of the kind of social order that will be introduced after victory. This is not an insurmountable obstacle. A careful study of the programmes of the various organisations discloses no basic differences, and in some cases there are even remarkable similarities, a fact which removes the only grounds on which our experiences in jail may be considered inapplicable to the situation in which the liberation movement wages battle. What people usually lose sight of is that the finer details of our future social order will not depend merely on abstract theorising but will be the product of empirical conditions at the moment of victory. Our preoccupation at the present moment should be the overthrow of the oppressor, and the issue of the precise social order is secondary as long as we agree that it should be stripped of racial discrimination. In addition we are already united by a common hatred of oppression and the desire to be free. There is general agreement that all effective means should be used in fighting the enemy. The ANC has raised the largest liberation army in the country, which has fought in Zimbabwe and is ready to strike at the first opportunity. The PAC also has its trained men and may be expected to take the field in due course. The Communist Party, which has worked closely with us throughout its history of 55 years and which demands full equality between black and white, was amongst the first organisations to take the decision to wage an armed struggle. It has given the ANC its full support all the way. In 1970 the NEUM sent in a few men from abroad to start training people inside the country. Legally the Liberal Party does not exist and prior to its dissolution it renounced violence, but it is common knowledge that an influential section of its membership, including its Vice-President, Randolph Vigne, operated through the African Resistance Movement (ARM).

Thus there is a large area of agreement on the main issues. The next step should be fairly easy. A united liberation movement that enjoys the solid support of the oppressed people as a whole, which does not have rivalries to divert its attention, and which can devote all its resources to the single objective of crushing the enemy will be a turning point in the history of our country. However, although there are no basic differences in the present programmes, we cannot ignore the impact of world events. In particular the future attitude of our people will be influenced by the fact that whilst the imperialists are on the side of the enemy, the socialist countries are among those who support our struggle. The fact that we now have two socialist countries on our borders will have repercussions on our policies.

The unity we are advocating is a unity of existing political organisations in the movement, of those who are already waging the armed struggle, those who are still preparing to do so and even those who have no such plans. It is the type of unity that is imposed from above by that minority of conscious freedom fighters who are aware of the dangers of disunity and of the value of concerted action.

Stable political unity involves not only the mere amalgamation or co-operation of the various population groups on matters of mutual concern. In the final analysis unity must be the expression of what is actually taking place amongst the oppressed people and will go hand in hand with the acceptance of the idea of a full equality amongst them and those progressive whites who fight on our side.

The readiness of the more affluent blacks to share economic and social benefits with the less privileged sections of the population, the large-scale emergence of mixed activities like joint labour and parents' organisations, co-operative societies, promotion of joint trade enterprises and professional associations and sports and recreation bodies, the introduction of the principle of equal pay for equal work and the increase in intermarriage between population groups will all indicate that the message of unity has penetrated deeply into the ranks of the people. These developments cannot be set fully in motion until white supremacy is removed with all the legal restrictions and deep-seated social prejudices that accompany it. Only then will there be unlimited scope for tremendous possibilities, when through daily contact the common people will overcome their isolation and prejudices, and when a new generation living in the same residential areas and attending the same schools, playing and singing together, will have arisen. But there are areas where such restrictions do not apply and where it is possible to initiate such trends immediately.

Paradoxically, the independence of the Bantustans is a by-product of our own activities.[7] If we had not stubbornly resisted apartheid during the past 26 years, exposed its hardship and carried the fight against it, independence would have not come about. Apartheid was conceived as a means of preserving white supremacy forever. But when it became clear that we would resist it to the bitter end and that colonialism was in full retreat everywhere, the regime changed its tune and decided to grant self-government to the Bantustans with a view to ultimate independence. In this way the regime hoped to kill two birds with one stone. On the one hand, it would give them some constructive solution to offer to a critical world and, on the other, it would help deflect the demand for emancipation and preserve white rule outside the Bantustans.

This paradox throws some light on the position of these Bantustans *vis-à-vis* the white regime. With armed men of the national liberation movement poised across the borders, the Bantustans gain room to squeeze concessions from the Nat regime. This is an unavoidable spin-off but cannot be expected to last. Furthermore, the whole question of a cluster of independent Bantustans subserving the economy of white South Africa bristles with contradictions and points of friction.

The decision to resort to violence has brought its own problems. In a liberation movement that has for half a century used non-violent methods of struggle and included legal and illegal organisations working together, the decision to switch over to violence could not have been an easy one. Some may have opposed it on principle whilst others may have argued that the proposed switch-over was premature, and that it would merely afford the enemy an excuse to smash the movement. Nevertheless, the decision was taken and the new phase opened with a real bang. First there was the curtain-raiser on the Witwatersrand in October 1961, when power pylons were blown up and phone wires cut. This was followed by the sensational emergence of Umkhonto weSizwe (MK)[8] on 16 December of the same year, when acts of sabotage took place in Johannesburg, Port Elizabeth and Durban. In spite of what happened in October, the regime was caught unawares. For two years thereafter, white South Africa lived in fear. Apart from MK, the National Liberation Committee (NLC)[9] was also active and attacked selected targets. At last, after many reverses, we had taken the initiative and struck hard blows. We were elated by our initial successes. Even those who had first doubted the wisdom of the new line were swept away by the tide of excitement that accompanied this brief spell of activity. Few of our men had received professional training in sabotage. On the whole they acquitted themselves well and deserved the praise that has been heaped upon them. However, we were not strong enough to maintain the offensive. Within 24 months the regime had cracked down on us, crippled our organisations and stamped out the acts of sabotage. This was the first serious setback we suffered. We were forced to abandon activities that enabled us to come to grips with the enemy and could have paralysed the economy of the country, and that would have enabled us to speak from strength. When the blasting of the Pass Office buildings had ceased[10] and power pylons were no longer tumbling down and many of those who had made sabotage such a lethal weapon were jailed or driven out of the country, voices were again heard that we had acted prematurely and underestimated the strength of the enemy. Others even argued that we made a cardinal error by launching the acts of sabotage with inadequately trained men and by embarking on such acts without having trained our own armed units to defend our organisations when the enemy retaliated.

Acts of sabotage were snuffed out because, in our enthusiasm for violence as a weapon to strike at the enemy, we neglected the important work of strengthening the political organisations by recruiting new members, holding branch meetings, conducting political classes, and using legal platforms to reach the masses of the people. In almost all cases the members of the new sabotage organisations were recruited from the liberation movement, which, in the process, was drained of many of its most active and experienced functionaries. The net result was a weakened movement at a time when it should have been raised to its feet.

Having been forced to abandon sabotage, which was relatively easy to execute, we now concentrated on the more difficult preparations for the armed struggle. MK began sending out recruits for military training in 1962. Later other organisations followed suit. Both the ANC and the PAC have well-trained and disciplined detachments whose mere existence should be a source of pride to us all and which remind us of olden times when we commanded our own armies and could defend our freedom. MK has made several efforts to open a route for our men to fight in South Africa. The PAC made a similar attempt. All were foiled by the enemy with the result that 14 years after the first MK recruits were sent out, the armed struggle is still to begin inside South Africa. Even the independence of Mozambique and Angola is no guarantee that our problems in this regard have been solved. Newly independent states have numerous problems to contend with and they may find it quite difficult to do what they wish. The initiative is still in enemy hands and the most pressing task, after the question of unity, is to wrest that initiative from the enemy. I have confidence that this historic moment will come and that the results will more than compensate for the agonising moments of suspense and tension the movement has experienced for more than a decade. For some years the movement has been operating from abroad, where our people are doing magnificent work. They have isolated and weakened the enemy considerably and continue to pile on the pressure, forcing the enemy to defend its policy to a world that is alive to the dangers of racism. But inside the country we are paralysed by the imprisonment of hundreds of active freedom fighters, by many fleeing the country and by restrictions of all kinds. The movement is well aware of this and during the past decade has sent trained men into the country to reorganise the movement. The casualties have been heavy and many were caught before they carried out their respective missions.

Time is of the essence and we cannot afford to hesitate. One of the most burning issues in the country today is the independence of the Transkei and other Bantustans, and the whole question of our tactics towards apartheid institutions. Separate development is just another name for apartheid and the use of the phrase to describe the same thing must be taken as an admission by the regime that apartheid as a political concept is discredited. The liberation movement totally rejects separate development and has boycotted the elections to the legislative assemblies in the affected areas.

It is not possible to examine the merits and demerits of the highly controversial question of the boycott as a political weapon here. Suffice it to say that the very first elections held in the Transkei in 1963 revealed serious weaknesses on our part. The question of whether or not the elections should be boycotted was treated by some as one of principle rather than of tactics, and the actual decision taken bore no relationship whatsoever to the question whether we were in a position to carry out that resolution. Of course, tactics must flow out of principle if opportunism is to be avoided. The test is always whether the pursuit of a particular line will enable us to reach our objectives sooner or whether it will retard the struggle. It would have been correct for us to take part in the elections if this would speed up the defeat of apartheid. As it is, the tactics we used showed we were out of touch with the actual situation. We made no proper assessment of the position and were unable to predict the reaction of the people, and not a single organisation was strong enough to launch the boycott campaign. Although the majority of those who voted in the 1963 Transkei elections emphatically rejected separate development, they chose to use the legislative assembly as a platform to fight apartheid. Two other elections have since been held in the Transkei and there was a swing in favour of the Transkei National Independence Party (TNIP) and independence of the area. In other Bantustans the trend was similar.

Some may prefer not to say a word in regard to the mistakes we have made and the weaknesses shown in the course of our political work. The fact that apartheid institutions are in operation in certain areas is a reflection on us, and a measure of our own weaknesses. Of course, it is our duty to condemn and expose those who have gone over to the enemy and who believe that freedom can be attained by working within the framework of apartheid institutions. But merely to vent our frustration on all those who have gone into these institutions irrespective of their motives for doing so and the line they pursue inside these bodies is not only dogmatic and naive, but entails the danger of alienating potential allies. We should concentrate more on constructive self-criticism and on frankly and publicly acknowledging our own mistakes to our own people. Far from being a sign of weakness it is a measure of one's strength and confidence, which will pay dividends in the end.

The movement, however, faces an entirely new development: the independence of the Transkei, which will be followed by other Bantustans. The Transkei will have an independent legislature, judiciary and executive and may control its foreign relations. Such independence will be the product of separate development, a policy that we unequivocally reject. It will mean breaking up into small separate states a country we seek to free intact. The crucial question is whether we stick to our tactics and ask people to boycott independence or whether the moment has come for a review of the whole question. People in the affected areas will approach the question in a practical way. The heavy and visible yoke of white oppression will have gone. For the first time since conquest the people will run their own affairs. Now Africans will be able to be judges, magistrates, attorneys-general, inspectors of education, postmasters, army and police officers, and they will occupy other top positions in the civil service. Do we ask them to stick to the status quo ante – the maintenance of white supremacy in their areas – and refuse to accept these positions? If we were unable to carry the people on the boycott question before independence, can we hope to succeed after independence? Would it not be far better to consider independence as an accomplished fact and then call upon the people in these so-called free territories to help in the fight for a democratic South Africa? Would acceptance of independence as an accomplished fact limit our freedom of action when these territories apply for admission to the United Nations Organisation (UN) and the Organisation of African Unity (OAU)? It seems to me that to ask the people to reject independence would bring the movement into conflict with their wishes and considerably multiply our problems.

Some people have argued that the liberation movement is now preparing for armed struggle and that it is incorrect for us to waste valuable time examining tactics on the independence of the Bantustans and on the boycott of separate institutions. They regard all talk of independence as mere propaganda on the part of the regime and criticise those who consider such talk seriously. They refuse to examine the problems the movement has been grappling with for the past 14 years and will make no constructive suggestions as to how these should be solved. They insist that the reason why the armed struggle has not commenced is because the movement is planning to attack from bases located outside the country instead of trying to do so from inside. They further argue that the boycott question was settled 14 years ago and that it is wrong to reopen it now.

In matters of this nature, rigidity is as dangerous as wishful thinking and opportunism. The mere decision to wage an armed struggle does not mean that armed operations have already begun and can be no excuse for abandoning the vital work of organising the masses of the people inside the country. An armed struggle is not a question of simply acquiring a gun and shooting. The people should be drawn in and for every man in the front line there should be 10 others to help in the fight. From the beginning, the aim should be to develop the armed struggle into a people's war. Victory is impossible if we fail in this. Concretely, we should explain our policy carefully and tell the country why we have turned to violence; that separate development is no answer to our problems; and that all peaceful methods have failed to rid the country of white supremacy. Far from being a diversion from the armed struggle, mass mobilisation is an essential part of preparing the country for the struggle ahead. Moreover, tactical decisions must be reviewed from time to time and adapted to the changing situation. When subsequent events show that a decision previously taken was wrong, we should have no hesitation whatsoever in reviewing it. The enemy may speed up the independence of the Bantustans to improve its own public image and that of the Bantustan leaders. On independence the people of these areas may regard the Nat regime as a benefactor and the so-called Bantustan leaders as the messiahs who have liberated them without bloodshed. The traitors of yesterday may become the honoured redeemers of today. Independence will give South Africa a ring of buffer zones on its borders, where Africans will be able to govern themselves. When the armed struggle begins, will these independent areas fall within the sphere of our operations? Can we really hope to get the support of the masses in these areas? Will we not be playing into the hands of the enemy who would be happy to see black men massacre one another? Can our operations against the enemy ever be effective if these enclaves are excluded?

De facto acknowledgement of these fragmentary mini-states would not in any way oblige us to support their admission to the UN, the OAU and other world bodies. In fact, it will be our duty to oppose such admission because their acceptance as members of the international community will represent the final triumph of separate development.

A related problem is the emergence of several political parties in the Bantustans and amongst the Coloureds. This immediately raises the question of the relationship of the liberation movement to these new parties. It is easy to dismiss all of them as a collection of traitors with whom we will settle accounts one day. To brand them as sell-outs helps to divert public attention from our own weaknesses and mistakes. By all means, let us attack those who choose to work with the enemy and isolate them. But often in issues of this nature solutions are not so simple. Throughout its history the movement has drawn into its ranks many who once believed that their aspirations could be realised by co-operation with the government, but who were forced by truth and experience to change their views, and who later occupied top positions in our political organisations. We can reason with the pro-apartheid parties in the Bantustans and amongst the Coloureds and Indians and at least try to neutralise them. The anti-apartheid parties are amongst the forces inside the country that continue to expose the evils of colour oppression and in their respective areas fill the void that was left when we were driven underground or into exile. There may be plenty to criticise in the policies and tactics of the Democratic Party of the Transvaal, the Seoposengwe Party of Bophuthatswana and the Coloured Labour Party. A major criticism against all of them is that they confine themselves only to legal activities, when the limitations of such an approach have become all too plain. But which political organisation anywhere in history has been free from criticism? Can we afford to label anti-apartheid parties such as these as stooges merely because their tactics differ from ours? Would it not be in the interests of the struggle as a whole to work with them and give them encouragement in their efforts to defeat apartheid? Or better still, has the moment not arrived for us to establish our own political organisations in the Bantustans through which we can address the people directly and through which we can work with other anti-apartheid groups? But a divided movement in which freedom fighters fight among themselves cannot win over any substantial section of the population. Only a united movement can successfully undertake the task of uniting the country.

The success of the regime in carrying out its separate development manoeuvres highlights the weakness of the liberation movement, particularly in the countryside. Throughout its history the movement has been essentially an urban movement with hardly any significant following in the countryside.

The chiefs have played a key role in the acceptance of the regime's Bantu Authorities and Bantustan schemes. However, attempts to place all blame for the introduction of Bantu Authorities on them are made hollow by the introduction of the Urban Bantu Councils in the principal cities, where the liberation movement commands more influence. This emphasises the importance of looking at our own weaknesses and problems objectively and from all angles.

One of the major contradictions is that the Bantustans will be dismembered from the Republic of South Africa when economic forces demand ever greater cohesion between South Africa and the new 'homelands'. The major industrial areas of the country all fall outside the Bantustans and so far the whole border industries scheme has not lived up to the much-vaunted promises that it would stem the influx of labour from the Bantustans to the Witswatersrand, the Durban–Pinetown area, the Port Elizabeth–Uitenhage area and Cape Town and its environs. Moreover, the main network of rail and roads falls outside the Bantustans. It will require large capital reserves to solve these economic and financial problems. In the meantime acute social problems are likely to arise. Hardly any critical review of the policy of separate development has omitted the glaring contradiction of squeezing more than three-fifths of the country's population into less than 13 per cent of the highly over-populated and highly over-stocked part of the country, whilst the tiny minority of whites clings to the rest, monopolising the most fertile areas, its mines and industrial areas, which were built with our own sweat and blood. No serious comment on the whole situation can fail to point out that one of the weakest links in the whole scheme is the simple fact that more Africans live in the so-called white areas than in the Bantustans today, and no people will ever accept any system that gives them political and other basic rights away from their homes and places of employment. The banner that should be hoisted on all the rooftops of our country should declare that South Africa belongs to all who live in it, black and white, and that our country will never be prosperous or free until all our people live in brotherhood, enjoying equal rights and opportunities.

The campaigns we have waged since the present regime came to power in 1948 have been mainly in the cities. There have been some stirring demonstrations in the rural areas involving opposition to the Rehabilitation Scheme, the pass system, the dipping tanks and the Bantu Authorities Act. In some cases the movement inspired the demonstrations itself but, in the main, they were spontaneous. At no time did we reach the level of organisation in the country areas that existed in the cities.

In exploiting our weakness in the rural areas, the regime probably realised that the independence of each Bantustan would result in a sharp drop or total disappearance of whatever following we had there. Once people enjoy the right to manage their own affairs they have won the only right for which they could join the liberation movement. We would be very optimistic if, in spite of these developments, we still expected much support from an independent territory unless we devised new methods of neutralising them or drawing them nearer to us through the exploitation of some of their unresolved major grievances, such as the land question and economic independence. But an even more serious danger for us is looming on the horizon. Our movement is the product of the very social conditions against which we fight and is influenced by changes of these conditions. The emergence of no less than eight ethnic states requiring qualified men to fill the new positions that will become available will revive regionalism and clannish attitudes and cast a severe strain on a movement that is recruited from all the ethnic groups and that lives in exile under extremely difficult conditions, where divisions and quarrels can be very frustrating. Already the fact that some men who were once politically active have crossed over to the enemy should serve as a warning to us of the centrifugal forces future developments are likely to set in motion. If we do not iron out our differences and close ranks immediately we may find it difficult, if not impossible, to resist the divisive pressures once independence becomes a fact.

In this regard we can draw important lessons from the standards set by our Indian people. They are the only national group in the country that maintains a high degree of political unity. One central body – the South African Indian Congress (SAIC) – has for 56 years served as the undisputed mouthpiece of the entire community. In its manipulation of separate development, in so far as the Indian community is concerned, the regime indirectly acknowledges this fact. Although 'elections' have been held in almost all the Bantustans and amongst the Coloureds, the regime – realising the strength of the South African Indian Congress and the unity of the

Indian people – refuses to allow elections to the statutory body, the South African Indian Council, and relies partly on nominated members and partly on those 'elected' by electoral colleges. Of course, in spite of the numerous restrictions on the economic development of the Indians, they have made great progress in this field and class divisions are emerging. They are the only black group here that has produced a merchant class and now they are developing a class of industrialists relying on enormous capital and large-scale wage labour. Up to the present moment this particular development has had no significant effect on the unity of the Indian community.

A final word on the question of our weaknesses. Whilst the enemy has penetrated deeply into our ranks and uses our own people to retard our progress, we tend to treat him as a homogeneous group with a uniform and unalterable attitude on race matters, holding that no useful purpose will be served by trying to reason with him.

Feelings become particularly strong when our people think of the Afrikaner, the group that dominates the political institutions of the country, and sober discussion becomes difficult. The attitude is understandable, since it is mainly the Afrikaners who enforce the regime's policy and who, as soldiers, policemen, pass and poll tax officials and jailers, are in daily contact with the black man. It is mainly Afrikaners who serve us in the railways, post offices and other public services, often with contempt and discourtesy. In addition, although lately there have been exceptions, their literature portrays us in an unfavourable light and shows no proper respect for our history, culture, aspirations and for the role we have played in the development of the country. These things have made us bitter and reluctant to have any dealings with the Afrikaner. It may well be that the black man's hostility and contempt for the Afrikaner has also been influenced by the well-known hostility and contempt of the Englishman for this group. Be that as it may, in matters of this nature we cannot afford to be governed only by our emotions. Afrikaner politicians have no monopoly of their people just as we have none over ours. We ought to speak directly to the Afrikaner and fully explain our position. Honest men are to be found on both sides of the colour line and the Afrikaner is no exception. We have a strong case and the Afrikaner leaders will command undivided support only as long as their people are ignorant of the issues at stake. To penetrate their ranks enables us to be informed on trends of thought on current problems and to base our own actions on accurate data and not on mere speculation.

This also has relevance to the question of dialogue. We have always favoured peaceful settlement and urged our people to avoid violence. But the regime took advantage of our desire for peace and burdened us with more repression, forcing us to turn to violence. A violent clash is now unavoidable. When we have fought it out and reduced this country to ashes it will still be necessary for us to sit down together and talk about the problems of reconstruction – the black man and the white man, the African and the Afrikaner. But we are not interested in talks between Vorster[11] and Houphouet-Boigny[12] and any suggested solutions within the framework of apartheid would be an insult to us.

The problems facing us appear insurmountable only so long as we try to solve them through a liberation movement which is divided and which cannot rally the people to concentrate all their resources on the defeat of the common enemy. We will be able to consolidate past gains and to face the future with confidence only if we link up without delay. Within the country the vast majority of the people, including a significant section of the whites, are at war with apartheid. In Parliament the most forthright condemnation of apartheid has come from Helen Suzman, who until 1973 was the only member of the Progressive Party in the House. She has spelt out the numerous hardships it has brought to the black man. She has emphatically denounced detention without trial and called for the repeal of the Terrorism Act and the release of all political prisoners. The return to Parliament of six members of the Progressive Party during the 1973 general election revealed an increase in the number of whites who are in favour of a non-racial South Africa. In addition, the split in the United Party, the official opposition party in Parliament, the emergence of the Reform Party and its merger with the Progressive Party has strengthened the anti-apartheid forces in Parliament. Not only is the new party – the Progressive Reform Party – playing an important role in educating the whites on the evils of colour discrimination, but by condemning apartheid it is exposing the regime's propaganda that in opposing racial oppression the black man is merely responding to incitement by communist agitators.

Outside Parliament there is a wide range of influential individuals, groups and organisations who clamour for the total scrapping of apartheid. Industrialists, economists and other intellectuals, the Institute of Race Relations, the Christian Institute, churchmen of all denominations and other public figures have become more outspoken in their criticism of apartheid. The activities of student organisations like SASO and the National Union of South African Students (NUSAS) and students outside these bodies from the black and English universities are particularly noteworthy. They have shown tremendous initiative and courage in the face of difficulties and have staged successful anti-apartheid demonstrations. NUSAS has long been in the field. Since the early 1960s it has concentrated its main attack on the suppression of civil liberties and supporting the general demand for the abolition of detention without trial, the repeal of the Terrorism Act, the release of political prisoners and helping the latter with study funds. The links that NUSAS is trying to develop with Frelimo of Mozambique show that a rather remarkable development has taken place in the thinking of our white students. SASO and the BPC are comparatively new and entered the freedom battle when the enemy was at the height of its power. They have acquitted themselves well and are worthy comrades in the fight for democracy.

A significant development between 1971 and 1974 was the waves of strikes by black workers that erupted throughout the country. Their demands centred on higher wages and a general improvement in working conditions. There was hardly any evidence that the workers were now looking beyond the limited horizon of purely local and immediate interests. The speed at which the strikes escalated, the stubbornness of and solidarity among the workers, and their defiant attitude showed that in their respective factories they were no longer prepared to tolerate any kind of discrimination. In the struggle against apartheid the black workers will strike the most decisive blows. Without their participation the impact of the liberation movement must remain limited. Fortunately they are in the centre of the battle against racial discrimination and constitute the mighty force that will lead the way to a democratic South Africa.

The anti-apartheid forces are strong and vocal both inside and outside Parliament. Their continued existence during such a critical period and the rise of new organisations in place of those that have been driven underground show that the masses refuse to accept white supremacy and that in spite of the great damage the enemy has done, ultimate victory will certainly be ours. The enemy has reached the height of its power and cannot be stronger than it is now, whereas we are growing stronger and will ultimately outstrip him.

South African whites are making a fine contribution to the struggle. Since 1962 no less than 45 of them have been jailed for a variety of political offences ranging from sabotage to furthering the aims of a banned organisation. The majority of these belong to the COD, and the rest to the ARM. The severity of the sentences and the danger of being ostracised by the white community do not deter them. One was hanged for sabotage, two were sentenced to life imprisonment, whilst others are serving long sentences. In the case of the Weinbergs, both husband and wife were jailed together with their daughter.[13] The COD has since 1953 worked closely with the ANC, SAIC, CPC and SACTU and provides a platform for all those whites who fight for full equality between black and white. From the outset they were subjected to all forms of political persecution and no less than 23 of them were arrested for treason in 1956. The COD has brought to the movement a group of dedicated men and women who enjoy all the numerous advantages and comforts the whites are privileged to have, but have chosen to identify themselves with the struggle of the black man. Their record is impressive and right up to the present moment there is a hard core that mans the fortress of freedom in the firm conviction of the justness of the cause.

The ANC is part of a powerful alliance in southern Africa involving Frelimo, ZAPU, the MPLA and SWAPO. We cannot resist being optimistic that the prospects of a new era have been greatly advanced by the liberation of Mozambique and Angola. It is only a question of time before the ideal conditions exist which the movement can fully exploit to come to grips with the last racist regime in our continent. When that moment comes, the enemy may be forced to fight on many fronts.

The climax of our own struggle will begin at a time when the rest of Africa has been liberated from colonial oppression and when the African states can give us material and moral support. It is the African states and the OAU which make it possible for the liberation movement abroad to exist and to prepare for the struggle that lies ahead. That support is bound to grow as the African states gradually solve their economic and social problems, and the prospect of victory will be even brighter. The socialist countries have attempted to meet all our needs and to make available all the wealth of experience they possess in solving the kinds of problems we are sure to meet in future clashes with the enemy. Above all, the condemnation of racial discrimination by the whole world and the expulsion of South Africa from many world bodies are a crushing diplomatic defeat for it and a great victory for us.

Forced by internal and external pressures the regime is backing down on several fronts. Today there are so-called 'mixed' sports in the country and some theatre and other public facilities are being made available to blacks. Our main demand is the total abolition of all forms of white supremacy and the extension of the vote to all South Africans. These relaxations, clumsily made and bureaucratically controlled, do not at all remove our grievances. But at least they show once more that the government has become sensitive to pressure. We have consistently condemned the colour bar and maintained that no man of principle could surrender his dignity and submit to it. After persecuting and even slaughtering our people for more than 60 years for demanding these facilities, white South Africa is at last beginning to acknowledge publicly that our grievances were genuine and our demands reasonable, and that the government was wrong. In particular, the granting of independence to the Transkei shows that we were right to fight racial oppression and to demand the right to manage our own affairs in the country as a whole.

But we cannot exploit the strength of the anti-apartheid forces internally and externally without a strong and united liberation movement. A powerful movement that is able to rally and co-ordinate the political activities of all the oppressed people and with a firm grip on the course of future developments is the first condition for victory. The internal and external climate may fluctuate; today it may favour us and tomorrow the enemy. We will be safe only if we rely primarily on our own strength and if we concentrate our resources on building a machine that can vigorously prosecute the struggle and free our people from the evils of race oppression even if we are alone in the world.

The ANC can fulfil its historic mission single-handedly, if need be. It has survived the most ferocious onslaughts from the enemy, launched powerful campaigns from underground, rallied world opinion on our side and is now well poised for the beginning of a new era in the fight against white supremacy in our country. Its daring and initiative have encouraged new organisations to emerge and join the struggle. The PAC was hardly one year old when it launched its 1960 campaign, and a political organisation that was baptised by the fire of action would be a worthy ally. Few developments in the history of the liberation movement would assure victory more than unity between the ANC and the PAC. This is a crucial moment for big decisions and time is not on our side. I have confidence that my views on this matter are identical with those of Oliver Tambo[14] and Potlako Leballo[15] and feel certain that both of them will take the initiative to remove the disturbing uncertainty arising from the existence of two rival organisations and two rival armies competing against each other on important questions. I like to think that their lead will receive the support of Yusuf Dadoo, Reggie September, Rusty Bernstein, I.B. Tabata and Randolph Vigne.[16]

WHITHER THE BLACK CONSCIOUSNESS MOVEMENT? AN ASSESSMENT[1]

NELSON MANDELA

THE DEEP ROOTS OF OUR STRUGGLE

The editorial of a local English newspaper, commenting on the banning of 18 organisations by the Minister of Justice in October 1977, described the emergence of the Black Consciousness Movement (BCM) as the most important development in black politics in recent years. The editorial comment produced conflicting reactions. There are critics in all sections of the liberation movement who refuse to acknowledge the achievements of others. They seem to believe that such acknowledgement will be a sign of weakness on their part and a lack of confidence in their own organisations. More specifically, they say that in a country like South Africa, with a significant and vocal body of whites which is opposed to apartheid and identifies itself with the black man's struggle, the emergence of the BCM is a setback; that its slogan of 'Black is Beautiful' is racist; that its policy of communalism in an era of industrial capitalism and an ever-expanding socialist world is primitive – hence the contention that the movement is in the hands of reactionaries. These critics are suspicious of the support the movement enjoys from the imperialist countries, particularly the USA, as well as the movement's alleged hostility to Marxism. Some of the critics dismiss the movement as the brainchild of the American Central Intelligence Agency (CIA) and resist any form of co-operation with it. The youth demonstrations that began in Soweto in June 1976 are condemned for being badly planned, reckless and disastrous, exposing hundreds of innocent people to slaughter, arrest and persecution. The campaign fizzled out when the youth were jailed, fled the country in large numbers and schools in affected areas were closed.

Opposing critics go to the other extreme of exaggerating the role of the movement and claim that in the history of our country the BCM is a movement with a special mission of freeing the black man, that within a few years of its formation it eclipsed the older organisations, both legal and otherwise, that the older organisations are essentially reformist in outlook and methods. Earlier political struggles are denounced as adventurist and ineffective, a mere playing around with people's lives. The sabotage activities of the early 1960s are dismissed as a few bucket bombs that made no impact. They interpret the setbacks and political lull of the past 16 years, especially the delay in commencing armed operations inside the country, as evidence of the collapse of the older organisations, as incompetence of their leaders and as an absence of dynamic leadership. The BCM is hailed as a revolutionary movement with resourceful leaders, the Kennedys and Kings of South Africa.[2]

Such contrasting views demand the unprejudiced and objective analysis of an emergent youth movement. But to look at the political situation from prison tends to distort the very events one is trying to examine and makes an objective analysis far more difficult. However, the matter is sufficiently significant for us to run the risk of daring where the more cautious would hesitate.

The involvement of students in the freedom struggle is crucial and the emergence of a vigorous student movement is to be welcomed. To underestimate or exaggerate its role merely clouds the issue. The effect is either to discourage those who might be the country's leaders in future or, what is equally dangerous, to make them swollen-headed.

The youth and, more particularly, university and high-school students, are often the most idealistic and sensitive section of the community. At times they feel the stigma of oppression more sharply than the average worker. The worker has heavy responsibilities and maintains a family. He is reluctant to take part in any form of activity that may cost him his job. In the case of an African worker in this country, that hesitation is sharpened by the fact that strike action is a criminal offence. To make matters worse, an African worker who is unemployed may be deported from his area – a disaster which entails, among other things, the loss of a house and the break-up of his family.

Students have less responsibilities and respond more readily to protest calls, for they have little to lose by such participation. Political action provides a platform for their idealism and love of adventure. Their high literacy level tends to make them more conscious of social developments in other parts of the world and the need for change in their own country – all of which compels political critics to be objective in dealing with such a movement. A short historical sketch of the BCM may be necessary to explain its role in the country's politics, define the scope of its impact and place its achievements in perspective. Such a sketch may provide the reader with vital information in examining the important question whether the BCM will be able to overcome the difficulties of switching over from an open to a disciplined underground movement, of maintaining pressure against the enemy and the speed at which this will be accomplished.

During the mid-1960s there was no youth movement in the country that specifically catered for the needs of the black youth. Both the African Students Association (ASA), which was dominated by the youth of the ANC, and the African Students Union of South Africa (ASUSA), whose membership came mainly from the Pan-Africanist Congress, were defunct. The Transvaal and Natal Indian Youth Congresses (TIYC and NIYC) also ceased to exist. Many of the active membership of these bodies were involved in the acts of sabotage which took place during the period from 1961 to 1964 and were either imprisoned, confined to certain areas, or had left the country for military training abroad or for study. Although the Coloured People's Congress (CPC) had drawn into its ranks progressive and militant youths, it did not form any distinct Coloured youth organisation. The Cape Peninsula Students Union (CPSU) faded out in 1962 when most of the members were brought into the African People's Democratic Union of South Africa (APDUSA), an affiliate to the Non-European Unity Movement (NEUM). The ANC Youth

League, after campaigning for no less than 16 years, folded when the mother body, the ANC, was declared illegal in 1960, whilst the Young Communist League (YCL), which had active branches in Cape Town, Durban and Johannesburg, had been forced to dissolve when the Communist Party of South Africa (CPSA) was banned 10 years earlier.[3]

Three youth movements, the National Union of South African Students (NUSAS), the University Christian Movement (UCM) and the Afrikaanse Studente Bond (ASB) were still active. Although the first two were open to both black and white members, in fact, neither attracted a substantial number of blacks. Both were totally opposed to apartheid and their non-racial programmes clashed with the government's policy. Not only did the government constantly harass their members, but also the organisations were not allowed to hold meetings in black universities.

The ASB, according to its constitution, sought to promote the scientific development of its members and of Afrikaans culture on the basis of Christian Nationalism. Unlike NUSAS and the UCM, whose membership was mainly English, the ASB was exclusively Afrikaans and throughout the 63 years of its history has never had any significant contact with black student opinion. It has been indoctrinated by generations of conservative Afrikaner politicians and racial thinking has become deeply rooted within it. The progressive developments that have affected practically the whole world, and which have established the principle of the equality of human beings, have barely touched this body. Its members moved together with their people into the isolation of the laager. There are several other white and mixed youth movements that we do not specifically mention here either because they avoided politics altogether or identified themselves with the government.

In the explosive atmosphere that affected the country since the Nats came to power, especially from the 1960s onwards, an organisation whose membership was, for whatever reason, dominated by whites was not likely to enjoy black support. In spite of the firm stand that NUSAS took on important national issues and the successful campaigns it launched, there was a widespread feeling among the black students that they had social problems alien to their white colleagues; that the white students had a patronising attitude towards the blacks, which the latter deeply resented; that they were only interested in their black mates while they (the white students) were still at university, but that as soon as they left university they forgot about blacks and became oppressors just like all the other whites. The black students were also of the opinion that the constitution of NUSAS, which did not allow for individual membership, hampered them in making their influence felt in the affairs of the organisation and that its policy was determined largely by whites. For these reasons black students felt that NUSAS was not the best organisation through which to seek solutions, and that the moment was ripe for the formation of a student movement controlled in every respect by blacks themselves.

In the meantime, international events and developments on our borders were helping to stimulate the protest spirit among all students. America, the world's mightiest imperialist power, was being mauled by the small Vietnamese nation. The atrocities the American army was committing in Vietnam and the heavy casualties it was suffering there not only provoked protest inside America itself, but led to the realisation even in conservative circles in the West that imperialism was a threat to world peace.

Student bodies on both sides of the Atlantic were rebelling against parental, social, educational and governmental authority, staging huge protest demonstrations, many of which involved clashes with the police and loss of life. The largest of these demonstrations was held in the French capital, Paris, where close to a million students and workers marched through the streets. The demonstrators fought the police from behind barricades and the country seemed to be on the brink of civil war. In the USA and some South American states, in Italy, Spain and West Germany, the students were also up in arms. Although these demonstrations were finally crushed, they produced echoes on almost all continents.

On South Africa's borders the people of Angola, Mozambique, Namibia and Zimbabwe had risen against their respective oppressors, whilst armed detachments of MK had clashed with the enemy in Zimbabwe, forcing Prime Minister John Vorster to rush his army to the Zambezi.[4]

These events inspired our youth at black and white universities. Although NUSAS did not attract large numbers of black students, it was for some time the only student movement that was outspoken in its condemnation of government policy. It condemned detention without trial from its inception and called for the repeal of the Terrorism Act. It backed up its demands with action and, in some cases, there were collisions with the police. NUSAS gave emphasis to public issues, demanding the release of all political prisoners, raising study funds for prisoners, helping their families and publicly attacking specific government measures.

African students at Fort Hare and at some of the high schools were also active. Apart from taking part in specific campaigns as part of the liberation movement, some students even joined MK after its emergence in 1961, but they had no specific youth organisation and concentrated on student domestic matters.

The initiative taken by white students on many public questions, affecting blacks mainly, pricked the conscience of black students who realised the irony of sitting with folded arms while their white colleagues were on the attack. The result was the formation of the South African Students Organisation (SASO) in December 1968. Its chief aim was to unite African, Coloured and Indian university students. It also had the undeclared aim of creating conditions conducive to the operation of the underground organisations. Its constitution was modelled on that of NUSAS, but whites were expressly excluded from membership.

The success of any new organisation depends upon efficient machinery, a dynamic programme of action and the correct application of leadership skills. Soon after its formation, SASO evolved an ambitious organisational scheme to capture intellectuals and to mobilise mass support. Within a few years it spread its tentacles to practically every field.

The organisation of students in high, secondary and training schools was entrusted to the South African Students Movement (SASM), while working youth would be rallied, at a later stage, through the National Youth Organisation (NAYO).

The Black Community Project (BCP) would help people gain a variety of specialised skills.

Training would be run on professional basis and would include leadership training, administrative skills, research, writing and publication of literature. Several cultural organisations were established or taken over to spread Black Consciousness through art, drama, poetry and music. One of these was the Music, Drama and Literature Association (Mdali). A programme was drawn up for the rural areas, particularly those affected by the government removal schemes. The programme included the building of schools, health clinics, roads and dams, literacy campaigns and lessons in domestic science.

Education By Employment was a special programme intended primarily for the students' benefit. Arrangements would be made for students to get employment during their holidays and to come into direct contact with workers and to acquaint themselves with the problems of the black man at first hand.

Within the UCM doubts were being expressed as to whether, in the country's unique situation, a non-racial organisation like the UCM itself was the best way to take up the specific problems of each particular population group. The emergence of SASO brought this question to a head. In 1971 the UCM voluntarily dissolved and its white members were given the task of conscientising the white youth. Blacks were now instructed to develop Black Theology, a new body of religious principles, which would serve as another effective agency for the freedom movement. In this way, it was hoped to draw all the black churches and black nationalists in the white congregation into the new movement.

Although primarily a student organisation, SASO realised from the start that the problems of black students were mainly a result of a lack of political power. The dominant idea in almost all the activities of SASO is that of Black Power and it soon felt the need for a legal organisation to promote this idea. With this object in mind, SASO held a number of bilateral meetings with different organisations. In 1972 there was a conference of cultural organisations that met to form one co-ordinating body. The SASO delegation rejected the original idea and suggested instead the formation of a political body. The conference ultimately accepted this proposal and the Black People's Convention (BPC) was born in July 1972. Although it was meant to be the senior body giving political direction to the other organisations, SASO easily captured its leadership.

The BCM embraced all these and other local organisations, all of which are bound together by the idea of Black Consciousness. Besides these, there are other organisations, like the Black Allied Workers Union (BAWU), the Black Women's Federation and the Black Parents Association, which used the label 'black' but were not directly linked with the BCM. According to its policy manifesto, SASO is a black student organisation working for the liberation of the black man, first from psychological oppression by liberating himself from his inferiority complex, secondly from the physical one accruing from living in a white racist society.

The manifesto describes black people as those against whom the law discriminates economically, politically and socially and who identify themselves as a unit with the struggle for the realisation of their aspirations. SASO accepts that South Africa is a land in which black and white will continue to live together. But SASO believes that because of the privileges whites enjoy and because it regards all whites as oppressors, they are the main cause of the black man's suffering and must consequently be excluded in all matters relating to the people's struggle. Although law shall not prohibit it, personal contact between black and white must be discouraged, especially where such contact undermines cherished beliefs.

SASO regards the urge towards black awareness as the logical and significant means by which the black man will gain freedom. Black Consciousness is defined as an attitude of the mind and a way of life which calls upon the black man to reject all value systems that deprive him of basic rights in his own country. The concept implies black awareness of the power they wield as a group both economically and politically. Hence group cohesion is regarded as an important facet of Black Consciousness. This concept calls for total involvement in the struggle of the oppressed people.

SASO believes that a non-racial society in this country can only be achieved by blacks themselves. Consequently, blacks must first unite and fight as a group to free themselves from white oppression. They argue that integration can only be realised in a just and free society and not in an atmosphere of suspicion and mistrust. The manifesto expresses its lack of faith in the genuineness of multi-racial movements and in the capability of individual whites in South Africa to bring about social change. Self-reliance and the rejection of all forms of subservience and paternalism are the rock on which the BCM is grounded. The idea was well expressed by Barney Pityana, then President of SASO, in the following words: 'We must make blacks independent of whites as far as possible and make them realise that they are on their own. In order for a group of people to bring about change, there must be an identity that they seek to protect and promote. Black people must build themselves to a position of non-dependence on whites. They must work towards a self-sufficient, political, social and economic unit. In this way they will help themselves towards a deeper realisation of their potential and worth as a self-respecting people.'[5]

Three important points about the BCM already stand out in this short sketch: a shrewd plan, a powerful ideology and an able youth leadership. Certainly the founders of the BCM provided that movement with an impressive structure, and in a country where blacks are hungry for political power and where the practice of racism affects every aspect of their lives, the Black Power ideology is still likely to be a potent weapon. The ideology must have been chosen with the firm belief that it would appeal to Africans, Indians and Coloureds from all walks of life, to educationists, professionals and businessmen, the clergy, students, workers and people from the countryside. The whole plan set the stage for a powerful youth movement, which would make a significant contribution to black politics, fill the vacuum created by the banning of older organisations and prepare the ground for revolutionary forms of struggle.

For three centuries the whites have tried to tell the black man that he has no history, civilisation or identity to be proud of; that only whites have a past, a cultural heritage and a common awareness of their mission in life. Even the standard works of white historians talk of Asia,

America, South Africa and Australia as having been discovered by their forefathers, illustrating the same type of racism on a world scale. They refuse to acknowledge the black man's contribution to world history and civilisation. They would like us to believe that continents and people exist only if the white man has seen them.

It was blacks, the Abathwa, derogatorily referred to as Bushmen in white literature, who founded South Africa ages before Bartholomeu Dias saw our shores, and the Khoi-khoi (the so-called Hottentots) who welcomed him when he landed. Yet Dias is introduced to the world as the 'discoverer' of our country. Race prejudice is so firmly entrenched amongst the whites that even history works that are published today hardly mention the ANC and the SAIC – the organisations that in 1946 initiated the campaign to isolate South Africa from the rest of the world, which culminated in South Africa's expulsion from the British Commonwealth of Nations and other world bodies. Equally revealing is the almost complete silence on MK, whose armed units have had numerous engagements with the South African army and whose activities have turned the country into an armed fortress.

Whites regard themselves as superior and blacks as inferior, and teach that the only way the black man can advance is by imitating the white man. Influenced by this colour prejudice, whites refuse to accept the black man as an equal, preferring to call him a non-white or non-European, not referring to him by what he is but by what he is not, all this being intended to support the myth of white supremacy. The district magistrate, the schoolteacher, the parish priest and the local trader all tell the black man this fable.

For centuries, generations of black South African patriots have fiercely challenged this fallacy and asserted the ideal of self-reliance in the most concrete terms. Although in the early days social conditions forced each ethnic group to fight independently of other black countrymen, within the framework of that social system, each group was fully aware of its black identity and the power of united action.

The Abathwa and the Khoi-khoi opened the patriotic wars that raged until the end of the nineteenth century and produced martyrs which today's freedom fighters, themselves born and bred in a racist environment, hardly ever mention in their speeches and writings on the struggle of our people against foreign aggression. Abathwa and Khoi-khoi fought for their country and their people. In doing so, they were asserting their identity and love of freedom. That glorious heritage was greatly enriched when, from the second half of the eighteenth century, the Africans took their respective positions in the line of battle. In those patriotic wars our forefathers were in fact saying: 'We are black and are on our own. This is our land and we shall defend it to the bitter end!'

After colonial conquest of South Africa, the Natal Indian Congress (NIC), the African People's Organisation (APO) and the ANC, joined later by other sections of the liberation movement, rallied the Indians, Coloureds and Africans in disciplined political struggle around the same idea of the right of the black man to live freely in his country, to plan his own life and to draw inspiration from his own past and culture. Since 1921 the Communist Party has put forward the country's most radical programme of reform and fully identified itself with the struggle of the black man. It gave particular attention to the formation of black trade unions, not only to improve the material conditions of the black worker, but also to be able to back up its demands with economic pressure.

That feeling of unity enabled the ANC, the SAIC and the APO 30 years ago to bring together Africans, Coloureds and Indians in a common struggle against white domination and to sharpen the spirit of resistance. That unity has become the solid rock from which the people's struggle is directed. All organisations that now accept this principle are either legitimate heirs of the heritage created during that unforgettable period of Wars of Dispossession or offshoots who broke away because they rejected this very principle, but who were later forced by events to eat their words. Few things illustrate an organisation's ignorance of our history and struggle better than to imagine that in this country the crusade for black unity only began in the 1970s.

AN EXPLOSION OF ENERGY

Preparing a master plan and applying it are two different things. All over the world Utopian programmes are a common feature of many organisations. Perhaps many critics may have dismissed the BCM as no more than a movement of this type and its ideology of Black Power as a false dream. They may have reasoned that the enemy, which had given stronger and more experienced organisations a rough time, was too powerful and that it would easily put out the new fires that were beginning to lick our shores.

But the BCM quickly advanced beyond plan-making and took a bold initiative on a wide front. It began attracting attention and forced many people to take sides. Barely six years after its appearance it had made quite an impact and SASO, the driving force behind the whole movement, had won the respect of progressive opinion here and in many parts of the world. No other movement since the emergence of MK had caught the imagination of the youth as the BCM had done, undertaken so many positive mass projects, conducted its campaign with such enduring aggression and handled such a big budget.

The contribution of the BCM is even more striking if we bear in mind that when it was launched the enemy had become ruthless in dealing with its opponents; that many activists had been jailed, killed in detention, confined to certain areas or had fled the country; that the liberation movement was seriously crippled and mass political activity had been stamped out.

Equally significant was the fact that the youth that now resisted government policy so uncompromisingly were products of ethnic schools. They were a new generation of intellectuals who were trained to be spineless government tools, who would accept separate development without question, man its key positions and finally lead the black man away from solutions sought by the liberation movement. It must have been a grievous blow to Vorster to discover that blacks who had been groomed from primary school to think on tribal lines could work so hard to unite Africans, Coloureds and Indians and reject apartheid with such finality.

When SASO emerged, the government and its supporters welcomed the new movement as a rebuff to the white liberals generally and, in particular, to NUSAS, hoping that this was a development much in line with their own policy. By throwing open its membership to all blacks the BCM had cut across government policy, which seeks to restrict the development of each ethnic group within the framework of a separate enclave. But the important point for the government was that in forming a black student body, the black youth had finally broken the links with liberal white student opinion. For this reason, the government did not harass the new movement and allowed it to operate freely.

Professor Kotze, a supporter of separate development, wrote a critical but sympathetic review on SASO and the BCM in *Politikon*, issued by the University of South Africa in 1974. Similarly Dean J.J. Otto, President of the South African Students Congress (SASCON), another body which advocates separate development, writing in the *Die Huisgenoot* of 19 November 1971, said that the chief object of the organisations was to unite Afrikaans- and English-speaking students, to develop responsible contact with black students, and, in so doing, to stem the influence of radical elements at the black universities, and that SASCON was striving for co-operation with SASO. He declared war on NUSAS, describing it as the archenemy of SASCON and threatened to dismantle it in the coming year.

Dean Otto's statement that the development of responsible contact with black students would stem the tide of radical influence on the black campuses may be a shade naive. In fact, it is a timely reminder to us, since it is an application of the general strategy of the government and right-wing liberals. They welcome black reformist movements that believe in co-operation, or at least in peaceful non-violent solutions, because such movements can eventually checkmate the more radical movements whose policies are to fight violence with violence. The editorial comment referred to earlier expressly warned government that the effect of banning the BCM, which until then worked openly, would be to drive it into the arms of sinister forces that are a threat to the security of the country.

SASO exploited this benevolence. Before the government realised its mistake, the new organisation was shooting out roots in all directions and had established itself amongst students on all the black campuses.

The unusually large number of full-time functionaries in BCM employ was a new feature and indicated the seriousness with which it viewed its mission. During specific campaigns the ANC and its allies, more specifically the SAIC, were able to assemble an equally imposing full-time staff and, as an underground organisation, the ANC today has an even larger staff. In its heyday as a legal organisation SACTU had a fairly large staff. Nevertheless the size of SASO's permanent staff was certainly a new feature.

SASO had a full-time secretary general, a permanent organiser, a director of literacy, four regional directors, a cultural committee director and various administrative assistants such as clerks, receptionists and typists. The BPC also had a full-time secretary general, a national organiser, four regional directors and several administrative assistants.

To ensure that it would reach all shades of opinion the BCM produced no less than 15 cyclostyled publications. SASO's major mouthpiece was the *SASO Newsletter*, printed bi-monthly with a circulation of 4 000 and distributed among the black community at large. The *SASO Bulletin* was also printed bi-monthly with a circulation 2 500. It was aimed at students. Ten thousand copies of *Creativity and Black Development* were published. This was a compilation of the various papers delivered at the third general Students Council Meeting at Hammanskraal in July 1972. It was banned shortly after publication. A series of fact papers was also brought out which went in depth into particular topics. This material was also distributed chiefly among students. The *Freshers' Pamphlet*, with a circulation of 9 000, came out annually. In 1973, after the country-wide student demonstrations during the preceding year, *SASO on the Attack!* was issued. It was banned after publication. Apart from these there were several other publications such as 'reports of conference', commissions and seminars on particular topics as well as conference minutes.

The Black Community Project published an annual magazine, *Black Review*, which contained a detailed survey of almost every aspect of black community life in the country. The viewpoint of leading persons in the black community was set out in *Black Viewpoint*. Only one issue was published. *Black Perspectives* complemented *Black Viewpoint*. A work of particular interest was the *Handbook of Black Organisations*, which published important details of every existing black organisation in the country: its constitution and other policy papers, aims and objects, its members and date of formation. The idea was to collect essential facts on every organisation in the country for purposes of planning future campaigns and for quick reference.

The main organ of the BPC was the bulletin *Inkululeko YeSiswe*. The police repeatedly confiscated its material, with the result that the bulletin did not come out regularly. In 1975 it issued a policy statement which, in many respects, was similar to the Freedom Charter of the ANC. However, by and large the BPC concentrated on explaining the concept of self-reliance and attempted to give guidance to the community on day-to-day events.

These publications constituted a powerful propaganda machine and brought the BCM into close contact with various sections of the black community. Through these organs the views of the new movement and its activities were brought to the attention of the public. At the same time these publications created a forum for members of the public. The cumulative effect of all this was to enable the BCM to put its pulse on the feelings of the people.

The tag 'black' now spread to other bodies not directly influenced, as SASO was, by the USA brand of Black Power. Among these were the Black Women's Federation, the Institute of Black Studies and the Black Academic Staff Association. Progressive political critics, like Fatima Meer and the late Dr Rick Turner, began writing articles in which they assessed the new movement.[6] In spite of reservations about certain aspects of its policy, they generally felt that in the light of our present situation, its emergence was a natural development and that its policy reflected the mood of the oppressed people.

The BCM also developed sophisticated techniques of politicising the people and used art to achieve this goal. Other sections of the liberation movement had tried this method in the past and staged exciting shows that attracted large crowds. They realised that art is an effective way of spreading ideas and influencing the public, that it can take a man out of his shell into the wide world of human endeavour, where he can achieve the fullness of life by identifying himself with the struggle of mankind to create a better world, where he can be happy without making others unhappy, that by seeing a play performed, reading a novel, listening to music or poetry, he can discover what other human beings were able to achieve in similar circumstances, that in South Africa good art can inspire the black man to stand up and fight.

Two interesting innovations, launched before the formation of SASO, aroused much interest. One of these was the idea of taking theatre to the people in their *pondokkies* and backyards. This was a revolutionary step and, with full-time and able functionaries, efficient organisation and sufficient funds, it has unlimited possibilities.

Another new development was the children's Experimental Workshop, whose aim was the orientation of the children's outlook, so that at an early age they could think progressively and be able to resist all forms of racial prejudice. African, Indian and Coloured children were organised into mixed theatre groups and presented plays, sang or recited poetry together. In this way, a new generation of artists was being created, which was free of colour prejudice and which was bound together by the common desire to build a greater South Africa. The Theatre Council of Natal (TECON) and the People's Experimental Theatre (PET) did useful work in this field.

Several young artists were also involved in theatre work and, more particularly, in the productions staged by TECON. After the establishment of SASO these artists applied these innovations as part of the conscientisation campaign. Some of their performances were based on these experiments and were definitely catching on when the BCM was banned.

The press often reported that the BCM ran several clinics, some with full-time and qualified medical and nursing staff. It was also reported to be running other important community development projects in various parts of the country.

Full-time functionaries, good organisation, a dynamic policy and constructive community schemes give an organisation a tremendous advantage and may help it to popularise its plans and entrench itself. But what completes the picture and excites the average man is its record in the field of conflict against the enemy – the fact that it can fight and win victories, however small. This is what has kept the ANC alive for more than six decades and this is why in his report on the 1962 Paarl riots Judge Snyman warned that the danger to white South Africa would come from MK, the military wing of the ANC.

In its short history as a lawful movement, the BCM tried to combine ideology and planning with concrete action. If one bears in mind that SASO members were mere novices when they were forced to fight back, with members on average still in their twenties, they acquitted themselves well. It was mainly its open confrontation with the enemy that caught the public eye and put SASO on the map. The first of these clashes took place in May 1972, only 28 days after the organisation had been formed.

The late Ramothibi Tiro, a student at the University of the North (Turfloop) and SRC President from 1970 to 1971, spoke at the university's graduation ceremony.[7] In the presence of the Chancellor, Dr W.W.M. Eiselen, and other white dignitaries, he criticised Bantu Education. That a black man should have had the 'temerity' to attack their divide-and-rule master plan on such a solemn occasion was a kind of subversion the university bosses could not permit. Tiro was summarily expelled.

That was the flashpoint and the whole university was on fire, with the students demanding that Tiro be reinstated immediately and threatening not to write the June examinations. The authorities closed the university and sent all the students home. Their aim was to disorganise the students by dispersing them throughout the country and making united action difficult. Convinced that the recalcitrant students were sufficiently intimidated, the authorities sent new applications forms for readmission containing humiliating conditions, which the students resented.

Unfortunately for the enemy, all these manoeuvres had been anticipated. The students were able to draw on their own efficient machinery and the goodwill of the black community and of progressive whites. Student leaders from all the black campuses met in Alice. They decided to boycott the examinations and refused to sign the conditions. They called upon all those at institutions of higher learning to support their Turfloop colleagues and appealed to parents to form parent committees to assist the students. The Council of SRC Presidents was set up to direct the demonstrations, and each campus was asked to make local demands in addition to the principal demand for Tiro's reinstatement.

The response was swift and solid. Examinations were boycotted, with varying degrees of success, by students at all black campuses including Springfield College, ML Sultan Technical College and at the Transvaal College of Education. Although there was no intention to involve high-school students, some joined in. Meanwhile, white students at the universities of the Witwatersrand and Cape Town staged solidarity demonstrations. Black and white leading personalities publicly condemned the government. Although some students were expelled, it was a runaway victory that shocked the government. Black youth, whom they had strongly relied on to become puppets serving white interests, had overnight become an army of rebels on the attack.

The echoes of the student demonstrations had barely died away when, in October the same year, African, Coloured and Indian workers of Natal opened another front. The strikes spread to Pietermaritzburg, Hammarsdale, Newcastle and other centres in the province and continued until early the following year when they reached their peak. There was sporadic activity in Cape Town, Port Elizabeth and on the Witwatersrand. Opinions vary as to who organised these particular strikes. Some say the strikes were spontaneous. Others maintain that the hand of SACTU was clearly to be seen. Others swear that at some stage BAWU, other trade unionists and even NUSAS were involved. Perhaps all these versions contain some element of truth. What is quite clear is that in the trial of Harry Gwala and others, the state alleged that the accused had played an important role in organising the strikes. It is also true that during the strikes nine SASO officials were among those who were banned. Five of them were later arrested and charged for fomenting feelings of racial hostility. It was part of the state case that they had taken part in the organisation of these strikes. However, the court did not accept the evidence and they were all discharged.

Events beyond South Africa's borders were also setting the pace for political developments in the country and stirring the youth into action. In April 1974 there was a military coup in Portugal. A dictatorship that had lasted several decades and that the Portuguese people had accepted as a way of life was toppled and popular institutions were introduced. The new coalition government, which included communists and socialists, agreed to negotiate with the MPLA in Angola, Frelimo in Mozambique and the PAIGC of Guinea-Bissau and the Cape Verde Islands. The negotiations with Frelimo, which had been fighting the Portuguese for more than 10 years, resulted in the formation of a provisional government in Mozambique on 25 September 1974. SASO decided to celebrate this event on a national level, and, on the weekend of 22 September, announced its decision, adding that Frelimo speakers would be invited to address the rallies.

For more than a decade before this development, South African government spokesmen had denounced Frelimo as a gang of murderers in the pay of communist Russia. The political changes that were now taking place in Mozambique would force South Africa to retrace her steps and were a source of real embarrassment to her. By planning the solidarity rallies SASO was rubbing salt into a wound.

On the same weekend the press announced that the Minister of Justice intended to ban the planned rallies. The students were determined to defy the ban. The stage was set for another ugly confrontation. Indeed, on 25 September there were violent clashes between the students and police at Turfloop. Students were so determined that they forced police to release four students they had arrested earlier.

That evening a large crowd gathered around the entrance of Currie's Fountain singing freedom songs and shouting slogans.[8] The police had cordoned off the place after locking the gates. They followed the same tactics as at Turfloop, dispersing the crowd with dogs and charging them with batons. Several people were arrested. In country-wide raids, homes and offices were searched and many BCM members detained. By the end of the year, no less than 200 people had been detained. Many of them were subjected to torture and other forms of persecution. Many activists had to flee the country. In the meantime, the prestige of SASO and the calibre of its leadership was considerably enhanced.

Thirteen of the members of the BCM arrested from September 1974 (this number was later reduced to nine) were finally charged in the Supreme Court, Pretoria, for conspiring to overthrow the state by violence. It was a show trial full of fireworks. In the tradition of all freedom fighters, the accused carried the fight to the enemy, even inside his own den. They entered the awe-inspiring court packed with police, singing freedom songs, showing the fist, shouting 'Amandla', even exchanging blows with the police. At one stage they dispensed of their lawyers, conducted their own defence and asked the presiding judge to recuse himself. They used the court as a platform from which to explain their views to the people of South Africa. In December 1976 they were all convicted and given sentences ranging from five to six years.

The most important student demonstration and campaign, however, took place in Soweto in June 1976. From Soweto the uprisings spread to other parts of the country. In terms of the numbers of students involved, the nature of demands made, the strength of feeling generated and their duration, these demonstrations were unparalleled in the history of this country. Not even the Sharpeville massacre created such world-wide outcry and damaged the image of South Africa as much as the Soweto uprisings.

The pivot of these riots was Soweto, an African complex of about 38 square kilometres. Although its official population is estimated at 800 000, in fact about a million people live there. According to government policy, Soweto is an area where African workers are temporarily housed and from here they would be removed to the Bantustans upon retirement or upon losing their employment. For this reason trading rights are restricted to small businesses such as groceries, butcheries and dairies. For those who have more ambitious trading schemes facilities are offered in the Bantustans. The white municipality owns the land and Africans live there either as outright tenants or leaseholders.

When the disturbances started, there were 40 state-run secondary schools in Soweto with a total enrolment of 27 000 students. The average man earned between R60 and R70 a month and a woman between R30 and R35.

The term 'city' conveys the idea of a town with a large population, modern buildings and installations, industrial and commercial establishments governed by an autonomous authority that provides its residents with public amenities of various kinds. Although called a city, Soweto is far from that. It has no autonomous authority and is governed by a white statutory body. Apart from one or two special housing schemes where the well-to-do section of the people live, Soweto is an ugly and badly planned collection of matchbox houses consisting of two to four rooms. It is a place of poverty, slums, frustration, bitterness and crime, and about 15 murders are committed there each month.

Prior to 16 June 1976, the Bantu Education Department ordered African schools to use Afrikaans as the medium of instruction. Students, parents and teachers alike greatly resented this and several schools went on strike. A Black Parents Association (BPA) was formed to mobilise the community behind the students. The students demanded the withdrawal of Afrikaans as a medium of instruction, universal and free education for all, the release of all political prisoners, adequate salaries for their parents, and the abandonment of the Bantustan policy. The students demanded further that negotiations on the disputed issues should be conducted directly with the BPA and not with dummy institutions.

These were bold demands. By linking them with the question of the Afrikaans medium of instruction the whole controversy assumed a political character that involved every black.

On 16 June 1976 about 10 000 unarmed students from the primary and secondary schools, the majority of whom were under the age of 20, staged a protest march in Soweto to attract public attention to their demands. During similar demonstrations by white students from the University of the Witwatersrand in 1972 and the University of Cape Town the police were restrained and used relatively moderate methods of crowd control, even though at the former institution, the students were defying a magisterial order forbidding the procession.

But in this particular case involving African students, who had every justification to protest, the police were vicious. They treated the matter as if the liberation army being assembled outside South Africa's borders had broken through and reached the Witwatersrand. They immediately opened fire, killing a child of 16 and injuring many others. All hell broke loose as the enraged students retaliated with everything they could lay their hands on. They stoned the police, burnt down symbols of white power in the townships and boycotted schools. Whilst the first clash between students and police occurred at Naledi Secondary School, the lead in the planned demonstrations was taken by pupils at Morris Isaacson High School. Its principal was later detained. Although the demonstrations revealed widespread opposition to Afrikaans as the medium of instruction, not all the schools were involved at that stage. A Soweto Students' Representative Council (SSRC) was formed under the chairmanship of Tsietsi Mashinini from Morris Isaacson High School to rally all the students behind the demonstrations. This was a shrewd move that brought immediate results. The school boycott was total. Clashes with the police occurred daily as students improvised a variety of weapons, such as petrol bombs, catapults and choppers. Administrative buildings and other installations were razed, members of the Urban Bantu Council were forced to resign and students virtually took over the administration of Soweto as the white power structure collapsed in the area.

In spite of the massacre of several hundred people by the police and the arrest of student leaders, the riots quickly spread to other parts of the Transvaal. A wholly unexpected feature was the spontaneous response of the Coloured people in the Cape Peninsula. Although students at the University of the Western Cape played quite an important role after speakers from SASO and the BPC had addressed them, there was already sporadic and organised action amongst them, which was initiated by Coloured and African youths who were not connected to the university, but who distributed a large number of leaflets in many parts of the Peninsula.

The intervention of university students in co-ordination with secondary-school students and working youth produced even better results. The university students formed a disruption squad that brought lectures to a standstill, forcing the authorities to close the institution earlier than usual.

The Cape Peninsula was in turmoil and the Coloured youth were fighting side by side with their African comrades at a time when Vorster, the Prime Minister, was working hard to lure them away from the Africans.

An exciting aspect of the demonstrations in the Peninsula was the arrest of four Coloured women from the university for acts of sabotage. The state alleged that they had attempted to burn a building. Witnesses refused to testify against them, and those who did gave favourable evidence, which resulted in the collapse of the case for the state.

The demonstrations and riots engulfed the secondary schools in the Eastern Cape and the Orange Free State. Although the administration building was burnt at Ngoye, there were no disturbances in Natal. Solidarity action came from white students at Wits, Cape Town and Natal universities.

The police handled the riots with total disregard for human life. They cruelly shot down schoolchildren, tortured those who fell into their hands and ill-treated those who were jailed.

In Cape Town and Johannesburg the police tried to incite African migrant labourers to attack the demonstrators and the families of known freedom fighters. Innocent people were murdered and injured. Property was damaged or looted under the eyes of the police. The youth found an answer to this manoeuvre as well. They fought the police and the migrants, at the same time carefully explaining to the latter the real issues involved. The tactic proved effective and the police gave up the attempt.

Students learnt that even if the school boycott was a hundred per cent successful, they could not by themselves cripple the economy and bring the government to its knees. This could be achieved only if the workers were mobilised. In pursuance of this goal a general strike was called. The response was poor. Nevertheless, demonstrations continued throughout 1977 and revealed remarkable endurance on the part of the youth.

This country-wide sustained youth resistance movement was greatly encouraged when the authorities were forced to withdraw the instruction enforcing the use of Afrikaans as the medium of instruction. Their guns and paid gangsters had failed to coerce black students, teachers and parents into submission. The black legion had fought and won, in the process emerging as an important force in the country. With the collapse of white-controlled administration in Soweto, a people's governing body, the Committee of Ten, supported by the students and progressive opinion in the area, emerged under the chairmanship of Dr Nthatho Motlana, a well-known freedom fighter and former secretary of the Transvaal branch of the ANC Youth League. His committee at once overshadowed the statutory bodies that administered Soweto and the government repressed it and sent its chairman and committee members to jail.

These achievements indicate the important role the black youth, and especially the students, played during the 1970s, and the vital contribution they are likely to make in future.

Soon after the riots the Minister of Justice, J.T. Kruger, was haunted by the spectre of more than 1 000 embittered black youths who had fled the country and were now squatting in the neighbouring states. In spite of the slaughter of their parents, relations and comrades, they had fought bravely and were conscious of the impact they had made. Events at home had compressed into a few months the political awareness that would otherwise have taken years to develop. From these foreign states they could now see with their own eyes and convince themselves that separate development was indeed a false solution. In the neighbouring states Africans were free, managed their own affairs and lived harmoniously with other population groups.

This army of rebels was now in direct contact with the freedom movement on South Africa's borders and fully exposed to all progressive forces that white South Africa feared most. It is events like Soweto that make children think hard about their own future and that of their country, that drive them to vow to avenge their dead parents and friends, to discover their political idols and to model their own lives on those of past heroes. In these foreign countries they were free to read all kinds of revolutionary literature, to listen to radical political discussions and to the story of the pioneers of our own armed struggle, who fought and fell in Zimbabwe and Mozambique. Now they had the chance of being part of an army with the most cherished mission in life, that of liberating our people and our country. With guerrillas systematically infiltrating South Africa and with the bulk of our units biding time just across the borders, it was a disaster for white South Africa that so many schoolchildren were out of their ghettos. For the first time Kruger regretted his mistake when he realised that, in the course of a few years, he himself would be running away from the same youth that were fleeing from him now. He decided to offer amnesty to all those who decided to come back, but nobody believed him. All that Vorster could do in the circumstances was to squeeze more money from the South African taxpayer, increase the defence budget and strengthen the defence force on the borders.

In desperation, and with the aim of winning more votes in the November 1977 general election, Kruger took what he considered to be the final step to crush the BCM. He cracked down upon them, banning the movement and all its affiliated organisations. Able men and women who once led this army of young people, Ramothibi Tiro, Mthuli Shezi,[9] Steve Biko and others, are no more. They fell fighting, even though without arms, and have joined that long line of South African martyrs whose heroic deeds span the five hundred years of our freedom struggle.

PITFALLS AND FAULT-LINES

It has been said that the successes the BCM achieved have made its members swollen-headed, that the bombastic language that characterises many of their speeches and writings show that they have now lost their original perspectives; that we must guard against the danger of a new movement developing into a third political force which, in spite of its militant language and anti-whitism, will finally ally itself with the enemy as some organisations have done in Namibia and Zimbabwe.

Critics vehemently protest that the BCM should not be raised to anything higher than a mere patrol to scout the terrain, investigate the deployment of enemy forces and to harass its weaker units. It is also said that, although full of fight, it is barely equipped ideologically; that in the past it made headway simply because it was the only legal movement in black politics in the country and received solid encouragement and support from older organisations; that behind it was a seasoned liberation movement that has been in the field of battle for decades and whose growing army is now beginning to strike deep into enemy territory.

There is plenty of evidence to show that until the end of 1976 SASO openly acknowledged the seniority of the ANC and the PAC. There is also evidence that SASO considered its role to be that of filling a vacuum created by the banning of the two older organisations and even worked for their eventual unity. At the 1972 and 1974 SASO conferences the proposal that SASO should form a military wing was heavily defeated and those who were keen on military training were advised to make arrangements with the two organisations.

This healthy attitude prevailed among the members of the BCM when they first came to Robben Island and they exchanged warm fraternal messages with all political prisoners. For some time relations were cordial and we were able to discuss even delicate matters in a comradely spirit. This gave the impression that they were fully committed to unity and our relations were inspired mainly by this fact.

It is not at all clear to what extent the present attitude of the BCM in prison accurately reflects the attitude of the movement as a whole and it is sincerely hoped that the sharp turn in its approach is influenced purely by local factors. But the image the new movement once projected as a neutral body striving for unity has been ruined by the BCM's anti-ANC alliance with the PAC and APDUSA in prison. According to our information there has been a similar change of position abroad and that after an abortive attempt in London to bring together the South African liberation movement at the height of the protests when Steve Biko was murdered, the BCM moved closer to the PAC.

It may well be prophetic to say that the BCM will play the same role in this country as the collaborating organisation in Angola, Namibia and Zimbabwe. Certainly the government welcomed its emergence in the hope that it would ultimately neutralise or even kill any influence of communism and liberalism in black politics. The support the new movement enjoys from the imperialist countries has led to considerable speculation about its role in future. Its present hostility towards the ANC, which works closely with the SACP, gives rise to concern, especially since that hostility is not based on any fundamental policy differences. The main aim of the entire liberation movement in this country is to remove all forms of racism and to introduce a new social order based on the principle of 'one man, one vote'.

The present hostility of the BCM does not justify making harsh judgements and observations about its future role. As a political organisation our judgement should be based on concrete facts and these show that, in spite of its mistakes, the new movement is led by serious-minded political activists who are making a definite contribution to the freedom struggle. That is why Kruger has thrown them into prison, killed their leaders and finally banned their movement.

Few people will deny that there is plenty of arrogance in their speeches and writings and one cannot help but wince from sheer embarrassment at some of their statements. Speaking only to 10 of them, one of them headed his paper 'An address to the nation'. They have also made claims like 'The 1976 SASO case turned Pretoria into a Mecca and increased the radicalisation of the black man in this country', 'It was the result of our efforts that the relations between the ANC and PAC in prison improved', 'We are at the helm and we must be there first' (presumably the first to take power), and 'Only the BCM is known by the people outside prison'.

It is the prerogative of the youth to exaggerate the importance of their organisation and to flex their muscles for everything under the sun just as we did in our younger days. They will probably mellow with time. It also seems irrelevant whether or not commentators consider them to be a mere patrol or more. What is important is to see them as they are and to acknowledge their achievements: to accept them as a body of organised young men and women who are fighting hard for a new South Africa. Equally important is the fact that they had produced their own cadres, theoreticians, writers, theologists and artists and formulated their own policy and tactics. They consider themselves as an independent movement with their own thinkers and ideology, however nebulous it may be.

Their bitterness flows mainly from the assumption that every member of SASO, SASM and NAYO is automatically a member of the BPC, the political mouthpiece of their movement. They also claim as members all those who participated in the demonstrations from 1976 to 1978, and even try to force this ridiculous claim against those who expressly state that they are not members of the BPC. The Freedom Charter and the operations of the ANC today attract many young men and women in the country and this tendency is strong in prison. To the BCM youth who have been made to believe that they were at the helm, it was a real shock to discover only on Robben Island, where it is easy to count those who have common ideals, that after all, the BPC is far weaker than the ANC. Above all, many young people find it difficult to understand how any freedom movement in this country today can ever hope to destroy white supremacy without an army.

In a cosmopolitan environment where common sense and experience demand that freedom fighters be guided by progressive ideas and not by mere colour, the ideology of the BCM remains embryonic and clannish. By opening its membership to all blacks this movement seems well ahead of those that are organised on ethnic grounds. But, while they admit that South Africa is a country where both black and white live and shall continue to live together, they adopt a purely mechanistic approach and brand all whites as oppressors. For this reason whites are excluded from all matters relating to the black man's struggle.

This dogmatism flows from the fact that the concept of Black Consciousness advocated by the BCM is imported from America and swallowed in a lump without regard to our concrete situation, in which progressive whites, including Marxists, liberals, missionaries, professionals and businessmen form part of the liberation movement and fight the enemy with the most militant methods.

Since the early 1920s progressive whites have been active in the struggle, and some of them were charged with fomenting feelings of hostility between the different racial groups, incitement, public violence, sedition, treason and a host of other offences connected with their political activities. Since 1962 no less than 36 white freedom fighters were given heavy sentences for furthering the aims of banned organisations, committing acts of sabotage and for so-called terrorist activities. As far back as 1965 John Harris, a white member of the Liberal Party and the African Resistance Movement (ARM) was executed after committing an act of sabotage. What more can a white man do to identify himself with the black man's struggle than to buy freedom with his own life? To dismiss such martyrs as oppressors is a crime most South African freedom fighters find difficult to excuse.

Such superficialities are peddled by youngsters who entered politics only in the 1970s, who confined themselves to non-violent forms of struggle, who have never committed any significant act of sabotage, nor recruited a single man for military training. The BCM organisations were banned in 1977, almost 30 years after the CPSA, where the most radical white politicians are to be found, was declared illegal. It is true that the South African revolution will be victorious only if the Africans take the lead, and if the African masses are fully mobilised. But the true story of our struggle shows that the fight against racial oppression is not the monopoly of the black man. The founders of the PAC made the same mistake when they defected from the ANC on the grounds, among others, that they were against co-operation with communists, Indians and whites. Later they turned right about, admitted Indians and whites and even sought assistance from foreign communist parties. Now they claim that the PAC has long been a Marxist–Leninist organisation.

Liberation movements in Africa and Asia have used nationalism, which inspires the BCM, to mobilise oppressed people against foreign domination, and this is the main inspiration of the ANC. But in the best traditions of progressive thought the ANC preaches a dynamic and progressive nationalism that seeks to unite Africans, to co-ordinate their struggle with those of other sections of the people at home, including whites, a nationalism that aligns itself with the progressive forces of the whole world. In its work the ANC is guided strictly by the principles set out in the Freedom Charter. Those who help to perpetuate white supremacy are the enemies of the people, even if they are black, while those who oppose all forms of racism form part of the people irrespective of their colour. A freedom movement that rejects this basic principle does so at its own peril.

The idea of Black Consciousness that dominated the BCM comes from the USA, where it has had a long history with many variations. The mechanical manner in which it has been applied to South Africa by the BCM has led to serious policy errors. Black Consciousness is in essence a rehash of Garveyism, a militant form of nationalism, which serves as the rallying point of black opinion in the USA. The Black Muslim and Black Panther movements are today the principal exponents of Black Consciousness in the USA, and, in their struggle to unite blacks, they have turned the idea into a powerful weapon. Its influence was greatly boosted in the 1960s when the world heavyweight boxing champion Muhammad Ali, himself a Black Muslim, refused to fight in Vietnam and chose to be jailed instead. The militant Black Power leader Stokely Carmichael was another prominent American citizen in the campaign against the Vietnam War. The Black Panthers went further to guarantee protection to blacks from whites. With a view to gaining a hold on sources of power and making its influence felt in the country's politics, it contested and won seats on various government organs. All these developments portrayed the Black Power movement as a dynamic concept that helped the black man to advance.

The similarity between the Black Power movement in the USA and in South Africa is striking. The principle upon which it was founded is that the black man must control his own affairs, develop pride in his own history, culture and blackness and reject the moral and cultural values of whites.

Quoting from *Black Power* by Carmichael and Hamilton, Austin Rauney in his book *The Governing of Man* says that the basic tenet of Black Power in America is that blacks must have the singular conviction that they are different from whites, that 'Black is Beautiful', that blacks should reclaim their history and identity from destruction by whites. Although blacks may be willing to accept financial and other forms of aid from whites, black organisations should be led by blacks only and whites must take a subordinate role. No matter how liberal a white person may be, continues Rauney, still quoting Carmichael and Hamilton, he cannot escape the over-powering influence of his whiteness in a racist society. Blacks must abandon all delusions that they can make progress by voluntary surrender of power by whites. Only by mobilising black votes and economic power can this be done. Blacks will never advance by working within the white man's parties or by playing them off against one another. Finally, the American Black Power movement completely rejects the policy of integrating blacks into white society. It is these ideas which SASO took over almost word for word from the book *Black Power* and embodied them in their manifesto without modification. By adopting such an exclusive philosophy the whole BCM assumed the character of a racialistic sect which blindly bundles a section of the progressive forces with the enemy.

A foundation member of the BCM declared that the outlook of the movement is existentialist; that they 'have no time for the dusty manuscripts of Marx and Engels'; that their fight is for a social order based on black communalism. In this statement the BCM seems to be urging South Africa to return to the community of potentially self-sufficient agriculturalists that existed before whites came to our country. Under that system we should live as our ancestors did then, with the land held in common, each household producing its own food, clothing and tools, building its own houses and with no incentive to produce more than was needed for consumption. The emphatic rejection of Marxism by the new movement seems to confirm this view. Although its remnants are still to be found in isolated parts of the country, primitive communal society has been completely shattered by a more advanced capitalist system and to hope that South African society can return to it is a mere pipe dream.

The declaration also suggests that the BCM embraces the philosophy of existentialism. According to this doctrine the individual, in association with his fellow men, his creator and the universe, is the key to the understanding of humanity, history and the universe itself. Even in Europe, where this philosophy began, it has many variations, but substantially all of them embody the above idea.

Another spokesman of the BCM who was well aware of the policy declaration made by his colleague later explained that the declaration expressed the opinion of the individual who made it and not that of his movement. According to him the expression 'black communalism' was a convenient cover for scientific socialism, which the movement embraced right from its establishment, but which it dared not state openly on security grounds. He insisted that the BCM had no intention of going back to the old ways of our forefathers, except to take from our past the humane principle of a man sharing what he has with his fellow men. He, however, challenged the Marxist doctrine, which states that the most crucial contradiction of modern society is its division into two main classes of workers and capitalists, adding that society is far too complicated to be sufficiently explained with such a simple statement. He argued that when Marx formulated these principles he was chiefly concerned with analysing conditions in Europe, which in some respects were fundamentally different from those of other continents, and that Marxism is a vibrant philosophy, the application of which should be dictated by the conditions. Discussing the matter particularly in regard to South Africa he disagreed with the proposition that economic factors are primary and that racism is of secondary importance. To him the position is the other way round and he considered racism to be primary in theory and practice and economic issues secondary.

Finally he pointed out that the term 'existentialism' in the BCM policy documents did not refer to the doctrine of existentialism as explained above, but was intended to stress the fact that the actual application of socialism in any particular country should be determined by the existing conditions and not just follow the formal rules laid down in any particular philosophy.

I readily accepted this explanation on the meaning of existentialism and was certainly happy to know a little more than what appeared in the policy documents of the BCM. But many critics will wonder how it came about that in a considered policy statement in response to a request made by leaders of other sections of the liberation movement such a top BCM member did not take his own colleagues into confidence on such an important issue. The context in which the concept of black communalism appeared and the categorical manner in which the author of the policy declaration rejected Marxism, the basis of scientific socialism, suggests to me that what was at issue was more than a question of caution. If a policy-maker of the BCM is ignorant of the views of his own movement on this issue, how would the masses of the people ever know?

The PAC also spoke with different voices on vital questions. The PAC was barely a year old when it was banned, its leaders restricted and scattered before they could clearly formulate a coherent approach on many pressing issues like African socialism, dialectical materialism, co-operation with other population groups and their attitude towards the SACP and its members. Frequently, enthusiastic spokesmen do not find it easy to admit to outsiders that on a particular point their declared policy needs to be reconsidered.

It is not possible to discuss these questions at length in this essay, but it is reassuring to know that the doctrine of existentialism is not part of this movement's outlook, since it is a philosophy of superstition, individualism and chaos, which can never be used as a basis for solving important social problems. The efforts of all truly radical social reformers are directed towards removing all social evils so that all men can lead a full and happy life. But in a progressive society the welfare of one person is measured by the welfare of society as a whole. Existentialism is really a bourgeois philosophy that cuts across this vital principle and that places the welfare of the individual above that of others. It is the epitome of individualism and anarchy and the antithesis of scientific socialism based on collective effort.

With regard to the 'dusty manuscripts of Marx and Engels,' no serious-minded freedom fighter would reject ideas in theoretical manuscripts that are a blueprint of the most advanced social order in world history, that have led to an unprecedented reconstruction of society and to the removal of all kinds of oppression for a third of mankind. Not even the most headstrong imperialist despises the socialist countries. On the contrary, in the war against Hitler the capitalist countries sought the co-operation of the Soviet Union. That co-operation is taking place today in world bodies, sports, scientific projects and in numerous other fields. Not only does scientific socialism bring security to all men in the form of a just distribution of the country's wealth and the removal of all sources of national and international friction, but the socialist countries are the best friends of those who fight for national liberation. They are giving enormous support to freedom movements all over the world in the form of military and educational training, unlimited quantities of weapons, ammunition, funds, medicine, clothing and other types of help. In world bodies they have condemned colonialism and racism in unequivocal terms and are helping the people of Namibia, Zimbabwe and South Africa to get rid of their racial regimes. Why would a committed freedom fighter have no time for literature containing the outline of a social system that is playing such a key role in the struggle for the liberation of mankind? Is it not significant that an increasing number of African and Asian states are either adopting scientific socialism or emulating important aspects of it? Western countries also help liberation movements in one form or another to prosecute the struggle. But such help is limited to funds and hardly any of them have given arms or military training to liberation movements.

In challenging Marx's theory of the division of society into two classes and the class struggle, the BCM spokesman appears not to have understood the theory at all. *The Communist Manifesto* states that there are two main classes in capitalist society, workers and capitalists, with smaller ones in between, that the fundamental contradiction in contemporary society is the clash of class interests and that the struggle against capitalism will be led by the working class. As the most reliable social force in the fight for socialism, this class will continue to grow whilst the other will be destroyed by the very development of industrialisation. The class struggle is the driving force in the development of society and to sharpen it is the duty of all revolutionaries.

The history of our country bears out Marxist theory. Before the industrialisation of South Africa, Africans were a simple community of peasants who lived by ploughing the land. The process of industrialisation led to the growth of the working class and the corresponding decline of the peasantry, until today the workers have become the biggest single class in the country. This is the revolutionary force on which the liberation movement relies, the force that will eventually overthrow the capitalist system. It is the force to which the Soweto students had to turn at the most critical moment during the 1976 demonstrations. It is this same force that provides MK with the bulk of its soldiers.

With regard to the primacy of economic or spiritual factors, the approach of the BCM spokesman may have been clouded by the fact that at this stage of the struggle the liberation movement is faced with the dual problem of national oppression and class exploitation. The concern of the liberation movement and its immediate task is the removal of the former evil, not because national oppression is primary, but because its destruction will pave the way for the eventual elimination of economic exploitation. This is a question of strategy. The fight against racism demands the maximum unity of all the people, who may differ fundamentally on the type of social order to be established after liberation. For this reason we deliberately do not stress the economic aspect.

In this country racism has been exploited by the white capitalist class to defend its economic interests and to secure the support of the whites as a whole for the maintenance of the system. The removal of white supremacy with all the racism that accompanies it will put political power in the hands of the people. The mere disappearance of racism will still leave intact many social evils. The white man will still be in control economically, monopolising all the resources of the country. But the destruction of class society will itself go a long way towards eliminating racial thinking. This is one of the reasons why racism cannot thrive in socialist countries. A final point is that although economic factors are primary over the spiritual, ideas also react on economic factors. In our country racism, even though it forms part of the superstructure, has been an important factor in shaping the economy. The fabulous wealth accumulated by whites and their high standard of living is a result of the pitiless exploitation of the black man.

Political critics have expressed concern over the support the BCM enjoys from the USA and over the movement's hostility to the Soviet Union. In this regard the new movement is again in a position similar to that of the PAC, the formation of which brought a new element into South African politics. The US State Department even inflated the number of its membership and deflated ours to boost the PAC. Officials from the American embassy in South Africa held regular discussions with leaders of the organisation and even paid them friendly visits in prison. At the same time American writers praised the extreme nationalism of the PAC, openly stating that its ideology was the best guarantee against a communist take-over in South Africa.

The PAC and BCM members have been equally critical of the close co-operation between the ANC and the SACP, as well as of the help the ANC receives from the Soviet Union. They have joined Western spokesmen and conservatives in accusing us of being a communist front and the tools of the Soviet Union. In actual fact, the ANC welcomes support from both the capitalist and socialist countries and has many friends in the West who give material and moral support. But as already pointed out, the support we receive from the Soviet Union and other socialist countries is far greater than what our Western friends have so far offered.

In helping the ANC and other freedom movements, the socialist countries are motivated by the desire to see all human beings running their own affairs and living happily. If they have any ulterior motive in helping us it is simply the knowledge that the freedom of any oppressed nation is a blow to imperialism and an advantage to socialism, a worthy motive that accords with the aspirations of any freedom-loving people throughout the world. This is why the Soviet Union plays such an important role in the struggle of the Vietnamese people against American aggression, of the people of Angola, Mozambique and Portuguese Guinea against Portuguese colonialism. The support the socialist countries are giving SWAPO, the Patriotic Front of Zimbabwe and the ANC is similarly motivated. In all these countries the USA has been on the opposite side. In Vietnam she was the aggressor, in Angola and Cabinda she supported the FNLA, FLEC and now UNITA, in Mozambique Adelimo Gwambe's Udenamo, all of which were anti-communist. It is appropriate to ask what imperialist America's ulterior motive is in supporting the PAC and the BCM now. Is there something in their policies and activities that encourages the USA to believe that the victory of these organisations can also advance their imperial interests?

A related question is that the amount of funds an organisation possesses and the way they are derived are normally an important yardstick to measure the strength and independence of an organisation and to assess its real as opposed to its apparent policy. An organisation is definitely in a commanding position if a substantial part of its budget comes from its internal sources, from the activities of its own members and from the public in general. This will give it greater scope for independent action. For one thing it will show that the masses of the people identify themselves with its aims and objectives.

Delicate problems may, however, arise if practically all the funds are donated by a single or small group of generous benefactors. It is not easy to investigate this aspect of an organisation's affairs: it is far better if it is volunteered. What is quite clear is that despite its 10 years of existence as a legal movement, the BCM never embarked on a serious drive for funds from the black public – yet it was swimming in money. Almost all its funds came from external sources. The size of its revenue and expenditure could not, therefore, be used to gauge its popular strength.

At best the size of its funds merely indicates that its policy and activity are acceptable to those who subsidise it. A political movement that puts forward a realistic and thoroughgoing socialist programme, as several liberation movements in southern Africa now do, or which closely work with the SACP, is no investment option for American big business. Many political observers believe that American imperialism has chosen to support the BCM in order to stem developments towards socialism.

Although on ideological questions the BCM speaks with an uncertain voice, the movement is clear as to who the enemy is and has rightly concentrated its attack on separate development, Bantu Education and dummy institutions. Despite the fact that its achievements in this field are far less than those of older organisations, it has nevertheless done well.

A controversial question is which organisation should receive credit for the 1976 demonstrations and whether the aftermath that was still erupting in 1978 was the work of the same organisation. In spite of all its setbacks that campaign scored notable victories. The withdrawal of Afrikaans as the medium of instruction has already been mentioned. In Soweto the demonstrations led to a closure of the schools, followed by large-scale resignation of teachers. The riots also led to the abolition of Urban Bantu Councils and forced the government to establish the new machinery of Community Councils, though with limited powers. So effective was the resistance to these dummy institutions, that only 3 600 of the 60 000 registered voters, mainly the older people, went to the polls. The so-called mayor of Soweto managed to gain only 97 votes.

The very success of the demonstration had made the question as to who organised them even more complicated, with several organisations and many individuals making conflicting statements. But there are concrete facts that cannot simply be brushed aside in searching for an answer.

The Minister of Justice tried to justify the banning of the BCM on the grounds that, although the BCM had first worked well, it was later infiltrated by the ANC. The Minister is the political head of the department, one of whose functions is to deal with questions of state security and to watch developments in black politics. He is expected to know what he is talking about, but his statements should be treated with caution for they may be plain propaganda to frighten whites to support the Nationalist government.

In a London television interview Tsietsi Mashinini, Chairman of the SSRC, told the world that, although the demonstrations had started spontaneously, the ANC subsequently stepped in and directed the campaign. Few people would ignore the considered statement of a man who played a leading role in planning and directing the demonstrations. For once in the course of the disturbances Kruger and Mashinini spoke the same language, a fact which adds some weight to Kruger's statement.

According to evidence given before the Cillié Judicial Commission on the Soweto riots, people like W.B. Ngakane and Winnie Mandela, whose association with the ANC is well known, were members of the Executive Committee of the BPA, which also featured prominently during these demonstrations. In fact, Kruger deported Winnie Mandela to the Orange Free State on the express allegation that she had incited the youth to riot.

The comment of *Die Burger* shortly before the November 1977 general election, on the review of the Soweto disturbances by the London office of the SACP, also indicates that the ANC and SACP were deeply involved. The newspaper report is obviously slanted, but it also contains interesting quotations and observations. According to a report, Soweto disappointed the ANC and the SACP for they had hoped that the demonstrations would mark the beginning of a people's revolution. Apparently the analysis posed the important question why the ANC after 16 years of a preparation for armed struggle was not in a position to arm the people and to ensure that the demonstrations would be backed up by effective action against the enemy army and the police. 'The greatest obstacle to an armed rebellion is the extremely difficult and unfavourable internal and external conditions under which we had to work ... When Soweto burst out our military structure was not strong enough.' In my view, in the light of the present situation among the African people in this country, the SACP could not have seriously hoped that a peaceful demonstration of unarmed African schoolchildren could have led to an insurrection. But it is clear from the report that the SACP approached the whole issue as an involved party having expected better results than those actually achieved. Apart from Mashinini's statement and others referred to above, there are the first-hand accounts from individuals who were directly involved in the demonstrations in various parts of South Africa and who were sentenced for taking part in them. Amongst these are ANC members who are also members of SASM, the organisation that led the demonstrations. One should remember that the ANC is an illegal organisation and if any of its members joined SASO, SASM, NAYO or any of the organisations claimed by the BCM, they would not burn their fingers by disclosing that fact to outsiders. In 1977 young people like Naledi Tsiki and Elias Masinga were charged under the Terrorism Act and evidence indicated that they were members of the ANC as well as SASM. A leading member of the internal wing of the ANC put the matter in a nutshell when he said: 'The ANC did not initiate the uprising but found itself in control.'

It is now common knowledge, especially on Robben Island, that the majority of students and working youth who took part in the demonstrations were not even members of SASM. In fact the SSRC was only set up after the first part of activities in the area because it was realised that, up to that stage, SASM was not representative of all students in Soweto schools. Many of those who later came in merely joined a student movement and had no political affiliations at all. Even more important was that they did not consider themselves members of the BPC – the political mouthpiece of the entire BCM. This was the position in other areas as well, especially in the Eastern Cape. The BCM people were shocked to note that the youth who were sentenced for their involvement in the riots and whom they wrongly assumed were their members, were in actual fact more inspired by the activities of MK and were keen to join it. This discovery made them aware of their shaky positions as individual organisations and is the main cause of the strained relations between the ANC on the one hand and the BCM and APDUSA on the other. Although the exact scope of the anti-ANC alliance here in prison, as well as that of the PAC faction abroad with which the BCM now works, is not altogether clear, the step may prove disastrous for the BCM because part of its success was due to the goodwill and co-operation it got from the ANC, a fact which members openly acknowledged on arrival on Robben Island.

This is an appropriate moment to point out that the ANC has used the slogan 'Amandla' and the clenched salute since 1960, when the ANC was banned. People frequently ask how it came about that the BCM, which emerged in the early 1970s, uses the same slogan and salute. This issue has led to considerable speculation. Some feel that the BCM uses the slogan and salute as part of its exotic outfit of ideas, imported lock, stock and barrel from the USA. Others regard it an action of men who considered themselves heirs of an organisation they dismissed as defunct. Maybe our members working in the BCM induced them to do so.

There are several questions on which the BCM ought to examine its approach to fulfilling its mission as part of the country's liberation movement. One of these is its policy on Afrikaans. Like many people inside and outside the liberation movement, BCM members have strong objections to the use of Afrikaans. The objection is quite understandable since Afrikaans is not only the language of the oppressor, but has also produced a literature that portrays the black man in a bad light. However, Afrikaans is the language of a substantial section of the country's blacks and any attempts to deprive them of their language would be dangerous. It is the home language of 95 per cent of the Coloured population and is used by Indians as well, especially in the country *dorps* of the Transvaal. It is also widely spoken by the African youth in the urban areas. Even if only Afrikaners spoke the language it would still be unwise to abolish it. Language is the highest manifestation of social unity in the history of mankind and it is the inherent right of each group of people to use its language without restriction. Not only would its abolition be out of step with progressive developments in the enlightened world, but also it would be inviting endless strife. The question of minority rights has been of major concern to progressive forces throughout history and has often led to sudden and violent strife from the aggrieved community. Today South Africa has almost three million Afrikaners who will no longer be oppressors after liberation but a powerful minority of ordinary citizens whose co-operation and goodwill are needed in the reconstruction of the country. One can think of no better way of turning South Africa into turmoil than to implement this proposal.

Precisely because Afrikaans is the language of the oppressor we should encourage our people to learn it, its literature and history and to watch new trends among Afrikaner writers. To know the strength and weakness of your opponent is one of the elementary rules in a fight. Past mistakes in the liberation movement – the contempt for the Afrikaner, over-confidence on our part and expectations of easy victory – have all been a result of our ignorance of this group and have led to disillusionment on our part. With proper planning and better knowledge of Afrikaans we can speak directly to a wider audience and win more Bram Fischers, Jack Simonses, Piet Voegelses and Breyten Breytenbachs.

It is better to draw a clear distinction between the oppressive policies of a dominating racial group and the language in which those policies are enunciated. We fight the former and not the latter. The German language has been used in committing the greatest atrocities in human history and for the perpetuation of the most offensive theories of race superiority. During the Second World War almost all nations rallied to resist Nazism and its atrocities. Yet nobody has suggested the abolition of that language. It is today the official language of the German Democratic Republic, which was founded on the ruins of Hitlerite Germany, and it is freely spoken in some of the socialist countries bordering the GDR.

Contrary to Afrikaans, English is an international language and to master it is in our own interests. While our people are repelled by the crude racism of the Afrikaner, they are attracted by the well-established tradition of liberalism in British political thought and by the fact that Britain has for centuries provided asylum to all kinds of political refugees. However, the English are still important partners in our oppression today. Why should our people not be invited to boycott the English language also and to demand its abolition after liberation?

Our English background has aggravated our strong feelings against the Afrikaner, and we inherited certain attitudes from the English who have their own reasons for despising the Afrikaner. Our forefathers eulogised Queen Victoria and her successors, were baptised and educated by English missionaries, bought their goods at English stores and were until recently ruled by English magistrates. English is the common language of the liberation movement and many of our political refugees sought asylum in England, from where our own affairs were directed for some time. In the process we have become 'black Englishmen', and that has many advantages.

The superficial manner in which the BCM has handled the Afrikaans question is very similar to the fanaticism with which they harp on the word 'black', and to their attempt to show that it is politically incorrect to speak of Africans, Coloureds and Indians. There is merit in saying that in our present situation, where the enemy is trying hard to split the oppressed people into small and parochial ethnic units, we should stress, wherever possible, those concepts that help us discover a common identity and to avoid those that may fall into the hands of the enemy. In this regard the positive concept of 'black' is of immense significance and is far in advance of the negative 'non-white' or 'non-European', which describe us in terms of what we are not, instead of what we are. This positive approach is used in the opening sentence of the preamble to the Freedom Charter: 'We, the people of South Africa, declare ... that South Africa belongs to all who live in it, black and white ...' But any form of fanaticism on political questions is undesirable and may blur the importance of ideas that are otherwise widely welcomed by the liberation movement.

To say that race is a myth and that in our country there are no Africans, Coloureds and Indians, but only blacks, is to play with words. The main ethnological divisions of mankind are acknowledged by bourgeois and Marxist anthropologists and those from the so-called uncommitted world. People can observe them with the naked eye. Physical characteristics – the colour of the skin and the texture of the hair – can be observed by merely looking at a painting of Chaka and one of Napoleon, at Tambo and Dadoo, Kotane and Reggie September. In addition to the colour of their skins and the texture of their hair they differ in historical origins and in their culture and languages. What is a myth is the theory that there is a pure race, for miscegenation has taken place throughout the world since the dawn of history. It has also affected this country, and many leading white families who are so obsessed with the idea of racial purity are themselves of mixed blood. Science and experience have also shown that no race is inherently superior to others, and this myth has been equally exploded whenever blacks and whites are given equal opportunity for development. But race as such exists in the world, and in our country there is nothing wrong with using the terms African, Coloured and Indian in appropriate cases.

Linked with the above issue is the charge that, far from developing non-racial thinking, the Congress structure – which embraces separate organisations for the four different population groups – entrenches racial thinking since it is a perpetual reminder that we differ from one another.

The Freedom Charter is the most radical programme ever proclaimed by the national movement in this country, and the historic mass campaigns of the last three decades, in which all the national groups joined, were inspired by the Congress movement. Among the better known of these campaigns are those of 26 June 1950, the 1952 Defiance Campaign in which 8 500 volunteers were jailed, the 1955 Congress of the People, which 3 000 delegates from all parts of the country attended, the 1956 anti-pass demonstrations to Pretoria in which 20 000 women took part, the 1958 Witwatersrand general strike which also affected Pretoria, the Eastern Cape, Durban and other areas, and the anti-pass campaign of 1958 to 1959 in which about 4 000 African and Coloured women were arrested in various parts of the country.

The effectiveness of the Congress structure is also shown by the number of people from all national groups who have either appeared before the courts or who have been imprisoned for political offences. Of the 156 people involved in the Treason Trial from 1956 to 1961, 105 were African, 23 white, 21 Indian and 7 Coloured. Freedom fighters from the Congress movement who were imprisoned during the period from 1968 to 1977 for MK activities, furthering the aims and objects of the ANC or SACP, include no less than 28 whites, 20 Indians and 8 Coloureds. The number of Africans runs into four figures.

No Coloureds or Indians have actually appeared in court or been jailed for PAC activities, but 3 Coloureds were associated with this organisation while serving their respective sentences on Robben Island. From the NEUM a total of 2 Indians, 2 Coloureds and 11 Africans were convicted for political offences during the same period. Between 1963 and 1973 there was, however, a splinter group from the NEUM called the National Liberation Front with 9 Coloured prisoners and 9 Africans, which voluntarily dissolved before its members left jail. But during the period under review only 2 Indians and 8 Coloureds were convicted for activities of the BCM.

Political trials alone and the racial composition of people who are convicted for political offences are not by themselves decisive in determining the effectiveness of a political structure.

But linked with the mass political campaigns mentioned above, the figures show that our machinery for joint action is the best in the country and suits our unique situation. Abroad, where conditions are totally different, the membership of the ANC is open to all groups and the innovation is working well. Even inside the country all groups are free to join the ANC, but internal conditions affect the full implementation of the experiment.

The history of the struggle in this country, over the last 30 years, demonstrates that there is no substance in the allegation that the Congress structure encourages racist thinking amongst the people.

The BCM criticises those who refer to our country as South Africa and to this island as Robben Island instead of Azania and Makana Island respectively. All its members scrupulously avoid the former two names and consistently use the latter. Whilst it is not clear why the name Azania was chosen, there is nothing wrong with the liberation movement giving a new name to our country, and in doing so, the movement is following the example of many countries on becoming independent. Ghana, Mali, Namibia, Zimbabwe and many other names are associated with the independence of these countries. The change was inspired amongst other things by the natural desire to cut all links with the imperialist countries that had previously ruled these countries or that still ruled them and to enter the international community in their own name and right.

But in all these countries the names were carefully chosen and formed part of their history. The names Ghana and Mali are taken from ancient kingdoms of precisely the same names and on whose ruins new African republics were established, while the Namib desert and the Zimbabwe ruins are prominent in the geography and culture of Namibia and Zimbabwe respectively. None of these countries have chosen an exotic name couched in a language unknown even to our intellectuals. 'Azania' has very little connection with our country's history and means nothing to our people. In his book *Old Africa Rediscovered*, Basil Davidson quotes from the old Greek pilot book, *The Periphis of the Erythraen Sea*, which he says contains fairly detailed information on the African coast. It describes the coast of Azania as that of Kenya and Tanganyika. It is clear from Davidson's account that Swahili was the language of this particular coastal region and that by the seventh and eighth centuries AD the culture of the area had become Islamic. The author also describes the longest Azanian road from Kenya that linked the head of Lake Nyasa with Arusha and Nairobi. Quite clearly this account confines Azania to East Africa and does not include southern Africa. Swahili has never been our language and Islam reached our country only when the Malay slaves were imported during the seventeenth century and through the Indian community during the second half of the nineteenth century.

It may well be that the naming of South Africa as Azania was influenced by the fact that, somewhere during our journey from the far north and our stay in the vicinity of the Great Lakes, as legend says, we were known as Azanians. But at one time or other in history many famous kingdoms were established around our route – Egypt, Cush and Nubia. Precisely for what reason must we choose to call ourselves Azanians and not Egyptians, Cushites or Nubians? Our country is rich in its own history and there is no need to venture out into the mists of ancient Africa, Greece and Arabia in search of a name.

As far as Robben Island is concerned, it is understandable that Xhosas in the past may have called it after Makana, since in those days they thought as Xhosas rather than as Africans and even much less as blacks. After all, Makana was a leader who commanded an army of 18 000 in 1890 and who devastated white areas for several months. His people were greatly disappointed by his banishment and deeply shocked by his unexpected death when trying to swim from the island to the mainland. They knew very little or nothing of the history of other indigenous peoples of South Africa or about the men who were deported here long before Makana's time.

It is not clear why in the twentieth century a political movement could endorse the use of a name which ignores the contribution of heroes who were the first to be associated with Robben Island or who at least equally deserve to be so honoured. Quite a number of people, including condemned prisoners or rebelling crews of passing ships, were sent to the island from the beginning of the seventeenth century. In 1658 the first black patriot, Autshumao, known to white historians as Harry the Strandloper, was banished here. After living upon the island for 17 months he escaped to the mainland. He was followed in 1742 by Sheik Motura, who had fought the Dutch in his homeland, Batavia. He lived on the island until his death in 1754 and a shrine that brings his followers to this island regularly hallows his memory. Why would Makana's name be preferred above these prisoners? It cannot be because Autshumao, as a Khoi-khoi chieftain with a small following, was regarded as inferior to the Bantu-speaking army leader, nor could it be owing to the fact that the other was a Muslim religious leader from a foreign country. Freedom fighters cannot be subjected to such discrimination and have been honoured by progressive forces in other parts of the world. All they need to do to deserve honour is to suffer or die for a great cause. That is why distant countries have honoured men like Albert Luthuli, Bram Fischer and Patrice Lumumba.

The naming of the country is an important matter and ought never to be approached from a competitive point of view. It requires maximum unity and careful consultation, not only with all sections of the liberation movement, but also with the masses of the people. The whole liberation movement and the entire world may enthusiastically brandish a new name, but if the masses of the people feel that it is a meaningless foreign importation, it can never catch on. It is worse when a political organisation, which is locked up in faction fights abroad like the PAC and which is conducting no effective struggle at home, seeks to impose such a far-fetched name unilaterally.

It is equally regrettable that the BCM should seize upon the name and wave it about in practically every speech. When the liberation movement finally agrees on a suitable name it would be advisable to use it sparingly at first as part of a campaign for mass mobilisation and to prepare people for contemplated changes in the history of the country. To the average man, as opposed to the intellectual or propagandist, the new name will assume real significance only when the struggle has reached an advanced stage and especially when certain areas have been liberated and a people's government is in power there. Otherwise many critics will rightly say that the use of the name is nothing more than creating a revolution by word of mouth.

The great divide in South Africa is the demand for full democratic rights for all people, for the removal of all racial discrimination and for total rejection of separate development. On this, the liberation movement speaks with one voice. Following in the footsteps of other South African freedom fighters, the BCM has from the beginning made the overthrow of apartheid its chief plank and it is today among the most uncompromising opponents of white supremacy. All its important campaigns have revolved around this issue. They firmly realised that real progress in this country will be made only after separate development has been completely smashed.

The liberation movement has not only rejected separate development in principle, but has also fought it through concrete action. The liberation movement has resolved to boycott all elections to dummy institutions and has urged the nations of the world not to grant diplomatic recognition to the independent Bantustans. Our campaign on the international level is not only intended to isolate South Africa from the rest of the world, but is also a means of forcing her to abandon separate development at home and to accept the principle of one man one vote without qualification. Fighting separate development involves the use of the boycott weapon, a controversial issue that has aroused heated debate in many countries where the weapon has been used. Freedom fighters naturally object to discriminatory institutions and do not want to be associated at all with them even for strategic reasons. Moreover, the boycott weapon can also be a severe test for any political organisation and its success or failure can affect the future of that organisation. It is the type of weapon that can easily recoil and show that the organisation has no mass following and thus boost political parties that collaborate with the enemy. Because the enemy controls its dummy institutions and the entire voting machinery and therefore has considerable scope for all kinds of political manoeuvres, the weapon requires sustained initiative and flexibility on the part of the organisation using it, demanding that it should remain on its toes all the time. These problems have at one time or another faced us.

In this regard the ANC and the NEUM have always been poles apart, the latter treating the whole question of the boycott as one of principle and refusing any exception. Those who for any reason work within these dummy institutions are to the NEUM not just politically wrong, but traitors. Presumably, this would be the case even if the organisation that may elect candidates to these bodies on a boycott ticket is the most advanced in the country in terms of waging guerrilla warfare and committing acts of sabotage and even if it succeeded in crippling or destroying such institutions from inside. In its approach to this question the NEUM is guided not by concrete results but by abstract principle. Those who stand aloof and merely fight separate development and its institutions by word of mouth are considered as revolutionaries by the NEUM. But those who go further to capture and use them to reach the people and to prevent the people from using them as originally planned or who kill and paralyse them in the process are deemed collaborators.

The BCM has also taken this inflexible line and has gone further by inserting a clause in the constitution of the BPC that expressly prohibits members from taking part in the elections to government institutions. Like the NEUM it also recognises no difference between principle and tactics and does not fully appreciate the value of combining legal and illegal work.

A banned organisation depends for its existence on its illegal work and it is vital for it to build efficient underground machinery. Almost all its resources should be concentrated on this task and from time to time it must publicly announce its existence through various forms of political activity. This is the approach of the ANC and the correctness of that approach has been shown by results.

Though banned in 1960, the organisation has never been completely silenced. Various forms of activity demonstrate that it is much alive even though it might be acting under a different name. In March 1961 it held an All-in-Africa Conference attended by 1 500 delegates from all over the country. It called upon the government to summon a National Convention of all South Africans to draw up a democratic constitution. Two months after that conference the ANC called a general strike, followed in December 1961 by acts of sabotage, which continued for three years.

As numerous court cases have shown, in spite of the ban, the ANC continues recruiting members and holding secret meetings, sending out recruits for military training and for study purposes, broadcasting to the people of South Africa, distributing various forms of propaganda material and preparing for armed warfare. Our men have fought the enemy in Zimbabwe and are now doing so inside the country and on its borders. In spite of the counter-measures taken by the enemy, our operations are growing and our fighters are gaining experience and confidence. Government spokesmen, including the Ministers of Justice and Defence, the Commissioner of Police and the head of the Security Police, have repeatedly warned white South Africa about the impending civil war. Our underground work within the country is our trump card and the stronger that underground machinery becomes, the nearer will freedom day be.

At the same time, the ANC has not ignored the legal forms of struggle and, through legal organisations, we are constantly striving for mass activity on a large scale, trying to mobilise all anti-apartheid forces, even those outside the liberation movement, in spite of the fact that their fighting methods may fall short of ours. We will use dummy institutions once we are convinced that to do so will strengthen the struggle and hasten the enemy's downfall.

It is important to remember that the situation in the Bantustans changes from time to time. Though we reject the Bantustans, it will be disastrous if our tactics in fighting them remain stereotyped. Two Bantustans have already become independent and the rest may soon follow. It is correct for liberation movements to campaign against their diplomatic recognition and to claim them as still part of our country. It is also correct to say that these areas will remain caricatures of independence and not real states. In fact, few things illustrate the meanness with which the government carries out the scheme of separate development, and its contempt for the black man who is collaborating to make the scheme work, better than the fragmentary nature of each Bantustan. By May 1972 only QwaQwa was composed of one block of territory, while the others consisted of a number of fragments, in one case scattered over three provinces. KwaZulu had then as many as 29 and Bophuthatswana and Ciskei 19 each. Although some measure of consolidation has since been attempted, these areas still remain hopelessly fragmented. For the people of these territories that independence means something. At least they now have their own independent organs of government, their army and police, their education and health schemes and they control their external relations. They can own freehold land, have access to sources of capital, invest in big business and hold top jobs in the civil service. We cannot expect them to throw away the opportunities they now enjoy, come back to the present racist South Africa with their Bantustans and be subjected to all the evils of apartheid again.

Prior to 26 October 1976, when the Transkei obtained independence, many people inside and outside the liberation movement doubted whether the Nat government would ever grant such independence on the grounds, among others, that an independent Bantustan might give bases to freedom movements from which to attack South Africa. This is a possibility that has occurred in similar circumstances in other parts of the world. Who would have thought that Tunisia and the kingdom of Morocco, both of which were once considered, rightly or wrongly, as the puppets of France, could offer bases to Algeria to fight France?

In *Die Burger* of 25 April 1978, Chris Vermaak disclosed that it was the opinion of South African security experts that, should the Transkei carry out its threats and offer bases to freedom fighters, this would constitute a serious bridgehead for subversive activity. He added that should the territory allow the ANC presence with a view to strengthen its case for recognition by Africa, this would shorten the ANC's logistic lines and thus remove a great deal of the ANC's burden on Mozambique. These are possibilities which should not be ignored and which must, short of diplomatic recognition, influence our tactics towards any independent Bantustan. People in these areas can also be mobilised to join in the demand for majority rule in this country and for the eventual return of all Bantustans to a free South Africa.

Our strategy on separate development must also be seen in the context of the world situation and be related not only to the international forces on our side, but also to forces that try to checkmate militant liberation movements. Free elections have become a fetish in the West and the older generation of Western-educated freedom fighters has been taught to regard such elections as an acceptable method of settling major national issues. Common sense and experience have taught us to approach this question realistically and not idealistically.

An election involving a liberation movement that has been waging an armed struggle for years against a colonial and semi-colonial power and its black puppets is a critical affair, and freedom fighters are likely to insist on the fulfilment of the most stringent conditions before they can participate in such elections. An illegal or semi-illegal organisation enters such an election at a serious disadvantage. Usually its leaders will have been jailed or immobilised, or they will have been forced to flee, with the machinery of their organisation destroyed. The organisation will also have to overcome the stigma, projected for many years through various enemy propaganda agencies, of being an organisation of criminals who only want to murder and rape, of acting under the orders of some foreign communist power. To win an election under such circumstances would be a difficult task, since the organisation would have to start from scratch and depend for victory on a voting process still controlled by the enemy, whose limitless funds and propaganda machinery would be at the disposal of its stooges.

In Angola and Mozambique the imperialists tried this tactic, and in the latter country Frelimo, which was in a commanding position with almost all the country's leading freedom fighters behind it, promptly rejected the proposal. In Angola the imperialists were caught unawares by an entirely new development in the history of the struggle for national independence in Africa when Cuba and the Soviet Union intervened on the side of the people.

In Namibia and Zimbabwe the imperialists are trying desperately to forestall what happened in Angola and are using the technique of 'free' elections under a UN peace force. This move is creating problems for our allies there.

When Namibia and Zimbabwe have become independent and our own armed struggle is intensified, the imperialists might use this strategy in an even more sophisticated manner, requiring us to streamline our own tactics and intelligence. The central idea is to entrench ourselves firmly by involving the masses of the people inside the country in our own programme and, with this in mind, no organisation or individual fighting against racial domination should be alienated. In this way, the ANC will easily become the country's strongest organisation in armour and negotiation, behind the ramparts and at the ballot box.

THE CHALLENGE OF ILLEGALITY

The BCM emerged 30 years after the banning of the CPSA, 10 years after that of the ANC and PAC and 36 months after the ANC had started armed operations. Eight months after this historic development a PAC unit of 12 armed men on their way to South Africa, escorted by the Mozambique Revolutionary Committee, fought with a Portuguese patrol in Mozambique. In 1973 the Natal Supreme Court convicted 12 NEUM men and gave them sentences ranging from five to eight years on the allegation that they were engaged in preparations for guerrilla warfare.

These events should have made the BCM aware that the liberation movement has a long and proud record of struggle that dwarfs its own successes. For decades the liberation movement agitated and campaigned against racial discrimination, waged countless militant battles and made some notable gains. In this context, the contribution of the Indian community has been impressive and in the course of its struggle it built an organisation that up to the present remains its mouthpiece. The government's hesitation to have a freely elected South African Indian Council springs from the fear that the Indian people might paralyse this dummy institution, just as the Asiatic Land Tenure and Indian Representation Act was torpedoed in 1946.

The first Indians to arrive in this country were indentured labourers mainly of Hindu origin, who worked on the Natal sugar plantations. They were followed later by businessmen and other Indians, chiefly Muslims. The labourers were badly treated, underpaid, frequently flogged for minor offences and imprisoned for absence from work. They suffered many other indignities. At that time the business class kept aloof from the labourers and believed that close co-operation with the ruling class was the best way to advance their interests and those of the community.

This was a typical middle-class attitude, but in the South African setting it contained numerous contradictions. Because Indians offered economic competition, the government imposed various restrictions and discriminatory practices on them. Opportunistically the ruling class welcomed collaboration from the Indian segment of the oppressed, so that it could concentrate its attacks on the African people, whom it considered the real threat to white supremacy. Although class divisions, caste, religion, language and other differences divided the Indian community in South Africa it was spared the Hindu–Muslim communal strife that tore India apart. As the smallest community here they realised that it would be suicidal to be divided among themselves. The quest for unity was given expression by Gandhi when he formed the Natal Indian Congress in 1894. It was through the conscious efforts of the NIC, the TIC and, since 1920, the South African Indian Congress that the Indian community was finally welded together as a political force.

One of the tasks the NIC, as the oldest political organisation in the country, set itself was to unite the Indian community in the fight against racism. It inculcated in the people a spirit of self-reliance and dispelled the illusion that collaboration with the ruling class would serve their interests.

From 1906 the NIC and the TIC launched a series of passive resistance campaigns which drew wide support. These culminated in the 1913 mass campaign, when Natal Indians crossed into the Transvaal in defiance of provincial barriers and, simultaneously, Indian coal miners in Natal went on strike. These and other mass campaigns further united and politicised the Indian community. The workers' level of political consciousness, their emphatic rejection of racial discrimination and their readiness to make sacrifices to win their demands were firmly laid in those days. In initiating passive resistance they forged a powerful weapon, which was effectively used later by other sections of the oppressed people.

The SAIC was foremost in drawing world attention to the evils of racism in South Africa and actively campaigned against the oppression of all blacks. This culminated in the Xuma–Dadoo–Naicker Pact of 1948. Although traditionally associated with non-violence, Indians also saw the need to change to more effective methods of political action when conditions demanded this. The SAIC is still a lawful organisation, but some of its members were among the first to join MK and are today playing an important role in its activity.

Attempts to unite black political organisations have also been made by leading figures from other sections of the oppressed, notably by Dr Abdullah Abdurahman, the President of the APO. In 1927 and in 1933 he called conferences of leaders for this purpose. Although the proposal was not accepted, the issue had been thrown open to the public and occupied the minds of the far-sighted.

The APO was far ahead of all other sections of the liberation movement in this regard. Though the APO was ostensibly an organisation for Coloureds, it was also open to Africans and Indians, and its very conception indicates a strong desire for wider unity. To its founders the word 'African' meant not only the Bantu-speaking people, but all those who had made Africa their permanent home.

The present generation of youth mistakenly thinks that the quest for black unity was unknown before their emergence. In fact, black unity has a long history going back as far as 1795, when the Amagqunukhwebe Chief Cungwa and the Khoi-khoi leader Klaas Stuurman jointly attacked the Vanderleurs army in the Zuurveld. When the Xhosa army was locked in battle against the English during the Eighth War of Dispossession in 1850 another Khoi-khoi leader, Willem Uithaalder, seized the opportunity and led his people from the Kat River against the common foe and took Fort Armstrong. The efforts made by Moshoeshoe and Cetshwayo in uniting Africans against white aggression are well known.

Perhaps Abdurahman, aware of this background, consciously made this move at that particular time because in 1927 there was great agitation among Africans, especially at the passing of the Natives Administration Act. The law gave powers to the governor-general to break up and move tribes, and to deport people arbitrarily. It curbed freedom of speech under the pretext of a so-called fomenting of feelings of hostility between the various racial groups.

But Abdurahman was ahead of his times. By insisting on a single organisation to unite all the oppressed people, he encroached on the delicate problem of the independence of the organisations involved. A lot of spadework has to be done before realising this superstructure. This is the practical problem the BCM overlooked in its crusade for black unity, and this is why there is a hollow ring to its sermons on this issue. Apart from specific problems that affected black students at the various campuses, the BCM as such did not attract significant support from the Coloured and Indian communities, and is predominantly an African movement.

The APO faded out in the 1940s and from the early 1950s the Coloured People's Organisation (later Congress) became the main channel through which the ANC and its allies reached the Coloured people. The Coloured People's Congress (CPC) inherited the tradition of its predecessor and although it concentrated on organising Coloureds it made the question of unity with Africans and Indians a major one. Some of the national issues in which the CPC was involved were fighting the removal of Coloureds from the common voters' roll, the 1961 campaign for a National Convention and fighting race classification and job reservation. Its members are active in MK and some even fought the enemy in Zimbabwe.

The CPC has been paralysed by bannings, arrests and the flight of its members out of the country. As mouthpiece of the Coloured people it has been overshadowed by the Labour Party. Nonetheless the liberation movement's consistent standpoint on the issue of black solidarity is manifest even within the Labour Party itself. It also regards the idea of black unity as crucial and has allied itself with Inkatha and the Indian Reform Party.

In present-day South Africa it is by no means easy to win whites over to the liberation movement. This group occupies a dominant position economically, politically and socially, and regards the black man, particularly the African, as inferior and a threat. Whites earn high incomes, live in comfort and enjoy all the best facilities this rich country offers. They have little reason to risk those comforts by meddling in black politics and exposing themselves to victimisation. The matter is complicated by the rigid separation of black and white in almost every sphere of life, making meaningful contact between the two groups virtually impossible. To get a hard core of whites who are totally committed to the freedom struggle is a Herculean task. Yet this was achieved when the Congress of Democrats (COD) emerged.

The COD, which is part of the Congress movement, has white members who are prepared to break with their own racial group, surrender their valuable privileges and fight on the side of their oppressed countrymen. Moreover, the Congress developed a unique structure that embraces all those Africans who are welded by a common ideology. No other section of the liberation movement provides a better structure, comprising the different racial groups that jointly implement a common programme, and has produced such positive results in a fight for a non-racial South Africa. At the time of writing, news has reached us that white democrats are appearing in court in various parts of the country for political offences associated with the ANC's fight against apartheid – Helen Joseph, Barbara Waite, Illona Kleinschmidt, Jacqueline Bosman, Tim Jenkins, Stephen Lee and others.

Like the CPC and COD, the South African Congress of Trade Unions (SACTU) was not formally banned, but was paralysed by bans on its officials. At the height of its strength, SACTU galvanised the workers and ably implemented the policies of the Congress movement. Black and white trade unionists jointly tackled common issues. In some of its clashes with the government and employers it enlisted world support and brought powerful international institutions to their knees. SACTU has been a thorn in the flesh of the government, the reactionary Trade Union Council and employers. It played an important role in ending South Africa's membership of the International Labour Organisation (ILO) and in popularising the international boycott of South African goods.

On numerous occasions critics expressed concern that top communists held key positions in the ANC and the SACP. We have repeatedly tried to explain the all-embracing nature of the Congresses in speeches, in formal conversations and in writing. A section of the liberation movement is drawn into this trap and has joined in the witch-hunt. The BCM sneers at our association with the SACP with equal contempt. In a sense this fear of communism is genuine, for there are not many nationalist movements that are so broad in their political outlook as to welcome communists to their ranks and to entrust them with important responsibilities.

The history of the ANC demonstrates that its openness in this regard is not something new. It is a tradition going back as far as the 1920s when people like Walter Thibedi, John Gomas, Gana Makabeni, Johannes Nkosi, Albert Nzula and many other communists were members. Yet the ANC has been dominated throughout its long history by non-communists like Samuel Makgatho, Z.R. Mahabane, Alfred Xuma, Selepe Thema, Z.K. Matthews and many others.

In working closely with the SACP and welcoming communists into the ANC and its allies the Congresses are doing no more than the capitalists themselves are doing when they consider it in their interest to co-operate with the socialist countries and communist parties. Such co-operation is taking place in many fields today in several European countries. Bourgeois political parties have formed alliances or coalitions with the communist parties and communists occupy key positions in the army, civil service, commerce and industry. No serious liberation organisation can ignore the existence of a powerful ally in the communists. Had Churchill and Roosevelt not formed an alliance with Stalin during the Second World War, the history of the world may have been different. In our life and struggle the communists have proved faithful allies, fully committed to the principle of human equality and democratic government. Our long-term objective and the SACP's short-term aims are the same. The basis of our comradeship is the determination to overthrow colour oppression and to establish a united and democratic South Africa, where all its people will live as equals.

It may well be true that infiltration is a common method of spreading communist influence. In our own case there is no need for alarm or for communists to use underhand methods. For more than four decades the ANC has welcomed communists with open arms. No limits were put on the members that may be admitted and on their membership rights. They were always free and, if they so wished, they could have taken over the entire organisation by using the normal platforms and procedures of the Congresses. But they did not do this. Since the formation of the SACP in 1921, the communists moved to the forefront of the struggle and thus proved to be amongst the staunchest Congressites.

For our own part, we have confidence in the strength of the ANC and its ability to defend its policies and freedom of action. We are certain of mass support. History is on our side. We do not fear the judgement of posterity. We can tame the most ultra-leftist radical just as we can rebuff the rightist elements who glibly warn us of communist danger and who at the same time collaborate with our enemies.

Organisations and individuals should be judged by what they stand for in life and by their actual record in the liberation struggle. More specifically, their success or failure is measured by their service to humanity in general and their country and people in particular. By this token, no honest person will deny that the achievements of the SACP are impressive. From its inception the SACP singled out the special dangers: the evils of class exploitation, racism and aggressive wars.

Because they stand for a classless society, the communists are the most persecuted politicians and the SACP was the first political party to be declared illegal when the Nats came to power. Communists continue to preach human brotherhood and peace, although they are regarded as seditious in South Africa, where racism is firmly entrenched in all spheres of life. The white communists were the first to break away from the other whites and to cast in their lot with their downtrodden black countrymen. They were the first to form African trade unions and they pioneered adult education among urban blacks.

An equally important aspect of the SACP's work has been its influence on the international socialist movement, especially in the socialist countries. The SACP drew the socialist world closer to the aims and aspirations of not only the oppressed people of South Africa, but to suffering humanity the world over. From the time of the controversial Black Republic issue through to the national liberation struggle in Africa and Asia the SACP's theoretical contributions have been immeasurable.

THE ANC AND THE FREEDOM STRUGGLE

An account of the freedom struggle in this country is not complete without the mention of the ANC, which is proving to be the oak tree of South African politics. In its turbulent history of 60 years it has shown unusual resilience. It survived the crippling blows of the last 16 years. Though it has suffered heavy casualties and still faces a multitude of unknown challenges, the tremendous endurance and initiative shown by our men in the ever-sharpening struggle have won us more and more supporters, giving us the hope and confidence that whatever counter-measures the enemy may still take, victory will be ours.

Although the ANC existed in at least two provinces before 1910, it only became national in 1912, when its membership embraced Africans from all over the country. From its inception it stressed African unity based upon the fact that Africans have a common history, tradition, culture and aspirations. It strenuously resisted every encroachment on the people's rights and demanded among other things full franchise rights, adequate land, free and universal compulsory education, the right of free movement in the country and the repeal of all oppressive legislation. Its main blows were directed against the oppressive pass system. The ANC as a dynamic organisation with an equally progressive outlook uses militant methods of action to achieve its aims. In 1949 it formulated a militant programme of action and most, if not all, of the mass campaigns waged since then were the conscious application of that programme. In 1953 the ANC went further and brought together the widest spectrum of political opinion to draw up a democratic constitution for the country. This move finally took shape in June 1955 in the form of the Freedom Charter. The Freedom Charter is the ideological foundation of the Congress movement. With the exception of the political programme of the SACP it is the clearest and most advanced non-racial programme of principles ever formulated in this country.

In fighting for a non-racial South Africa the ANC is influenced by its undying love for democracy and by the important fact that the fight is not against a foreign power but against a firmly entrenched white minority in our own country. The staying power of the ANC is enhanced by its ability to adapt quickly to changing conditions. Within 21 months after it was declared illegal, it launched a series of acts of sabotage and began training a freedom army that is active today in various parts of the country. Our freedom army has forced the government to place the country under a perpetual State of Emergency.

The influence of the ANC reaches beyond our boundaries. It has led to the formation of similar congresses in many parts of southern and East Africa, including countries like Northern and Southern Rhodesia, Nyasaland, Tanganyika and Uganda. It was one of the foundation members of the Pan African Congress, which first met in Europe in 1919. In 1953 the ANC contacted independent African states and political organisations and suggested holding a Pan African Congress on our continent. This proposal culminated in the first All African People's Conference in Ghana in 1958. We consider the establishment of the OAU in 1963 to be the triumph of the idea contained in our proposal 10 years earlier.

But the history of the liberation movement is much wider than that of the ANC and its allies. Throughout its history the ANC faced serious challenges from a variety of political organisations. Some of these were originally formed for non-political reasons, whilst others, though inspired by political motives, were mere *ad hoc* bodies formed to deal with particular situations. Whenever new organisations emerged, many people, especially the government and its propaganda agencies, prematurely wrote off the ANC. This was the case, for example, when Clements Kadalie's Industrial and Commercial Workers Union (ICU) was established in 1919. Within 10 years the ICU was reported to have a membership of 30 000, and it reached a record figure of 100 000 by 1926: a fantastic achievement by the standards of those days. From a mere trade union body whose primary task was to organise the workers, it considered itself the African people's mouthpiece. Its militant campaigns provoked the government of the day to take drastic measures to curb its activity. However, by the end of the 1920s the ANC had regained its position as the country's premier African organisation. In 1930, working together with the CPSA, it organised the successful country-wide pass-burning campaign. The second challenge came in 1935 when it was felt that the ANC was not strong enough to rally Africans against the Hertzog bills. An *ad hoc* committee, the All African Convention (AAC), was therefore created with the special purpose of fighting the bills. That body brought together the country's leaders who were capable of uniting the African masses.

For almost three years, the AAC appeared to have eclipsed the ANC. Again the prophets of doom prognosticated that the ANC was a spent force. Although the AAC was an *ad hoc* committee expressly formed to fight the bills, certain elements tried to make it permanent. But by 1938 the AAC had lost momentum and those who had joined it expecting quick results became disillusioned.

In 1943 another newly formed organisation that attracted much attention was the African Democratic Party. According to its manifesto, its programme would differ from that of other organisations in the methods of struggle. It claimed that its programme covered immediate and pressing issues and that it would use militant methods to win its objectives. It never fulfilled any of these claims and became defunct within a few years. Since then several smaller groups have appeared – the nationalist block in the Transvaal and the Bantu National Congress in Natal. But all these soon fizzled out.

Although it has always been a small organisation of intellectuals confined mainly to the Western Cape and the Transkei, the Non-European Unity Movement has been vocal in emphasising black unity. It has played some part in the polarisation of the oppressed people. But it spent as much of its energy, literature and speeches on attacking the ANC and its allies, with the result that it unconsciously served as a divisive element in the liberation movement.

A more serious challenge came in 1959, when the PAC broke away from the ANC. In March 1960 it launched its anti-pass campaign with the slogans: 'No bail, no defence, no fine!', 'Freedom by December 1963!', 'Unity of Africa from Cape to Cairo, from Morocco to Malagasy!' The slogans had their impact especially on the youth and even the sceptics felt their hearts beat faster. There were unprecedented demonstrations in Cape Town and the Sharpeville massacre triggered off fierce condemnation from every part of the world, whilst foreign investors hurriedly withdrew their money. Police Commissioner Rademeyer temporarily suspended the pass laws and no less than four senior cabinet ministers made statements promising urgent policy changes.

Overnight the PAC found itself setting the pace in African politics and was to revel in sunshine and warmth for several months. The 'Voice of Africa' describes Robert Sobukwe as a Christ carrying the cross to Calvary. Indeed, in some circles March 1960 aroused the hope that the target the PAC set itself might be reached in time. After all, the campaign had started off with a big bang. But March 1960 passed into history, leaving the Nats on the rampage. The ANC and the PAC were banned and the magic slogans came flush against the concrete realities of life. All the flowery slogans were thrown to the winds and during the campaign the PAC paid bail and fines, engaged lawyers to defend members and appeal against convictions.

Potlako Leballo surprised everybody in 1963 when, speaking from Lesotho, he announced plans by PAC forces to invade South Africa. No armed attack followed and no explanation was ever given for the failure to implement the sensational declaration or to liberate the people before the end of 1963.

At the 1962 Pan African Freedom Movement for East, Central and Southern Africa (PAFMECSA) Conference in Addis Ababa, a PAC spokesman dramatically told delegates that his organisation had ordered all members who were abroad to return to South Africa and report directly to their National Executive before the end of June that year. Again nothing came of this 'order'. Members of the PAC continued to leave the country like other freedom fighters.

There are several other examples of these fanfares that may have damaged the public image of an organisation whose initial showing certainly made some impact. A sizeable number of PAC members have been imprisoned for various political offences including acts of sabotage, and it is regrettable that their contribution to the cause should be marred by such unrealistic propaganda. When the organisation was banned its internal machinery collapsed and although it still lingers, it is a shadow of its former self and its membership split into warring factions.

The latest splinter group to emerge was the so-called 'pure' ANC of the Mbele-Makiwane group in 1975. Unlike the PAC, which broke away, this group was expelled from the ANC and included men who held top positions in the organisation. Some of them were Marxists of fairly long standing and two of them were imprisoned on Robben Island for political offences. When they advocated racist and anti-communist standpoints and resorted to the slander of the leadership, they antagonised even those who might have given them a hearing. Many dissident groups have tried this tactic in the past and in every instance the effect was the same: to unite Congressites as never before. The dominant impression this group left was that of a clique of self-seeking, irresponsible and undisciplined men who were determined to wreck the organisation. Almost all were capable men who served the organisation and made sacrifices. It is up to them to recant their false stand, which only plays into the hands of the enemy, and to rejoin the organisation.

No political organisation is free from internal conflicts and we have not been spared this problem. But the endurance of the ANC has been demonstrated over the past 60 years by its continued growth and influence against all odds. The heavy casualties that we have suffered, the constant flow of men into jail and the vigour with which the ANC prosecutes the internal struggle and the campaign to isolate South Africa from the world indicate in-built resistance.

Many splinter groups have landed on the rocks. Those that still remain are but caricatures. This should be sufficient warning to all those sections of the liberation movement, particularly the new ones which may wish to venture in a different direction and which may cherish the hope of leading the people. Experience tells us that the road to liberation is not an easy, romantic wish, but a practical and complicated undertaking that calls for clear thinking and proper planning.

The ANC welcomed the formation of SASO, SASM and NAYO as organisations of students and working youth. As a banned organisation which operates from underground, the ANC realised the enormous value of a legal body that could work openly among the students and working youth and rally them behind the liberation movement. Almost all the major problems of black students, even those relating to education, the powers of student representative councils and diets, are basically political. They can never be removed before a political settle-ment is achieved. Consequently, any black student who fights for his rights as a student is auto-matically drawn into the struggle against racial oppression. This is one of the reasons for empha-sising the political aspect in the manifesto of SASO.

Furthermore, the establishment of these student bodies also contained the important lesson that despite the ruthless counter-measures taken by the enemy, it is still possible to form a legal organisation inside the country auxiliary to our underground work. In this situation it was natural for the ANC to make resources, expertise and experience available to all these bodies and to assist them in every possible manner. Whether or not the slogan 'Black is Beautiful' had any scientific basis, and whether a broad-minded organisation like the ANC, which fights for a non-racial democracy, should be associated with organisations whose ideology was basically chau-vinistic, is not the issue. Of immediate importance was the fact that the black student had found his feet, his slogans appealed to the black man's emotions, flattered his national pride and inspired him to assert his identity with confidence.

The ANC was able to work out a suitable formula to co-ordinate the efforts of the students with those of the organisation. These efforts bore fruit, especially during the 1976 uprisings, when the bulk of the young people who were involved identified themselves with the ANC. Meanwhile, the enemy and other sections of the ruling class tried to drive a wedge between the liberation movement and the youth organisations. They hailed the latter as a new political force that accurately interpreted the mood of the black man, and with whom a peaceful settlement should be sought. Unfortunately, a minority of the BCM fell into this trap and now sees itself as the prophet of a new South Africa.

But like all emotional slogans, 'Black is Beautiful' has lost its original appeal. The BCM must now come up with something fresh and concrete to gain the initiative. It will find that now that it is an illegal organisation many agencies that once patronised it will lose interest because they do not want to be associated with an organisation that is deemed subversive. Even more impor-tantly, it will discover that the real reason a section of the press hailed its emergence as the most important development in black politics in recent times was mainly to discredit and minimise the role of the underground, which undoubtedly is the main threat to the existing white power structure. The observation that emerges from an objective review of the short history and role of the BCM is that, in spite of all its weaknesses and mistakes, the BCM attracted able and serious-minded young people who acquitted themselves well, appreciated the value of unity, and whose main efforts were directed towards this goal. Realists amongst them accepted that the enemy would not be defeated by fiery speeches, mass campaigns, bare fists, stones and petrol bombs, and that only through a disciplined freedom army, under a unified command, using modern weapons and backed by a united population, will the laurels be ours.

WALTER SISULU

Walter Max Ulyate Sisulu was born in Engcobo in the Transkei on 18 May 1912, the year the ANC was founded. He became active in the political struggle in the 1930s and rose to prominence in 1944, when he, together with Oliver Tambo, Nelson Mandela, Anton Lembede and others, founded the ANC Youth League. At the 1949 conference of the ANC the Youth League successfully proposed the adoption of the militant, mass-based Programme of Action. At this conference, Dr Alfred Xuma stood down as President and Reverend James Calata relinquished his post of Secretary General. Dr James Moroka was elected President and Sisulu Secretary General.

Sisulu, together with Yusuf Cachalia, served as joint secretary of the Defiance Campaign, which was launched in June 1952. He was first accused in the Defiance Campaign trial. He was guest of honour at the 1953 World Youth Festival in Bucharest. During this trip he visited Israel, the Soviet Union and the People's Republic of China. He was served with his first banning order in 1954. Despite these banning orders he was part of a group of leaders who clandestinely continued their political activities.

He was arrested for treason in 1956 and was among the 30 accused whose trial lasted until March 1961, when they were acquitted. He was placed under house arrest (first for 12 hours a day, and later for 24 hours a day) in October 1962. He was arrested and sentenced to six years imprisonment for participating in ANC activities. He appealed against his sentence and, while out on bail, went underground. He was arrested at Rivonia on 11 July 1963 and sentenced to life imprisonment.

As part of the negotiation process initiated by Mandela from prison in 1986, Sisulu and other Rivonia trialists were released on 10 October 1989. Sisulu was elected Deputy President of the ANC in July 1991. He has since retired from official positions in the ANC.

The triumvirate of Mandela, Tambo and Sisulu is widely acknowledged for the formation of the ANC Youth League in 1944, steering South Africa towards democracy and bringing the ANC to power in 1994.

WALTER SISULU
BY DAVID KOLOANE

PROFILE

Ambition is an accepted part of the human psyche. Perhaps because politics is about power, there is the perception that all who engage in political activities have personalities dominated by personal ambition.

Walter Sisulu's life and personality run completely against any such stereotype. He and his wife, Albertina, individually and as a couple, today enjoy veneration and warmth from South Africans that is surpassed only by that accorded to Nelson Mandela.

His unwavering commitment to the struggle for freedom sits comfortably with an absence of personal ambition. He exudes an aura of calm, careful judgement, deliberation and empathy.

All of us in prison, irrespective of which political organisation one belonged to, always sought and gave the greatest weight to his opinion. One sought his counsel because one was secure in the knowledge that he never made a hasty conclusion or decision. This careful weighing, be it of situations or people, drew all, including intellectuals and professionals, to seek his views.

When I left prison, Mandela and Sisulu had given me assignments that necessitated my going into exile. The tasks also required that I work with Oliver Tambo, the President of the ANC (known as 'O.R.'), in close trust and confidence. I was concerned that O.R. may have reservations about this, given that I was a communist. I raised the matter with Mandela and Sisulu and asked their advice on how I should respond if O.R. were to ask me whether I was a communist. Mandela felt that I would not be asked such a question. Sisulu tended to go along with this view but came back to the issue the next day.

It was still his opinion that O.R. would not raise the subject, but added that if the question arose, I should without equivocation acknowledge that I was a communist. He maintained that this would be the only way I could hope to create a workable trust.

I was struck by the fact that he had gone to such lengths in weighing the issue. As it happened, O.R. never asked the question.

In our discussions and during the political classes we conducted among ourselves, Sisulu specialised on the history of the struggle and the ANC. There was a consistent thread in everything he said: we, as freedom fighters, had a fundamental obligation to the people, the masses. Whatever our differences and disagreements, he said, we must never mislead or divide the people. Our task must always be to unite the people.

On reflection, this is the core value that explains his personality and his greatness. It gives him a unique place in the history of South Africa.

WE SHALL OVERCOME!

WALTER SISULU

Every organisation engaged in national liberation constantly has to isolate, analyse and search for solutions crucial both to its continued existence and growth, and to the success of the struggle as a whole. Stripped to its bare essentials the national liberation struggle reduces itself to a struggle for political power – a struggle born of irreconcilable interests. No ruling class has ever relinquished power voluntarily and we dare not bury our heads in the sand in an effort to escape the problems simply because they appear intractable. Indeed, there are no insoluble problems. Some problems may appear so: more often this is so not because a problem is insoluble but rather because it has been posed incorrectly.

In a certain sense, the story of our struggle is a story of problems arising and problems being overcome. It is understandable that many of the problems should generate much controversy and emotion. However cool and detached we may strive to be in our analyses, the fact remains that we are deeply involved and interested parties and the solutions we adopt are solutions we ourselves have to implement. It requires a strong sense of revolutionary discipline for one to implement with zeal what one has vigorously opposed and disagreed with in debate. While it is not always possible to control the degree of emotion generated, it is possible and necessary to maintain a sense of proportion. Problems should be examined against the background of the nature of our struggle and in terms of their interactions with the general struggle if they are to be seen in their true dimensions.

Furthermore, in evolving solutions we should avoid that style of thinking that gravitates towards 'final solutions'. There are no final solutions. Solutions must always be open to modification and adjustment on the basis of experience and fresh evidence – sometimes they may even have to be discarded. It is in this spirit that an attempt is made here to isolate and examine certain problems that are important to our struggle.

The central feature of the revolution in South Africa is that it is an African revolution. In the first place, the oppression and exploitation of the African people is the pivot around which the whole system of white supremacy revolves. There are other oppressed minority national groups in South Africa, and to characterise our revolution as an African revolution is not to gloss over the oppression of the other national groups, nor is it to ignore or minimise their contribution to the unfolding revolution. To speak of the African revolution is to emphasise a fundamental aspect inherent to the structure of oppression, namely, that the liberation of the African people is a necessary condition for removing the oppression of all other national groups in South Africa. This is not the case if the liberation of any one or several of the oppressed minority national groups is characterised as the pivot. The concept of the African revolution reaches into the heart of the mechanism of the system of oppression as it obtains here and projects a vision of a free South Africa, which is assured of the complete elimination of national oppression of all groups. That such a broad expanding outlook is inherent in African Nationalism is not derived from idealistic notions born out of abstract considerations, but from the concrete conditions giving rise to it. It is verifiable by an examination of African Nationalism as an historical process both in South Africa and in Africa as a whole. Different organisations in the national liberation movement in South Africa have reached towards this facet of our revolution in different ways and with varying degrees of accuracy. Nowhere has it been so tersely and compellingly set forth as in the Freedom Charter, which embodies the basic policy of the revolutionary forces headed by the African National Congress.

Ours is not an isolated struggle. If it were, the prospects of victory in the near future would be gloomy – not so much because of the inherent strength of the white minority racist regime but because of the underpinning it enjoys from the most reactionary imperialist powers. This support flows out of objective relationships. But reality is many-sided and the very conditions that create a community of interests between the ruling classes in South Africa and the imperialist powers also result in the inextricable interweaving of our movement with the national liberation and other progressive movements throughout the world. Such a perspective fully justifies the conviction that the enemy cannot long forestall the victory of our revolution.

The development of capitalism stamps the character of our struggle and is central to the creation of these interconnections. Plunder and loot from the colonies played a significant role in the process of primary capital accumulation that led to the emergence of capitalism. As capitalism established itself as the dominant mode of production in several Western European countries its dependence on the colonies increased. Towards the end of the nineteenth century the first phase of industrialisation of the Western world was nearing completion and capitalism entered the phase of imperialism. This phase marked significant changes in the structure of capitalist economies. Inter-imperialist rivalries became a dominant feature, with embittered struggles for investment outlets, markets and sources of raw materials. Capitalism spread its tentacles to every nook and cranny of the globe, tying up the whole world in a tight system of ruthless oppression and exploitation.

However harsh and evil the consequences of this process, it was in the nature of capitalism to unleash forces that made our world one world. The insatiable appetite of this system effected this without design and without regard to the fate of peoples and nations. Autarchic economies were destroyed, nations and peoples subjugated. Imperialism and colonialism created a unified world in their own image – a world enslaved to serve the interests of the ruling classes of a handful of imperialist countries.

Wherein lies the unity of the world?

Within the imperialist states capitalism forged two nations – the exploiters and the exploited – eyeing each other across the chasm of social revolution. Across state boundaries, imperialist states, driven by the common pursuits of wealth through exploitation at home and abroad, have been and continue to be locked in rivalries that are the powerhouse of world wars. The trade routes from the colonies and former colonies to the imperialist states, along which the super-profits are drained out of these areas, are sign-posted with national and social revolutions. The epoch of imperialism ushered in by the First World War is the epoch of wars, of national and social revolutions.

The unity of the world is not to be found in any community of interests between imperialists, nor can it reside in any hopes of harmony between oppressed and oppressors. The unity of the world is embedded in the forces striving against exploitation and oppression, against imperialism. The struggles of the oppressed and exploited, issuing in national and social revolutions, are giving birth to a new world, the world of peace and friendship between the peoples of the world, of freedom and national independence. And every blow struck against oppression and exploitation hammers out the new era. These are the forces whose community of interest rests neither on rivalry nor oppression nor exploitation, but on the realisation of humankind's humanity.

The period that marked the crisis of capitalism and manifested its inherent tendencies towards stagnation, economic and political crisis, and imperialist conflagrations, also ushered in the era of triumphant national and social revolutions. Even as the world of imperialism signalled its bankruptcy with the senseless slaughter of the First World War, the new world heralded its birth with the triumph of the October Revolution of 1917 – a revolution which, in an age of great social and national revolutions, still stands as perhaps the greatest revolution of all times. The October Revolution broke the chain with which imperialism girdled the world and gave socialism, whose core is the drive to end the exploitation of man by man, a home. A lone child in a singularly hostile world, it survives not only through the blood, sweat and tears of the Soviet people, but also because it was founded on the unity of all oppressed and exploited peoples within and outside the Soviet Union. That this unity was the essential condition for its triumph was clearly understood and stated by V.I. Lenin, the architect of the October Revolution and one of the world's greatest revolutionary strategists and tacticians.

The triumph of the October Revolution became the opening shot of the world-wide socialist and anti-colonialist revolutions. How significantly the world has changed since then! In many ways the Second World War was but a continuation of the First World War and marked a new peak in inter-imperialist rivalries. At the same time it differed radically from the First World War in that revived German imperialism, under the banner of Nazism, set out not only to re-divide the world and establish its dominance, but to reshape the world on an avowedly anti-democratic basis. This altered the character of the war and stamped the efforts of the Allied powers a defence of democracy.

Two important consequences attended the aftermath of this war. These were the emergence of the socialist camp and the growth of the national liberation movements, with the ultimate emergence of independent states in the former colonial areas. That these two consequences should be linked is not fortuitous. The two processes are intertwined and inseparable. Both developments reinforce each other and together continue to reshape the world.

Thus by the end of the Second World War the liberation of the colonial peoples had become a practical proposition. The oppressed peoples by their own struggles placed the issue of national liberation on the agenda and in the post–Second World War world the flames of freedom spread like a veld fire, leaping across continents. The age of independent national states in Asia, Africa and Latin America became a reality.

The interconnectedness of these two processes has been highlighted at the Bangdung Conference of 1956, the Afro-Asian Solidarity Council that followed, and the Tri-Continental Conference held in Havana in 1966.

In this process it is useful to see the advance of the national liberation struggle on the African continent and the emergence of independent African states in terms of a continent-wide African revolution. By doing so we do not in any way overlook the interrelations with, and the unity of, the national liberation struggles throughout the world, as well as with the advance of the socialist camp. On the contrary, on precisely this basis, we are able to give meaning to the idea of the African revolution by highlighting the particular features that are present in the African revolution.

From its inception the national liberation struggles in Africa have been marked by the recognition by all leading organisations that the liberation of the African people is a single process. This fact has been translated into practical form through the series of pan-African conferences that originated from a meeting in 1900. It has been carried through into the phase of independent African states by the creation of the Organisation of African Unity (OAU). The OAU seeks to harmonise the interests of the independent states and thereby to facilitate their progress and development, and also to liberate the remaining areas of Africa that are still trapped in the maws of colonialism and white minority racist regimes.

Furthermore, despite the diversity of colonial and imperialist powers that have made our continent their hunting ground, the common history of our peoples is imprinted with a particularly traumatic experience, which colonialism seems to have earmarked for our people – the wholesale slave trade that ripped open and destroyed the fabric of African societies. Slave-owning societies have existed before in many parts of the world and are related to a particular stage in the historical evolution of human society. But the slave trade that transported millions of our people into slavery in North and South America in particular, and killed many more millions in the process, was associated with developing capitalism and was practised on a scale that has never been equalled.

Finally, while it is common practice for the colonialists and imperialists, in the process of subjugating and maintaining their rule over the colonial peoples, to denigrate the culture of our peoples, in our continent this practice was carried to its ultimate limits. In Africa, imperialism completely denied our cultural past and history and applied the theory of race superiority so as to stamp our peoples with the mark of permanent inferiority.

This, of course, happened to be convenient as a device for rationalising the most inhuman practices to which our peoples were subjected. In the period of the slave trade, those who profited from trading in human beings therefore lived with intact consciences. So, too, did those who built plantations on slave labour. (It is no accident that the Deep South of the USA remains even to this day one of the bastions of racist views.) And, even after the end of the slave trade, this pernicious racist doctrine was entrenched in southern and central Africa.

Again this was no accident. Imperialism requires a social base in each dominated area to serve as its agent and to facilitate its exploitation of the people. It has never hesitated to recruit such forces from the local population. But in the case of that curve stretching from the south up to central Africa and culminating in what has long been known as the 'White Highlands' of Kenya – areas which proved climatically suitable for permanent white settlement – it was not necessary to recruit these forces from the African people. That social base was available in the form of white settlers at a price that was to make these white settlers and their descendants the world's repository of racism.

The African revolution matured rapidly in the post-war period and resulted in a number of independent states. The price paid for independence has not been small and each state's road to independence is rich with experience and sacrifice. Fired by the desire for freedom, our peoples have joined the forces of progress and are engaged in translating their political independence into meaningful social and economic terms. This process continues unabated.

Even as this elemental force swept through our continent, the colonialist and white minority racist regimes in southern Africa were shaken by the struggles inside these areas. The Portuguese colonialists, backed by NATO arms, clung to power and forced the peoples of Mozambique, Angola and Guinea-Bissau into a long war for freedom. British imperialism, temporised in Northern Rhodesia, Nyasaland and Southern Rhodesia, put forward elaborate schemes for a Central African Federation in search of formulas to assure the whites of their privileged position. It ended by yielding to the liberation forces, which established Zambia and Malawi, but succumbed to the politics of skin colour and racism in Southern Rhodesia. Thereby it paved the way for the illegal racist regime of Smith that has forced Zimbabweans to an armed struggle for freedom. South Africa, long wishing to swallow Namibia, found its path checked by the people of Namibia and the progressive forces of the world, but holds on to the veto in the United Nations Security Council of the US, French and British governments. Nevertheless, the Namibian people have taken their destiny into their own hands and have taken to arms too. And South Africa, bastion of racism in Africa, turned a deaf ear to the horror of the post-Hitler world, instituting a reign of terror in an effort to crush the liberation forces, thereby driving our people onto the inevitable path of the armed struggle.

The African revolution that swept through the continent knocked at the doors of southern Africa. The doors remained bolted. It has become the historic mission of the African revolution to batter these doors down and force entry.

When we in South Africa grasp the content of our revolution in this way, we are able to recognise its inner unity with the continent-wide African revolution, as well as with the anti-colonial and progressive struggles throughout the world. To see our revolution in terms of its nature and these interconnections is of special importance in our situation. It is only in this way that we can reach towards an understanding of what is unique and particular to our situation, and what is general to the national liberation and other progressive movements. This is also the basis on which we can absorb the experiences of the struggles in other parts of the world and creatively adapt these in charting the path of the African revolution. Such an understanding also helps us to recognise who are our friends and who are our foes.

In broad outline the main features of the way in which society in South Africa is ordered may be set out as follows:

- The South African economy is a developed and industrialised capitalist economy with a developing machine tool sector and harnessing sophisticated modern technology.
- At the same time this economy is sharply etched with colonial features. Its industries, mines, agriculture and commerce are built and dependent on sweated black labour. Black workers, by legislative and administrative fiat, are confined largely to unskilled and manual jobs. Cheap black labour is the source of the super-profits that make South African enterprises such an attractive proposition to both local white and foreign investors. The core of this labour force consists of Africans. Africans, and to a lesser extent Coloureds, provide the agricultural labour force. Mining is totally dependent on African labour, which is largely employed on a migratory basis. In industry and commerce, while Indians and Coloureds are granted limited opportunities in skilled jobs, the general norm is that black labour and African labour in particular is confined to manual and unskilled work. Equal pay for the same work is unheard of and the wage differentials are extremely wide.
- In all spheres the condition of black people is similar to that of oppressed peoples in the classical modern colonial set-up. They are politically subjugated, economically exploited, socially discriminated against and treated as inferiors.
- Political power is monopolised by the whites. The whites control the economy. Socially the life of the whites is so organised that blacks are admitted into it only to wait at their tables, nanny their children, and as domestic servants.
- The colonial model breaks down here in the sense that no foreign country remains as the colonising power. The whites in South Africa constitute this power. South Africa's capitalist class is drawn from its white population.
- At the same time, foreign investments play a substantial role in our economy, with British and US capital investments holding the field against more recent penetration by West German, French and even Japanese investment.

Where, then, does racism fit into this model? Racism in South Africa has deep roots going right back to the early days of colonisation by Europeans. We do not propose to make any lengthy examination of this phenomenon here. It is our purpose to stress that racism on its own can never survive as a significant force in the life of a country for long, unless it is buttressed by the way in which the material conditions of life are ordered. In South Africa this objective basis for the entrenchment of racism came about via imperialism's resort to the whites as the social base through which it set out to maintain its exploitation of our country. This provided the basis for racism to develop into and hold the dominant position it now occupies. The South African ruling class has barricaded itself by erecting social, economic, political, legislative and psychological barriers between white and black. Racism is the gospel to herd the whites into a laager. Racism serves to perpetuate the privileged existence of the whites, and apartheid, which is racism in its most virulent form, is the ideology founded on and giving expression to this privileged way of life.

It is this interplay between the way in which the material conditions of life of the whites is structured and racism that has made racism such a powerful and dangerous force in the life of South Africa. By means of it, the social and economic forces that would tend to bring about a closing of ranks between the blacks and sections of the white population are muzzled and distorted, and every section of the white community is nurtured with the idea that its position is threatened by the blacks. Thereby racism has become a material force in its own right and prevents any sizeable section of the whites from being drawn into the national liberation struggle.

The appeal of racism, buttressed as it is by such a privileged way of life, places those few and brave whites who ally themselves with the black man's struggle under constant and tremendous pressures to return to the laager. Racism and the maintenance of the privileges the whites enjoy have become so hopelessly intermeshed in the life and thoughts of the whites that a reactive anti-whitism as a phase in the development of the political consciousness of individual blacks is almost unavoidable. The fact that non-racialism is a leitmotif in the programmes of almost all the forces in the struggle becomes an outstanding testimony of the maturity of their political and philosophical outlook and also points to deeper economic factors that are at play, and which rise above and beyond the constraints of racism.

If the objective conditions of the whites put blinkers on their vision and thereby confine their outlook to their short-term interest, the mainstream of thought among the blacks, and African Nationalism in particular, has consistently risen above such constraints.

This caste-like division of our society into white and black renders it all the more necessary for us to be clear at all times as to how and where we draw the lines between the enemy and the people in our revolutionary struggle. The drawing of such lines, if the process is to be meaningful and of service to the revolution, cannot be allowed to be simply an outlet for bottled-up emotion. It must rest on the prevailing objective conditions and the long-term forces at work within the system, while taking into account the views and actions of the different sections of the population.

Objectively we, as the oppressed people, possess by our overwhelming majority a strategic advantage over the enemy, an advantage that guarantees the victory of our revolution. The enemy, by drawing the lines between white and black and, on this basis, attempting to make inroads and sow divisions among the blacks, hopes thereby to assure itself, first, of the undivided loyalty and support of all whites, and, secondly, to weaken what it regards as the strategic strength of the revolutionary forces.

Monopoly of power has helped and does help the enemy to look with confidence to enjoin the support of the majority of whites. Whatever strata of the white population we look at, we can clearly mark out real and tangible benefits that accrue to it by virtue of the existing system. But to treat the matter solely on these terms is to hand to the enemy a gratuitous and unjustifiably inflated strength at the strategic level.

For any revolution to succeed, it is essential to pare away the strength of the enemy and to pin it down to the narrowest limits. Revolutions triumph not on the basis of absolute strength but on revolutionaries gaining a position of relative superiority over the enemy. Furthermore, signs of fissures and cracks in the unity of the ruling classes are one of the most reliable indicators of the stage a struggle has reached. Every reduction of the enemy's strength has a much greater effect than absolute numbers. At this level there are two aspects to weakening the enemy – that of winning sections onto the side of the revolution and that of neutralising sections of the enemy camp. To achieve both we have to take account of the fact that white supremacy benefits all sections of the whites. This means we have to look more closely at the structure of their societies and the different forces and currents of thought among them to devise appropriate tactics.

This means that we must be alive to the contradictions among the white population group. Consider, for example, the National Party and its image as the authentic voice of a united Afrikanerdom. Significant changes are taking place among the Afrikaners. They have gained entry into and become an integral part of South Africa's capitalist class. This came about through the opportunities that opened up for them, particularly from the beginning of the Second World War. In addition, the National Party made use of political power since it became the ruling party in 1948 to speed up this process and force the entry of sections of the Afrikaners into a class that was once much the preserve of the English-speaking section. As a result, the Afrikaner community has become fully stratified and the National Party has begun to show signs of difficulty in projecting a convincing image to the Afrikaner that it represents all Afrikanerdom. It must continue to appear to serve all strata among the Afrikaner while in reality control of the National Party belongs to that section of Afrikanerdom that has become increasingly integrated in the capitalist class, either as fully fledged members or as bureaucrats and technocrats serving that class's interests.

The difficulties have not become unmanageable, but ripples are visible on the surface. Among the Afrikaners there has emerged a small group of intellectuals who are raising in their literature matters of a nature that are extremely disturbing to our rulers. There has grown a school of thought that actively espouses 'commitment' in literature, and the powers of the state and Afrikanerdom in general have reacted angrily. We need only refer, for instance, to the fact that Jan Rabie's *The Agitator* and André Brink's *The Saboteur* were refused publication. Brink's latest book was banned after publication. It is noteworthy that, in the field of literature, Afrikaner writers appear to be rapidly showing themselves more forthright and outspoken on questions of oppression and racial discrimination than their English-speaking counterparts, who have delved somewhat delicately into such questions over a longer period.

Furthermore, white students and other intellectuals have begun increasingly to question the foundations of apartheid. Perhaps this is partly a result of the fact that as students they are in a phase of life in which their consciousness of the economic and other benefits they derive from the system as whites is less constricting on their thoughts and actions and that in later life they eventually succumb to the corrupting influence of the system. But this is not an invariable law. The activities of these students are important – many will carry into their lives the lessons of these experiences. They show, as students, an awareness of the gap between themselves and their counterparts in other parts of the world, and are doing something about it. Recently even Afrikaner students at the Afrikaans universities have been showing signs of some independent thinking. They are pulling away from the Afrikaanse Studentebond (ASB), while at the English-speaking universities, the tendency towards a radical outlook and activities is becoming more pronounced.

At a general political level there are also signs of incipient, often very hesitant, new alignments among which we have the setting up of the Progressive Reform Party. South African whites show themselves extremely sensitive to every triumph in the anti-colonial struggle and their concern arising from the triumph of Frelimo in Mozambique and the MPLA in Angola has a touch of hysteria. The laager is increasingly proving to be a source of nail-biting insecurity.

All these are important signs. Small and insignificant as they may appear, our task is to look beneath them and find ways to exploit these fissures, widen them and whittle away the enemy's strength. This is supported by the experiences of other countries. There we are often able to see how developments in the colonies and the metropolitan countries interact to the advantage of the anti-colonial and the progressive forces in both countries. We have an example close to us in the recent triumph of the revolutionary forces in the Portuguese colonies in Africa and the democratic forces in Portugal. The experiences of the Portuguese soldiers in defending colonialism in Mozambique, Angola and Guinea-Bissau were an important part in their awakening and their overthrow of the Caetano regime. In its turn the April coup in Portugal and its subsequent development considerably speeded up the victory of the liberation forces in the three colonies. Similarly, the struggle and triumph of the Vietnamese against the leading imperialist power showed a close interaction between the Vietnamese struggle and the anti-war forces in the United States. Vietnam won its freedom. Inside the United States the effects of the defeat are still at work in that society.

The enemy rallies the whites on the basis of their survival being at stake. This is false. What is at stake is their privileged position. The clearest way of reaching the whites (and all other national groups too) is for the liberation forces to explicitly state their position with regard to the whites. We recognise all people as belonging to our country and the Freedom Charter states this in no uncertain terms. This approach will help divide the enemy camp, for it exposes the falsity of its propaganda.

We can rally all sections of our people and make inroads into the white community by raising the banner of 'Destroy Apartheid', for this is the crucial and immediate task of our revolution. Along this path we will be able to work with the widest and most diverse forces among all population groups and link up with the anti-apartheid forces inside and outside government institutions. Those who fear that such a wide platform is purely negative misconceive the situation. They are correct in demanding that as the vanguard of the revolution we must place before the people positive goals, a clear vision of not only what we are against, but also what we are for. We hold that this is essential and that this is precisely what the Freedom Charter does.

With regard to the black people we wish to give attention to the divisive forces at work because these are the factors that prevent us from realising and giving effect to the potential strategic superiority that belongs to our revolution. Our emphasis will be to show the basis on which these divisive forces exist and to pinpoint the need for our constant and conscious effort to overcome them. In other words, we focus attention on the fact that such divisive tendencies are the direct product of the enemy manoeuvres.

At first sight, racism and the system of national oppression of all blacks objectively place all blacks into one camp. Whatever their class position, all blacks are denied the power to determine how our country is governed and are denied equality of opportunities. Nonetheless, while this is valid for the overall picture, the enemy has been unceasing in its efforts to drum racism into the thoughts and style of life of the blacks. We must face the fact that the enemy has made inroads. A vast array of measures that differentiate one black group from another is built into the apartheid system. While these measures were in existence long before the Nats came to power in 1948, the accession to power by the Nats heralded a steady increase in such measures. The basis of the differential treatment is the division of the black population into three groups: African, Coloured and Indian. In present-day South Africa differential wage scales apply to these three groups and jobs are reserved for one group or another. Coloureds and Indians may belong to recognised trade unions. African trade unions are not recognised by the law. Africans, Coloureds and Indians have to live in separate residential areas and go to separate schools and universities. These and many other measures provide an objective basis for the enemy to inject the poison of racism into our people. The manoeuvre is patent: let the different black groups see each other as threatening each other's position, isolate the different segments of the black people, drive them apart, detract their sights from the common enemy.

Whether between white and black or black and black, one of the ways in which the system indoctrinates the people and attempts to sugar-coat the pill of racism is to premise its differential treatment on the heterogeneity of the different population groups. The questions it evades are the questions that must be asked if we are to find our way out of this jungle: Who created this system? In whose interest was it created? Whom does the system benefit? The heterogeneity of the cultures of our people is our wealth, which ought to cross-fertilise and broaden the humanity of our people. Instead it is abused at the altar of white supremacy.

The enemy has also set out on a consciously designed path of dividing the African people along tribal and ethnic lines. Again, it bases its appeal on drawing fine distinctions of culture and tradition and tribal lineage and to hold out the promise of each ethnic group's destiny outside the framework of the whole. This is one side of its many-pronged design that lies behind the Bantustan policy. The aim is clear: divide the African people to deal with them piecemeal.

Finally, in its arsenal of divide and rule, we have the time-worn and world-wide technique of anti-communism. On a world scale, in our own lifetime, we have been witnessing how the reactionary forces of the world drummed up a crusade against the socialist countries through the Cold War. The real aim of the Cold War was not only to destroy the socialist countries, but also to halt the progress of the anti-colonial revolutions and to keep those countries that had gained political independence within the imperialist fold.

It is no longer open to doubt that the imperialists have long used the cloak of anti-communism to impede the struggles of the colonial and former colonial peoples. Many have been deceived by its appeal, but the passage of time continues to unearth incontrovertible proof. In the midst of the Watergate scandal and its aftermath is there anyone who can point with confidence to any struggle of the oppressed and exploited and say: here the CIA kept out; here the CIA refrained from its notorious activities? The murder of Patrice Lumumba. The fascist coup in Chile. Numerous attempts to assassinate Fidel Castro. There is no need to catalogue the instances. The hand of the CIA is visible.

In our own struggle the gospel of anti-communism is preached and used by both the racist rulers of South Africa and foreign imperialist powers. To give but one example of the latter: in the early 1950s, and even before the Nat regime dared to openly dub the ANC and its allies communist organisations, the foreign office of a well-known imperialist power had drawn up a list of 'communists' active in our organisation and treated our organisations as such. As for the white racist regime of South Africa, anti-communism has been a long-standing technique to divide our people and movements. To them every effort of the black people to liberate themselves is nothing but the work of 'communist agitators' and 'terrorists'. Its standard weapon for attacking, persecuting, banning, torturing and imprisoning freedom fighters is the Suppression of Communism Act.

Those who may be tempted to say that the racist regime in our country has so overplayed its anti-communist propaganda as to make it palpably unbelievable may have a point, but it would be dangerous to underestimate the extent to which the enemy indoctrination has penetrated our people's movements. We cannot ignore that much of the disunity among the organisations has been around the question of communism and communist participation in the struggle. John Vorster has already set out to present the presence of Cuban troops and of Soviet assistance given to the MPLA government of Angola as proof that communism is the threat to all Africa. Of course, Vorster is trying to deflect attention from the activities of his own racist regime and to breach African unity, which has solidly opposed the Vorster regime. The presence of the two states, Mozambique and Angola, on our borders, whose ruling parties openly declare themselves Marxist, and the way in which South Africa has set out to whip up anti-communist hysteria around developments in Angola, may well turn out to be the opening phase of a new high peak in the racist's internally directed anti-communist crusade.

The power of anti-communism lies in the way in which even well-meaning people succumb to it. Thus the late George Padmore, knowledgeable as he was, in his book *Pan Africanism or Communism*, instead of setting out the African revolution in terms of Pan-Africanism versus imperialism and colonialism, posed the issue in terms of Pan-Africanism against communism.

The majority of the black people are wage earners in one form or another, and it remains true even for present-day South Africa that workers and peasants constitute practically the whole of the black population. The black working class is at the forefront of our struggle. We, in the national liberation movement, can neither ignore this nor close our eyes to the fact that Marxism explains the nature of exploitation in a way that enables the worker to give meaning to his condition. The ANC and its allies in the Congress movement have consistently supported and assisted the organisation of black workers. The task of the national liberation movement is to unite all our people, irrespective of their class positions. National liberation is our goal, the unity of all classes and strata the condition for its attainment.

This is not something peculiar to the South African situation. Other countries waging national liberation struggles have faced similar problems. Achmed Sukarno made one of the clearest statements on this matter in the early years of the Indonesian struggle for freedom. In an article published in 1926 and entitled 'Nationalism, Islam and Marxism' he examined the diversity of elements to be found in the Indonesian struggle. After isolating nationalism, Islam and Marxism as the predominant elements he asks: 'Can these three spirits work together in the colonial situation to become one Great Spirit, the spirit of unity? The spirit of unity which can carry us to greatness?' He was convinced that this was possible and concluded that 'the ship that will carry us to free Indonesia is the ship of unity'. The achievement of Indonesian independence shortly after the Second World War was a product of that unity. While Islam is hardly a significant force in our struggle, African Nationalism and Marxism are.

We would seriously endanger the success of our revolution if we were to allow anti-communism to destroy the basis of the strength of our liberation struggle. The experience of the ANC confirms the value of the co-operation of these forces and shows this as the firm basis for our strength and resilience.

Racism, tribalism and anti-communism are the three most dangerous impediments in the path of realising our strategic superiority over the enemy. They are part of the divisive armoury deployed against our struggle by the enemy. We have to wage a constant struggle to remove all trace of these divisive ideas among our people. In one form or another they divide our organisations and create disunity within them. Precisely because there is some objective basis for their existence, we cannot hope to eliminate them overnight. Thus racism can only be overcome with the triumph of the revolution. At the same time the very existence of such differential treatment shows that we must not allow our attention to be deflected from the source of our oppression and our common enemy. We must recognise and handle the problems arising within our ranks within the framework of contradictions among the people. That is to say, our struggle to overcome them must be founded on educating and persuading our people. Men and women are drawn into the struggle not as ready-made freedom fighters. They come into the struggle covered with the scars and mire of an oppressive society. Within our organisations and in the course of active struggle and constant political education, it is our duty to wash off the mire, heal the scars and make them steeled fighters for freedom. We live in a society permeated with racism, where tribalism and anti-communism are drummed into our people in a thousand ways. Even inside our organisations and sometimes, regrettably, in individuals holding high positions, vestiges of such thinking survive and bedevil our work. Such ideas are incompatible with our goal and we must never relax our efforts to rid our organisations of them.

One of the promising aspects in this connection is the emergence of Black Consciousness, which has been championed by the South African Students Organisation (SASO) and the Black People's Convention (BPC). That these organisations, the majority of whose members are African, have reached out and made Black Consciousness an idea which draws in all black people – Africans, Coloureds and Indians – is a measure of self-confidence and increasing maturity of the awakening forces in our country. That most of their activists are students, products of the education in racially and tribally organised government schools and universities, shows how repugnant apartheid is to our people and how all the power of the enemy cannot overcome the long-term objective forces that have been and are shaping our people as one people, and our country as one country.

It would be appropriate to address a few remarks here to the specific question of the unity of the organisations in our struggle. The problems of unity of our people, unity of our organisations and unity within our organisations are interrelated. One of the essential standpoints of this article is that we are servants of our revolution, of our people, and whatever organisation we may belong to, we must accept that much of the disunity evident among the masses arises from the disunity of our organisations. Our task should be to enlighten the masses, not to confuse. Any organisation or member of an organisation who goes to the masses to vilify other organisations in the liberation struggle or uses arguments founded on racism, tribalism or anti-communism to gain the support of the masses, serves no other purpose than to confuse and sow disunity among the people, and thereby makes the task of unity between the organisations even more difficult to achieve. These, fortunately, are errors that the ANC has assiduously avoided. As far back as 1950 the ANC sought to bring about the unity of the organisations in the struggle and its record in pursuing this objective is second to none. The achievement of unity between the organisations would be a triumphant milestone on our road to freedom. However, we must be realistic in our expectations. Such unity cannot come about by the efforts of one organisation alone. It can only be the product of reciprocal action. The time is long past for speaking of the desirability of unity. We need to translate our desires into concrete terms. Our desires should be reflected in our actions. Our priorities should mark our realism. Our principal target must be: Destroy Apartheid!

We have a proud history of struggle behind us. Our people waged a long and bitter campaign of resistance from the earliest days of colonisation. Resistance was crushed by force of superior arms and organisation. The white man's conquest was made easier because our people had not reached the stage where the different tribes could be mobilised into one single mighty force, though there is evidence that already there were emerging individual leaders who were beginning to see the necessity for this. Resistance was crushed, but memories of those historic exploits remain to inspire us in our present struggles. In the present century too, we have accumulated a proud record. The path has never been easy. Moments in which we have been in a position to carry the fight to the enemy stand out as brief, brilliant flashes and beckon us to greater exploits.

We are living in one of the most difficult and challenging periods. Those short-lived days when, despite the enemy having driven our organisations into the underground, freedom fighters emerged in the dark night to unleash bombs that reverberated across the country are now part of history. Since then our struggle has been one of regrouping, reorganising and preparation, while the enemy has set out to execute a many-pronged offensive aimed at destroying not only our small tactical strength, but also our strategic superiority.

Someone who has been in prison throughout this difficult period cannot hope to make an adequate examination of the problems that have arisen. There are, however, two problems that lend themselves to some comment.

THE ARMED STRUGGLE

The first of these problems relates to the decision to wage an armed struggle for the liberation of our people. In particular, two possible divergent views are isolated here, which, it is submitted, do not grasp the significance of the armed struggle in a balanced perspective. One rests on treating the armed struggle as a form of struggle that is exclusive of other forms of struggle. The other, which is the reverse side of the same coin, ignores the reality of the armed struggle, and exhorts us to seek the realisation of our goals solely through forms of struggle that would exclude the armed struggle. To see the path of our struggle in either of these exclusive terms is erroneous and harmful.

The armed struggle is not a form of struggle which, merely by decision in its favour or by its commencement, automatically becomes the dominant form of struggle. There exist at all times a multiplicity of forms of struggle that a movement exploits as part of its arsenal of weapons. Any form of struggle, including the armed struggle, can only emerge to dominance over time and as a result of consistent effort. Nonetheless, even if a given form of struggle emerges as a dominant one, this does not mean that other forms do not co-exist. What it does mean in such a situation is that the other forms come to occupy a subsidiary place and are essentially reinforcing the dominant one.

Several organisations in South Africa have committed themselves to the armed struggle. The leading organisation in this respect is the ANC and it is clear that its decisions and activities are dedicated towards raising the armed struggle to a position of dominance. It is also clear that the armed struggle has become a reality. Armed guerrillas of our liberation forces have for some years been actively engaging the forces of the enemy. This has happened in Zimbabwe, where forces of the Vorster regime were present to assist the illegal Smith regime,[1] along the Caprivi strip and in Namibia. Our guerrilla forces are striving to overcome major difficulties in carrying the armed struggle right onto South African soil. There is every indication that this will become possible in the near future. Furthermore, the enemy recognises that the greatest threat to its continued rule emanates from our trained cadres who spearhead the armed struggle. All the efforts of the enemy are directed towards forestalling the growth of the armed struggle. In my view the armed struggle is destined to mature and steadily reach a position occupying centre stage in our struggle.

Within South Africa one of the most unreal aspects of political activity among blacks is that such activity totally ignores the reality of the armed struggle. This comment stands despite awareness of the rigid censorship imposed by the Vorster regime and the obvious slant that press reports must carry to depict all clashes as either being fairy tales or having gone against the guerrilla forces.

Under these circumstances one of the easiest mistakes would be for voices to emerge advocating that the liberation organisations should devote their entire energy towards the armed struggle, and desist from other forms of political activity which, along these lines, are regarded as diverting our energy and resources. Such a view misconceives the nature of our struggle and the relationship between other forms of struggle and the armed struggle. It amounts to ignoring the cardinal fact that the armed struggle, as we understand it, must develop into a people's war if it is to succeed, and as such depends for its success on the support of the masses, not only in providing guerrilla recruits but in a thousand other ways. The masses at this stage can only be drawn in by activising them through their day-to-day struggles against the Vorster regime in a variety of forms that may be conveniently described as non-violent. Further, such a view leaves the movement bereft of any guidance to the masses in areas where no armed action is taking place. When the masses, for example, ask what they must do about a given Bantustan government in their area, is it seriously suggested that the answer that this would be solved by the coming armed struggle can be treated as adequate, however much it may be backed by lengthy exposition of our struggle and its future course?

The responsibilities of our organisations should be clear. Thus, for example, the claim that the ANC is 'the sword and the shield of the people' can only remain valid as long as this is evident not only from afar, but is felt by the masses in all spheres of their lives, where they are confronted with practical problems of both an immediate and a long-term nature.

As for the opposite view, little needs to be said here beyond what has already been said to expose its policy. The importance of activising the masses – and this remains the most effective way to their politicisation – must take into account that the enemy has created a situation where the road to change by any means that excludes the armed struggle cannot lead us to our goal. The limitations of non-violent forms of struggle that, among other things, brought about the realisation of the need to prepare for and give effect to the armed struggle remain as valid today as they were then.

We face a powerful enemy and a long war for freedom and we would do well to draw lessons from the heroic struggle of the Vietnamese people. They have faced the power of France and the power of the almighty US and triumphed. One of the lessons of the Vietnamese struggle was that their victory was as much a political as an organisational one, achieved by building and maintaining a mass movement. One of the ways in which they succeeded in building up this political machinery was by setting up a structure of interlocking self-help organisations throughout South Vietnam. Without efficient political machinery in the country our armed struggle will always be walking on one leg.

THE BANTUSTANS

Much of the confusion surrounding the relationship and interaction of the armed struggle and other forms of struggle becomes evident when another problem, namely, that arising from the Bantustans, is considered. The above should help us to find correct answers. From several points of view the enemy's thrust along the lines of its Bantustan policy gives rise to some of the most pressing problems facing us.

Faced with the growing power of the liberation movement, the rising threat of the armed struggle, and the hostility of world opinion to its policy, the enemy set out on a long-term manoeuvre that finds expression in its Bantustan policy. The beginnings of this manoeuvre lie in its attempts to substitute the policy of what it calls separate development for apartheid. Fundamentally this is no shift in policy and the objective is the same – the preservation of white supremacy. What it does reflect is a measure of growing subtlety and sophistication on the part of the Nat regime's methods. Instead of crudities like 'Keep the Kaffir in his place' there is the glib talk of each group's 'national identity'. And in selling their policy the method of the carrot and the stick has been prominent. On the one hand they bludgeon the popular organisations, imprison their leaders, torture and murder some, ban and banish others, and ban the organisations. Having terrorised and intimidated the people they appoint those among the blacks who are prepared to play ball and dangle the carrot of 'homelands', 'independence' and talk of consultations with 'national leaders'. The dishonesty of this manoeuvre is self-evident: the basis must always be that you can decide for yourselves, but only what we, the Nats, have decreed. They who destroyed the culture of the African people, pose here as preservers of our culture and lecture us on the need for the preservation of our culture and traditions. Dedicated to fashioning their lives and living on the backs of the black people, they pose as our benefactors guiding us to 'independence'. And if anyone should see in all this a gross insult to the intelligence of the African peoples, why, such a person can be nothing else but a 'communist', a 'terrorist' and an 'agitator'.

But the Nats have never had it all their own way. The introduction of the Bantu Authorities Act met with the overwhelming opposition of the African people, including the chiefs. Those who voluntarily accepted the scheme were few and far between. Within the atmosphere of terror and intimidation, the racist regime forced Bantu Authorities on our people. It owes its successes in this respect to its relentless determination to force its policies on our peoples, the resources it commands by virtue of its control of the state, the weaknesses of our own organisations, and the presence of elements among our people who voluntarily agreed to play the game according to the rules laid down by the Nats and who, under the tutelage of the racist regime, have been elevated to the status of 'national leaders'.

In pursuing its objectives the Nat regime trimmed its policy to meet the developing situation, sharpened its propaganda offensive, but always kept a firm grip on its aims. In particular, it has long been evident that at the highest level the Nats had allowed for the possible development of the Bantustans to so-called political independence. That such a move was possible within the framework of its policy would have been evident to anyone who closely attended to the significance of the colonial model, as it has been adapted to explain the basic set-up in our country. Faced with the reality of the armed struggle, the resistance of our people and the hostility of the world, it has had to accommodate the idea of independence.

Today there can be no doubt that 'independence' for the Bantustans is coming and this adds a new dimension to the problems that confront our movement. Within the 'politics of the Bantustans' it is hardly possible to conceive of any successful legal opposition that would make anti-independence its platform.

This must be acknowledged, although we understand the depth of the feelings we have against the machinations of the racist regime. With 'independence' for Bantustans the Nats will have gone a long way in dividing our people along ethnic lines. Furthermore, the Nats have sown seeds that may well become a time bomb that will explode in our midst long after they and white minority rule have been vanquished. They have determined that if they are to fall, South Africa should nevertheless be plagued with tribalism and regionalism.

Further, in a limited way, by 'independence' the Nats will have effected a *de facto* partition and dismemberment of our country. They would be only too pleased if such a partition could be accepted as a complete solution and that thereby the whole question of blacks in so-called 'white' South Africa could be willed away. But this is a pious hope out of joint with reality.

Our anger is all the more exacerbated because we realise that all the objective and long-term forces that shaped the development of our country and fashion its future show that the only path to the unity of its people, to a harmonious and peaceful way of life free of the poison of racism and tribalism lies in one South Africa, one nation, based on 'one person, one vote'. What strains and difficult, painful moments 'independent' Bantustans will set in motion until we reach that goal are matters that lie ahead in the future. We shall only experience their full impact when the revolution has triumphed over apartheid. Nonetheless our vision of the future enshrined in the Freedom Charter remains unshaken and we shall carve our future out of the reality that will be inherited by the revolution.

In the meantime, we have to shape our tactics on the concrete circumstances. Specifically, this means that we cannot close our eyes to the fact of 'independence' of the Bantustans, and prosecute our struggle as if 'independence' does not exist. Bleak as the foregoing picture may appear to some, there are real and genuine grounds to make us confident that 'independence' of the Bantustans will in the process generate even greater problems for the enemy, whatever the problems it generates for our movement. That this will occur is evident in the latent and manifest contradictions present in the set-up, and the full effect of these will only come into play if we base our tactics on exploiting them.

Can it be done? When the Bantustans were introduced we decided to boycott the elections and hoped to kill the enemy designs in the cradle. In this we failed. The boycott was ineffective because we were never really in a position to effect it. Perhaps one of the vital points we overlooked in opting for the boycott is that its success depends on the complete and undivided loyalty of the people. We must examine the lessons of that episode and the subsequent developments with regard to the Bantustans dispassionately and clinically, and especially with a view to discerning our own weaknesses and errors. On the basis of those lessons we shall be in a better position to formulate and devise our tactics towards 'independent' Bantustans.

The broad outlines are clear. One of the important tasks of the national liberation movement is to work ceaselessly for the unity of our people. The future of our country lies in the first place in the unity of the African people, and as much in the unity of all our people. We have to work for this everywhere, even in the Bantustans. We need to bring the people of the Bantustans into the field of unity. This means that, while we uncompromisingly expose the fraud of these 'stans' and attack those leaders of the stans who kowtow to the white racists, we should at the same time unceasingly educate and persuade the people in the Bantustans to realise that their future is intertwined with the future of all the people in our country. They must be made to realise that as long as the white racists are in power freedom would be a mere word. These regions, even after 'independence', would remain colonies of white South Africa.

The readiness of the white racists to grant 'independence' to the Bantustans has become possible for the ruling class of South Africa because it can be accommodated within the basic framework of maintaining the exploitation of our people. It is also reflected in the so-called 'outward-looking' policy towards the rest of Africa that the Verwoerd–Vorster regimes have made much of in recent years. The kernel of this development lies in the fact that capitalism in South Africa has reached the point of expansion where it entertains imperialist ambitions for which overt and direct political control is not vitally necessary, as the experience of the other colonial and imperialist powers have shown. What it requires are investment outlets, markets, sources of raw materials and, in the case of the Bantustans, a reservoir of cheap labour. Hence its adjustments directed towards the rest of our continent are aimed at opening them to South African imperialist penetration, under the guise of helping them. Many African states, by virtue of the extremely low level of economic development and depressed conditions of life, may find this tempting. While Africa as a whole is fighting to establish its economic independence in the face of neo-colonialism, South African imperialism hopes that it can slip in through the back door and secure Africa as its preserve of economic exploitation. In the same way, by granting 'independence' to nine Bantustans occupying a mere 13 per cent of the surface of South Africa, and marked by the absence of any real possibility of economic viability, the ruling class see in their 'independence' no real disappearance of the exploitative bondage to which our black people are condemned. This shows not only that the white racists remain the controllers of the real destiny of the people in those areas, but also that South African capitalism and South African racists pose an enormous threat to the freedom of the whole continent. Already white South Africa puts out feelers for a wider grouping of southern Africa. The African states have a magnificent record with regard to giving support and assistance and are continuing to give to our liberation forces. They have been relentless in pursuing the goal of freeing the whole of our continent from imperialism, colonialism and white minority racist rule. In helping to bring about the success of our revolution they are helping not only the oppressed peoples of South Africa, but also assuring the whole of our continent of a future in which the freedom of our continent will be meaningful to its peoples. As long as the white racists rule in South Africa, all Africans remains in danger.

We cannot abandon our peoples in the Bantustans to the dictates of the white racists and to those who choose to kowtow to them in the Bantustans. White South Africa, in granting 'independence' to the Bantustans, hopes to win them over against the liberation forces. Cutting ourselves off from the people in the Bantustans would amount to playing right into the hands of the enemy. We have an alternative to offer to the people in these areas. We shall be able to offer it if we accept the reality of the political 'independence' of those Bantustans and set out to utilise every means available to expose the contradictions that make their 'independence' unreal and show them that their future lies not in co-operation and friendship with the white racists but in supporting and assisting the liberation movement, whose real target remains the white racist regime of South Africa. The Bantustans must never be allowed to become the buffers of white South Africa.

This is not an easy task. In devising our tactics, we shall be required to tax our ingenuity to the utmost. We shall have to display flexibility without succumbing to opportunism. But it can be done. We have the organisations, the leadership and the cadres capable of seeing the web of ramifications and relationships that make our struggle so complex and capable of prosecuting the revolution by drawing on the extensive armoury of methods and forms of struggle that belong to the arsenal of revolutionaries. Within the Bantustans there exist forces that sympathise with our goals. One of our greatest mistakes is to see in every man and woman who works within these apartheid institutions an enemy of the revolution. Many are open supporters of apartheid. Yet many others in these institutions do not accept the regime's policy. Of these, many will undoubtedly develop vested interests and lose their way. But at all times we must be able to isolate and distinguish their motives and link up with the anti-apartheid forces. Apart from those active in these institutions there are the masses in each of the Bantustans who are the storehouses of latent forces. We must activise them and draw them into the battle against apartheid.

In the course of a liberation war there are many long and dark days. The tiny nation of Vietnam, in a war that stretched over more than 30 years, faced many such bleak moments. But a people who want freedom, who are prepared to fight for it, are capable of super-human efforts. We face a powerful enemy, but never can it match the strength of the enemy the Vietnamese fought and vanquished. The hatred of our people towards apartheid is deep and enduring. The people are our strength. In their service we shall face and conquer those who live on the backs of our people. In the history of mankind it is a law of life that problems arise when the conditions are there for their solution.

AHMED KATHRADA

Ahmed Mohamed Kathrada was born on 21 August 1929 in Schweizer-Reneke. In 1941 he joined the Young Communist League. In 1946, he was one of the 2 000 resisters who went to prison as part of the Passive Resistance Campaign launched by the Indian Congresses. He represented the Transvaal Indian Youth Congress at the World Youth Festival in Berlin in 1951. He participated in the 1952 Defiance Campaign launched jointly by the African National Congress and the South African Indian Congress. He was one of 20 people charged for organising the Defiance Campaign (the case came up as the State vs. Sisulu and 19 others). All the accused received a suspended sentence of nine months. He was served with his first banning order in 1954. He was arrested in 1956 and charged in the Treason Trial and was one of the 30 accused who were acquitted in March 1961. Kathrada played an active role in Umkhonto weSizwe (MK) when it was formed in 1961. After he was placed under house arrest in 1963 he went underground and was arrested at Lillesleaf farm, Rivonia, on 11 July 1963. He was sentenced to life imprisonment in the Rivonia Trial.

In prison he completed the BA, B. Biblio., BA Hons. (History) and BA Hons. (African Politics) degrees.

He served 26 years of his sentence and was released together with Walter Sisulu and others on 15 October 1989. He was elected to the National Executive Committee of the ANC in 1991 and 1994, and declined nomination in 1997. He was elected to Parliament in 1994 and became Parliamentary Counsellor to the President during the presidency of Nelson Mandela. He declined to stand for Parliament in the 1999 election.

He serves as Chairperson of the Robben Island Museum Council and the Ex-Prisoners Committee and is a trustee of the Nelson Mandela Foundation.

His *Letters from Robben Island* were published in 1999 by Michigan State University Press, East Lansing, USA, and Mayibuye Books, UWC.

AHMED KATHRADA

BY BONGI BENGU

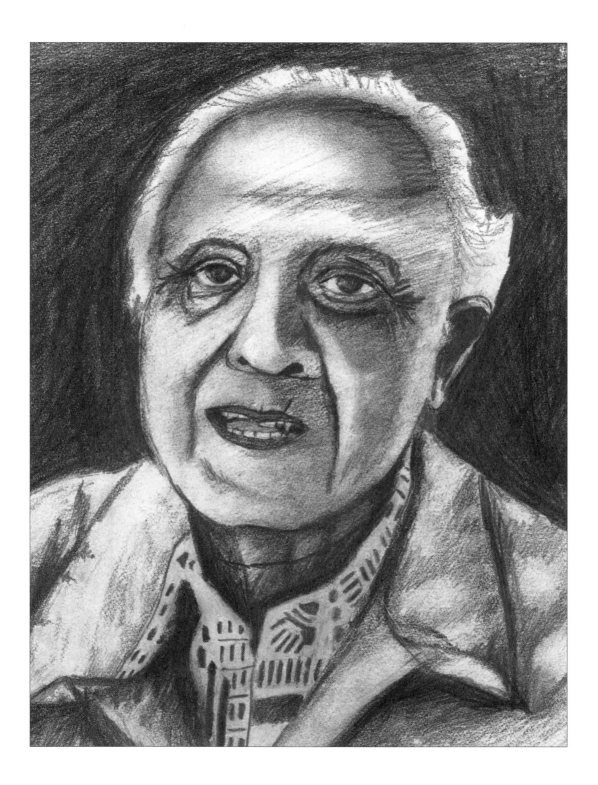

PROFILE

Kathy has a rapier-like tongue, a sharp wit laced with irony and sarcasm. To be really effective, this art needs to be combined with a deep understanding of human nature, the psyche conditioned as it is by culture and society.

Kathy spent the first ten years of his life in Schweizer-Reneke, a small *dorp* out in the platteland, where Afrikaners dominated. This gave him a facility with Afrikaans.

After his arrest in 1963, Theunis 'Rooi Rus' Swanepoel,[1] the Special Branch man who had already acquired a fearsome reputation as a torturer and brute, confronted him. Swanepoel threatened to make Kathy talk. In any tense situation, Kathy's voice remains controlled, but with an added whisper of a quiver. Visions of torture surfaced in his mind as he searched for a suitable retort. It came in the form of reciting an Afrikaans poem written by a noted Afrikaner poet, Jan Celliers:

Ek hou van 'n man wat sy man kan staan
Ek hou van 'n arm wat 'n slag kan slaan
'n Oog wat nie wyk, wat 'n bars kan kyk
En 'n wil wat so vas soos 'n klipsteen staan.

[I like a man who stands as a man
I like an arm that can strike a blow
An eye that never shies away, that can pierce a crack
And a will that stands steadfast as a rock.]

He had tackled Swanepoel on his own turf. Swanepoel had no answer and stormed off. His threats never materialised.

That was in 1963. Kathy would be the last to deny that he had got away because torture was not yet quite the stock-in-trade of the Special Branch at the time.

In the late 1960s, a head warder on Robben Island, Du Plessis (or Dup as he was known for short), was put in charge of us at work. He was a nasty specimen. It was practice that when we returned from work at the lime quarry, he would hand us over to the warder on section duty. This ritual involved stating the number of prisoners in his charge whom he was handing over.

As we prisoners trooped into the courtyard of the isolation section, Dup stood at the steel door impatiently looking for the section warder. He was nowhere in sight. Kathy had stayed away from quarry work that day because he needed medical attention and was exercising, walking back and forth on the concrete edge of the quadrangle courtyard. Dup stood at the top of the entrance ramp. As Kathy approached, Dup bellowed: *'Waar's die baas?'* (Where's the boss?)[2] He repeated the question, directing it aggressively at Kathy. Eventually, with calm deliberation, Kathy responded: *'Daar is niemand hierso met daardie naam nie.'* (There is no one here by that name.) Dup was livid. Kathy, after a pause, followed up with: *'Miskien bedoel u die beampte?'* (Perhaps you mean the official?) Kathy had used the polite form of 'you' and the very proper term 'official' rather than 'warder', which prison officials generally used. This was just too much for Dup. He flung the keys to the ground and left us in the section unguarded, without effecting the ritual handover.

Kathy employed his cutting tongue and sharp repartee even amongst us comrades. Behind it was a capacity to tell things as they were, rather than to put a gloss on something to suit the listener. Mandela, describing his friendship with Kathy, observed that many, especially leaders, tend to be surrounded by those who feel obliged to give reports based on what they think the listener would like to hear about himself. Kathy, he maintained, is a friend who holds up a true mirror to him so that he could see himself as he is, warts and all.

In Kathy these qualities combine with a fierce loyalty to the ANC, and to Mandela and Sisulu. This has made him stand four-square with the decision that, if the death sentence were to be imposed on them in the Rivonia Trial, they would not appeal against the sentence. The lawyers were convinced that he stood the best chance of being acquitted on appeal. Kathy would have none of it. All the Rivonia trialists refused to file appeals. Their releases, when they came in 1989, were part of the process leading to negotiations initiated by Mandela from prison, and never as the result of an appeal for clemency.

INDIAN SOUTH AFRICANS – A FUTURE BOUND WITH THE CAUSE OF THE AFRICAN MAJORITY

AHMED KATHRADA

In recent years we have witnessed a flurry of diplomatic activity and policy pronouncements by the apartheid regime. These developments have caused a renewal of speculation about détente and dialogue, about South Africa's outward-looking policy generally, and the possibility of the emergence of a new southern African grouping, which would include the Republic.

Within South Africa the doors of the prestigious Nico Malan Theatre have been thrown open to men and women of all colours. Black and white feature together in sporting and cultural events. Some 'Europeans Only' signs have been removed from lifts and park benches. The doors of learning are opening up to larger numbers of hitherto deprived children. Generally, prospects of improved living conditions apparently brighten the face of economic reality.

A number of people, including some blacks who perceive in these events a change of heart among the Nat politicians, are inclined to sit back as they see the beginnings of the end of problems that have plagued the country for centuries.

It would be short-sighted to ignore or dismiss these happenings. On the surface at least, there can be no doubt that the Nats are trying to project a new image. However, it would be a mistake to allow oneself to be carried away and only see the South Africa of 1976 through rose-coloured spectacles.

The National Party and white South Africans generally have a neurotic obsession with colour and numbers. Every white child is taught that the prerequisite to remaining happy, human and secure is to remain white; that the biggest threat to its future is the black man, who by virtue of his superior numbers is sure to swamp the whites and drive them into the sea.

In 1963, just before the Rivonia arrests, Dr Eben Dônges, then Minister of Interior, pinpointed the growth of African political movements at the time as the biggest threat to South Africa, meaning, of course, white South Africa. He appealed to whites, Coloureds and Indians to stand together in the face of this 'threat' and called for their 'five million hearts to beat as one'. This sentiment has since been echoed in varying degrees by people of different hues of 'verligte' opinion.[3] The bolder ones postulate the complete integration of Coloured and white; a few broaden this to include the Indians. The cynical ones advocate this tripartite grouping without significant adjustments to the existing politico-socio-economic position of the Coloureds and Indians.

A fair amount of Nat thought is today directed towards winning the Coloured and Indian peoples as allies of the whites. This follows the logic of apartheid reasoning. First, break the unity of the African people by dismembering them into ethnic groups and dispersing them among the nine projected Bantustans. Having done that, the whites would still find themselves outnumbered by Africans in the rest of so-called 'white South Africa'. Some sort of equilibrium would be necessary. Hence the Coloureds and Indians must be detached from the Africans and won over to the side of the whites.

In order to assess the prospects of the Nats seriously adopting this line of approach, it is necessary to review their policies and activities since 1948. In this essay we shall use Indian South Africans as a case study.

The National Party was swept into power in the 1948 elections on the slogan of *Die Kaffer op sy plek en die Koelie uit die Land* (literally: 'The kaffir in his place and the coolie out of the country').[4] The official policy was set out in a pamphlet, *Race Relations Policy of the National Party*, published at the end of 1947. It stated that 'the Party regards the Indians as a foreign element, which cannot be assimilated in the South African set-up. Not being native to the country they cannot expect more preferential treatment than an immigrant community. We accordingly have in mind the repatriation of as many Indians as possible ... With the Indians still in our midst a definite policy of Apartheid should be enforced between them and the Whites, and likewise as far as feasible between them and the indigenous non-white sections.'

We need not dwell on the 'foreignness' of the Indians and the calls for their repatriation. It is sufficient to state that almost one hundred per cent of the Indian South Africans were born in South Africa and know no other homeland. Even D.F. Malan (who became the first Nat Prime Minister in 1948) said in Parliament in 1946: 'Probably 85 to 90 per cent of the Indians in South Africa have been born in South Africa. In India they are aliens. Consequently, I take up the attitude that they form part of the permanent population of South Africa.'

As for repatriation, in spite of coercion, harsh legislation and the inducement of double bonuses for would-be repatriates, these proposals never got off the ground. Only Nat politicians and a few members of the South African Indian Council[5] believed and perpetuated the oft-repeated myth that Indians only became South African citizens in 1961 when Verwoerd announced the creation of a Department of Indian Affairs. The fact is that already with the arrival of the very first indentured Indians in 1860 it was laid down that after the expiry of their period of indentured labour those who chose to remain in Natal were to be regarded as full citizens and treated accordingly.

In 1961 the Nat regime was obliged to acknowledge the long established *fait accompli* that Indians were part of the permanent population. Former Minister of Interior, Senator Jan de Klerk, said that the attitude of successive governments had generated the 'feeling that [Indians] were being regarded as a foreign group that did not belong here'.[6] Referring to the change of attitude he said that the government had decided to 'start making use of a rubber and rub out what had been done in the past. One gains nothing by continually trying to play politics.' Benevolent words! And surprising, too, coming as they did from one who some years previously had reacted to India's anti-racist activities at the UN by referring to that country's UN ambassador, Mrs Vijayalakshmi Pandit, as '*daardie Koeliemeid*' ('that coolie maid').

Why did the Nats decide to adopt this 'new look' policy and what does it mean in terms of the everyday lives of the Indian people?

First, the Nats saw the need to have a more balanced population in terms of numbers. This is the essence of the Bantustan policy. It is also the reason why three-quarter million Indians and two million Coloureds are being wooed to form a common front with the whites.

Secondly, the National Party was no longer a parliamentary opposition. As an opposition party it could make extravagant statements and unrealistic promises for the purpose of winning electoral support. While white domination and *herrenvolkism*[7] still remain its basic tenets, as a governing party it has found that its public programme now has to be couched in terms that would project an aura of respectability and responsibility.

The National Party is no longer a party where farmers and farmers' interests and attitudes predominate. The post-war years have seen a radical change in the socio-economic conditions of the Afrikaners. There has emerged among them an industrial, mining and finance capitalist class. True, the farmers are still there, but to an increasing extent they, too, are no longer the bearded, tobacco-chewing, khaki-clad men whose thoughts and leisurely pace seldom exceeded that of the ox wagon they drove and whose vision of the world did not extend much further than the confines of their farms.

In the economic upsurge that the country still seems to be experiencing it is the bankers, insurance men and financiers, the supermarket operators, factory owners, mining magnates, scientists and technocrats who are exerting greater influence. While unwilling to abolish race oppression, their outlook is guided primarily by economic realities and their predominant interest is economic expansion and exploitation. Of necessity, they are more sensitive to pressures and developments, both local and international. For instance, with ever keen, almost colour-blind eyes, they see the giant African continent less as a monster to be feared and repulsed and more as a potential market and field of investment on their very doorstep, to be wooed and bought over. And in the process, if the need arises to parley with erstwhile Frelimo 'terrorists' over the electricity of Cabora Bassa, or with the Marxist MPLA over the Kunene River project, well, then parley with them they shall. Never mind the pledge nor the blood that is being spilt to 'ensure a communist-free southern Africa and to preserve it for the West'. Of course, in their business-orientated outward policy they are also eager to neutralise the neighbouring states against the use of their territories for guerrilla incursions against the Republic.

Another factor is the steadfast resistance of the Indian people. From the time their fore-fathers set foot on South African soil they have fought a relentless struggle against racial discrimination and for equality. In the face of the severest repression and victimisation, of boycotts of Indian businesses, starvation wages, blatant discrimination by legislation and open incitement to violence, they have persevered with dogged determination, not only to retain what they had gained, but also to win respect and human dignity.

In what condition, then, do we find the Indian community today?

Let us take education. In 1974 there were 366 Indian schools of which 287 were primary,

72 high, four nursery schools and three schools for handicapped children. Of these, 154 were built with funds raised by the Indian community itself. The total Indian school population in 1973 was 176 238. Between 1966 and 1974 the number of primary-school pupils increased by 4,8 per cent while the number of secondary-school pupils rose by 78,1 per cent. In 1974, 50 434 pupils were enrolled at high schools, 21 612 (42,85 per cent) of whom were female.

But according to Professor A.L. Behr of the University of Durban-Westville, of the 18 586 pupils who were in Standard 1 in 1966 only 9 339 remained to complete Standard 8 in 1972; of 172 141 Indian children at school in 1972 only 380 obtained Matriculation exemptions.

A survey of Indians in Natal and Transvaal carried out in 1973 by Market Research (Africa) Pty Ltd reported the following: 11 per cent of Indians over 16 had no education at all, 32 per cent of Indians over 16 had some primary education, 19 per cent over 16 had completed primary school, 7 per cent over 16 had finished high school and 1 per cent of Indians over 16 had some university education.

In 1973 compulsory education was introduced for Indians. It is expected that the drop-out rate will be reduced substantially.

In 1974 there were 112 410 university students in South Africa. Of these students 95 881 were white, 8 040 were African, 5 247 were Asian, and 3 242 were Coloured.

These figures look impressive. But they do not tell the whole story. They do not indicate that there still remains an enormous disparity in the per capita expenditure for whites, Indian, African and Coloured schoolchildren. The Minister told Parliament that the average unit cost for Indian children in 1968/1969 was R70 per pupil. The average for the same year per white pupil in the Transvaal was R191, while in Natal it was R285. The figures do not indicate the difference in facilities such as laboratories, libraries, sports fields, gymnasia, etc. One of the first actions of the Nat regime was to withdraw the school-feeding schemes for black children.

The figures do not show the hungry, barefoot children trudging to school each day, the majority from homes where the parents cannot make ends meet, where one or other necessity has to be sacrificed and children have to spend the afternoons playing in the streets because they are denied access to recreational facilities.

They do not show the disparity in the salary scales between white and black teachers and the ratio of pupils to teachers. The viciousness of race discrimination can be appreciated when looking at the salary position of the teaching staff at the University of Durban-Westville. Though this is an apartheid institution set up for Indian students, Indian lecturers' salaries are lower than those for their white colleagues at the same university and possessing the same qualifications. In December 1974, soon after Pik Botha, South Africa's delegate to the UN, promised to end racial discrimination, Vorster could boast to the South African Indian Council only of 'the very favourable ratio between salaries of whites and Indians' at the Indian university. His manner of ending discrimination was to announce that the government had approved that the university could 'out of its own funds, that is, funds not provided by the State, enhance the salary scales and further narrow the gap or bring it on par with the whites' (my emphasis). What cynicism!

In 1975 the South African Indian Council decided to make representations to the government that all educational institutions for Indians be opened to students of other racial groups. Even this separate development body was obliged to acknowledge the futility of the apartheid philosophy in education. Years ago the Congress organisations had expressed the universal desire of the black people in the Freedom Charter that the doors of learning and culture should be open to all.

Indian housing and living conditions are directly linked to the Group Areas Act, which was described by Malan as the kernel of apartheid policy. The people of South Africa – already classified, and often reclassified, into separate ethnic and colour compartments – are obliged to settle in their respective group areas. In conformity with the principles of the Group Areas Act the African people are being forced into nine ethnic Bantustans, which together make up barely 13 per cent of the surface area of South Africa.

The public has been accustomed to seeing photographs of luxurious Indian-owned mansions, huge supermarkets and department stores, the Oriental Plaza in Johannesburg, economic and sub-economic housing schemes, recreational halls, sports fields, clinics and other imposing buildings – all in Indian group areas (except in the Orange Free State, where Indians are not allowed to settle at all).

It is said that between 1966 and 1974, 33 561 housing units for Indians were erected. Much slum housing has been eradicated. According to figures quoted by Anson Lloyd, Chairman of the South African Sugar Millers Association, local authorities had advanced R53 million between 1966 and 1974 for building 27 000 housing units for Indians.

Very impressive! But again, this portrays only a part of the picture. Statistical data are notorious for the facility with which they allow themselves to conceal as well as expose conditions.

The application of the Group Areas Act in 1976 – cruel, unjust and oppressive as it is – seems almost benign when compared with what it was actually designed to achieve. Nat politicians made no bones about what it held in store. Indians were already living in segregated areas. The Act aimed at uprooting them and herding them into fenced-in locations under conditions not dissimilar to those to which the African people had so long been condemned. The greater portion of its venom was aimed at the Indian merchant class, which it sought to cripple and destroy. No provision was originally made in the group areas for alternate accommodation for displaced tenants and traders.

To facilitate the application of the pending legislation, a Nat-inspired movement was launched in the Transvaal in 1949 to boycott Indian businesses. Known as *Die Suid-Afrikaanse Beskermbeweging* (the South African Protection Movement), it initially received widespread support among whites in a few rural areas. It was allowed to propagate its racist policies of incitement and intimidation. In fact, one of its top officials was elevated to judgeship.

In 1950 the Congress of the federated Dutch Reformed Churches urged wholesale and immediate apartheid against the Indians, and that all Indians should be repatriated. A leading Nat politician prophesied that when the full effect of the Group Areas Act was felt, Indians would be only too happy to get out of South Africa.

What was the size of the 'monster' against which such big artillery was turned? In 1946 the total area of land held by Asians was about 150 000 acres![8] In relation to the size of the country and the landholding of the whites, the Indians could by no stretch of imagination be said to have presented a threat. The only explanation for Nat action was the sinister aim of destroying the economic position of the Indian community and reducing its members to the status of hewers of wood and drawers of water.

Past masters at euphemism, Nat politicians frequently boast that the text of their legislation does not mention any particular ethnic group or community but applies to all equally. By 1969, 108 767 families were deemed to have occupied premises in areas that were set aside under the Act for members of other racial groups. The disqualified families were made up as follows: 68 897 Coloured families; 37 653 Indian families; 899 Chinese families; 1 318 white families. Of these the following had already been forced to move out of those areas: 34 240 Coloured families; 21 939 Indian families; 64 Chinese families; 1 196 white families. Invariably the whites were least affected, and the few who were resettled, were resettled with the least inconvenience.

These statistics do not reveal the disruption, the agony and upset, the material and spiritual losses suffered by the Coloured and Indian people. Thousands were uprooted from premises they and their forebears had occupied and, under threat of imprisonment, they moved many miles away into group areas.

True, the Indian people have not been driven into fenced-in locations as envisaged, or into bare fields without alternative accommodation. True, the Act has been mellowed somewhat. But this was no generous gesture on the part of the regime. There were a number of contributing factors.

Foremost among these was the systematic resistance by the Indian people under the leadership of the South African Indian Congress (SAIC). From the outset the SAIC set out to oppose the Act by every means at its disposal. At almost every sitting of the Group Areas Board, the SAIC appeared and assisted the local communities to expose the gross injustices being perpetrated and to refuse to submit any plans or take any action that may be construed as willingness to cooperate with the nefarious activities of the Board. This was done side by side with a massive propaganda campaign throughout South Africa and overseas. Whenever the opportunity arose, Congress-briefed legal representatives challenged the Act in the courts, sometimes winning judicial relief, always causing obstruction and delay in implementation. Their actions often led to a modification of the Act. The Group Areas Act became one of the most amended pieces of legislation.

On 26 June 1950 the SAIC joined with the ANC (and the CPSA) to stage the first national political strike against, *inter alia*, the Group Areas Act and the Suppression of Communism Act. In 1952 the Congresses jointly launched the Defiance Campaign against Unjust Laws, with the Group Areas Act singled out as one of the six unjust laws for attack.

In addition, there were numerous acts of individual defiance. In this regard the Transvaal Indian Congress President Nana Sita stands out. Arrested, brought before court and jailed repeatedly, Nana Sita refused to move out of his premises and until his death symbolised the resistance of the Indian people.

So effective was the opposition that when the Minister of Interior Eben Dônges was criticised in Parliament for the delay in the implementation of the Group Areas Act he said, in a rare admission, that the delay was caused by the systematic obstruction organised by the Indian Congress.

This legislation is so repugnant and unjust that even the Nat-created Indian Council, having pledged to work within the framework of the policy of separate development, after years of efforts to seek amelioration, was in 1975 compelled to call upon the government to totally repeal the Group Areas Act and other legislation.

ECONOMIC POSITION

Let us look at the economic position of Indian South Africans. The Republic is the most highly industrialised country on the African continent and its economy has been steadily expanding. White South Africans can boast a standard of living that is among the highest in the world.

In 1969 the following figures were given in Parliament about the economically active persons in the different population groups: Africans – 4 800 000; whites – 1 438 000; Coloureds – 692 000; Indians – 157 000.

In 1974 Anson Lloyd of the Sugar Millers Association said that of a total Indian population of over 700 000 there were 202 000 who were economically active. Unemployment, which stood at 30 000 a decade ago, had been reduced to 1 250. From 1961 to 1974 the number of Indians employed in industry in Natal increased from 32 000 to 82 000, that is, by 156 per cent. This, he said, exceeded the growth of employment amongst whites, Africans and Coloureds.

H.C. Morecamve, President of the South African Federated Chamber of Industries, said (in 1974) that by 1970, 26 per cent of whites, 35 per cent of Coloureds, 41 per cent of Indians and 14 per cent of Africans who were economically active were employed in secondary industry. According to the Department of Statistics the number of people employed in the manufacturing industries in 1969 was as follows: Africans – 608 000; whites – 279 000; Coloureds – 196 000; and Indians – 74 000.

It is reported that 20 years ago the only industry in which Indian apprentices were found was the furniture industry. Ten years ago the building industry was added. With the growth of the economy and the concomitant shortage of skilled labour more and more avenues of employment have opened up for Indian workers. In 1973 the M.L. Sultan Technical College in Durban offered training courses to Indians in the following trades and vocations: plumbing, sheet metal work, radio, fitting and turning, welding, motor mechanics, building, draughtsmanship, surveying, medical technology, etc. In 1974, Indian telephone technicians were being trained.

A survey of Indians over the age of 16 in Natal, the Witwatersrand and Pretoria was carried out in 1973 by Market Research (Africa). The survey claimed a coverage of 327 000 Indians over

16 living in the above areas, that is 83 per cent of the total adult Indian population. It showed that 34 per cent of Indians were tradesmen and labourers, 18 per cent were salesworkers, 15 per cent were clerical workers, 8 per cent service workers, 7 per cent professional and technical workers, 6 per cent transport and communication workers, 2 per cent administrative or executive personnel and 10 per cent not gainfully employed. The above data show that significant developments have taken place over the last decade in the field of Indian occupation and employment.

In 1966 a Bureau of Market Research Report on Indians in Durban showed that the mean monthly household income was R95,78, but that the median was R77,30. Research workers pointed out that the median was more important to establish for Indians than for other communities since there is a small minority of comparatively wealthy professional men, traders and industrialists, but that the majority of the people live in poverty. This survey showed that just over half of the households had incomes below the Poverty Datum Line (PDL), and that 54,8 per cent of the heads of households earned less than R60 per month.

Figures relating to the manufacturing industry published by the Department of Statistics in 1969 confirm not only the continuing low income of Indian workers, but also the great disparity between black and white wages. The gross monthly income of white workers was R278, Indians R67, Coloureds R65, and Africans R48.

In 1969 the Natal Regional Survey carried out by P.W. Pillay and P.A. Allison studied a sample of 835 Indian households in Durban. The average number of persons per household was 6,9. They estimated monthly living costs at R73,51 per household. The survey found that between 50 and 60 per cent of the households had incomes below this amount. Of these 15,4 per cent had incomes of less than R40 per month.

In 1970 a survey of Indians in Durban was conducted by Media Community Research on behalf of the *Daily News*. It showed that 1 in 100 earned a monthly income of R400, while 14 per cent fell within the R150 to R400 bracket. The bulk, that is, 68 per cent, had incomes less than R150 per month. A breakdown of the lower income group showed that 14 per cent earned between R26 and R50 per month; 19 per cent earned between R51 and R75 per month; 18 per cent between R76 and R100 per month; and 13 per cent between R101 and R150 per month.

Finally, the South Africa Bureau of Statistics gave the following wage rates in the manufacturing industry for the years 1970 and April 1973:

	Whites	Coloureds	Indians	Africans
Average wage per month – 1970	R300	R71	R75	R51
Average wage per month – April 1973	R376	R97	R103	R67

The annual rate of increase was the highest for Indians. However, the salary gap between Indians and whites, though narrower, still remained large. Taking into account the inflationary conditions, and the high prices and rents, which invariably hit the lower income groups hardest, it is fair to conclude that a significantly large percentage of Indian South Africans still live in conditions of poverty.

Reference has been made to a developing minority of wealthy industrialists, traders and professional men among the Indians. Statements about the exact number of industrialists differ. Former Minister of Indian Affairs, Owen Horwood, said that in 1961 there were 161 Indian industrialists in Natal and these increased to 700 in 1973. Former Minister of Interior Theo Gerdner said that the number increased from 181 in 1961 to 527 in 1969. Anson Lloyd says there were 191 in 1961 and over 800 in 1974. M.B. Naidoo of the South African Indian Council said that between 1961 and 1973 there were 800 new industrial ventures among the Indians. It is clear that there has been a considerable increase over the last decade in the number of Indians who fall into the category described as 'industrialist'. It is believed that a few Indian-owned enterprises each employ close to 1 000 workers. At least one was listed on the stock exchange. Cottwall of the Natal Clothing Manufacturers Association said in 1974 that all in all there were 208 clothing factories in Natal employing about 24 000 people, 95 per cent of whom were Indians. Over half the manufacturers were Indians. It was not clear how many of the 24 000 workers were employed by Indian manufacturers. It is assumed that a considerable number, if not the majority, of the Indian 'clothing manufacturers' consisted of small cut-make-and-trim (CMT) establishments, each employing a handful of workers. This assumption is made on the basis of the type of undertakings included by Theo Gerdner as industrialists. His 527 industrialists included: 46 food processing establishments, 12 textile mills, 40 timber undertakings, 62 motor garages, 24 furniture factories, 24 printers and 72 laundry and dry cleaners.

In the agricultural sector Indian interests are negligible. B.M. Sutney of the Department of Agricultural Technical Services estimated in 1975 that 2 500 Indians were engaged in agriculture, 1 800 of these as registered sugar cane farmers. The median size of the farms was 7,9 hectares, far less than the minimum of 24 hectares regarded as an economic holding under sugar cane. The Indian farmers in Natal occupy a total of approximately 37 000 hectares.

It has been established that 81 per cent of the sugar cane farmers on the North Coast had net incomes of less than Rl 000 per annum. Of these, 62 per cent earned less than R500 per annum and 4 per cent had a net income of R300 per annum.

Some years ago it was estimated that 15 per cent of Natal Indians and 71 per cent of Transvaal Indians were engaged in commerce. This referred to the Indian retail and wholesale shopkeepers and presumably included the shop assistants. A considerable number of these, if not the majority, were small retail shops run by family members, employing few if any shop assistants. Another investigation found that a large number of these remained constantly in debt and were frequently on the verge of bankruptcy. Shop owners were in effect glorified workers who preferred to cling to some measure of independence. Also, the lack of opportunities, particularly in the early years, had left open few avenues for Indians apart from joining the unskilled labour force.

It was because of this lack of opportunities that Indians who could afford it gradually began to enter the professional sector, although even here the opportunities were severely restricted. Of the 9 152 doctors, lawyers, chemists, engineers and other professionals in 1936, only 25 were Indian, 23 Coloured and 14 African. In 1968 there were 385 Indian doctors, 59 interns, 14 dentists, 52 attorneys (in Natal) and five advocates. In 1974 there were 6 590 Indian teachers in South Africa. The minority of wealthy Indians, who constitute the bulk of the income taxpayers in the community, come from these latter groups.

To round off investigations on the extent of poverty among Indian South Africans the Market Research (Africa) survey of 1973 showed that 86 per cent of Indians in Natal, on the Witwatersrand and in Pretoria owned no property at all. Only 12 per cent owned their own houses and 30 per cent owned some other property.

In the economic plane it is apparent that the Indian people are somewhat better placed in relation to the other black groups, but their standard of living and economic advancement could by no stretch of imagination be compared with that of the whites. In fact, the surveys referred to show that about half of the Indians still live in conditions of poverty.[9]

Finally, what does the much-vaunted Nat change of attitude towards the Indians mean in terms of political rights? Indians, like Africans and Coloureds, do not have the vote in the municipal, provincial and parliamentary institutions of the country. In Natal, Indians were deprived of the parliamentary vote in 1894 and the municipal vote in 1924. In the Transvaal they never possessed the franchise. The handful that enjoyed the vote in the Cape lost it together with the Coloureds in 1955.

In 1946 the United Party (UP) government of General Jan Smuts passed legislation that offered the Indian community in Natal and Transvaal the right to elect three whites to represent them in Parliament. In addition, Natal Indians could elect two members of the Provincial Council who could be Indians. The Indian people, under the leadership of the SAIC, rejected these proposals and condemned them as an insult to their dignity and honour. United, they rallied behind the Congress demand for the extension of the vote to all the people of South Africa on a basis of equality. So powerful was the Congress-led campaign that the government was unable to implement the legislation. When the Nats came to power in 1948 they regarded even this sham representation as conferring too many rights on the Indians, and abolished it soon after.

In 1961 the Department of Indian Affairs, headed by a Minister of Indian Affairs, was created. This was followed by setting up the South African Indian Council and numerous local affairs committees in Indian group areas. The new department took over responsibility for some Acts of Parliament affecting the Indian people. In the implementation of these laws the Department works in close collaboration with the Indian Council. In 1961 the Department had 102 posts, of which Indians filled approximately 30 per cent. By 1973 the posts had increased to 648, of which Indians occupied 50 per cent.

The new dispensation allowed for the setting up of local affairs committees (LACs) in Natal. In the Transvaal and the Cape they were called consultative committees. Initially the committees consisted of five members, all nominated by the Provincial Administrator. Later most of the members were elected. These committees are supposed to provide local Indian communities with avenues of contact with the white municipalities, which retained all effective control. The law graciously required the municipalities to 'consider' any suggestions and comments made by these Indian committees.

The first LAC was set up in Glencoe in 1963. By October 1972 there were 21 LACs in Natal, nine consultative committees in the Transvaal and three in the Cape. When they reach a partly elected stage these bodies are called management committees. Under certain circumstances they can graduate to the status of 'local authorities'. They are then known as town boards, for example Verulam and the two Isipingos. With a few exceptions these are fully elected and have their own 'mayors', 'town clerks', etc.

Let us look briefly at the experiences of the Verulam Town Board, the first of the three town boards established in 1969. As a municipality it became a member of the UP-controlled Natal Municipal Association and sent two representatives to attend its annual conference. The two representatives 'voluntarily refrained' from attending social gatherings, but their attendance at the conference led to protests by the four Nat-controlled municipalities in Natal, which threatened to boycott the gatherings. Thereafter Verulam, presumably with the acquiescence, if not at the request, of the UP, refrained from sending delegates to the conferences although it was allowed to retain membership of the Association, after a motion supported by 32 local authorities against four.

Not all LACs can aspire to being raised to the status of town boards. This was made clear by the former Minister of Indian Affairs, Owen Horwood, towards the end of 1973. Only those that were financially viable could hope to become autonomous, he said. The Natal Ordinance conferring 'self-government' to Indian areas requires the fulfilment of the following criteria: size of the area, financial viability, number of voters, and availability of suitable people. From this it is clear that with the exception of a few areas with a large concentration of Indians (Umzinto, Durban, Stanger and Pietermaritzburg) the great majority of LACs are doomed to remain powerless bodies. They can be likened to toy telephones to be used by members to transmit messages to the white authority in the hope that somehow their voices would be heard.

The UP member and Chairman of the Non-white Local Government Administration Committee of the Natal Provincial Council, E.P. Fowler, saw great merit in this arrangement. Addressing the South African Indian Council in 1974, he said he was pleased the government was seeing to it that the Indians were receiving good grounding in local government through LACs, instead of being required to assume responsibilities for which they were not ready. He appealed to the Indians to work within the framework of separate development. This type of humiliation and insult should not be allowed to go unchecked. The Indian Council has been forced to take note of these feelings. As a result the Council resolved in 1975 that it would not be to the advantage of the Indian community to create small local authorities that had very little prospect of development and of adequately meeting the needs of the community. The

Council decided to recommend to the government that the present system of local government be replaced by one in which all the racial groups would be able to be represented by one local authority for the whole of a particular area.

On a national level, the South African Indian Council was established in 1964. During the 13 years of its existence it has concerned itself with questions such as the removal of inter-provincial restrictions against Indians, bilingualism (that is Afrikaans and English) in the hotel trade, employment of domestic servants, recognition of medical degrees from India and Pakistan, the establishment of training facilities and cultural organisations. It remained a body of 25 members, all appointed by the Minister of Indian Affairs. In 1972 the Chairman of the Council, H.E. Joosub, complained that until the Council became at least a partly elected body it would not be able to convince the Indian community that it was representing its interests adequately. He said there was a growing lack of faith in the Council. Eventually, Joosub withdrew from the Council because of the 'ineffectiveness', 'sterility' and 'impotence' of the body.

The State President and the Minister of Indian Affairs have the power to declare the body partly or fully elective. But because of the continuance of widespread anti-Nat feelings among the Indians, the call for universal franchise for all the people of South Africa, and as a result of its experience with the Coloured Representative Council (CRC) and the Labour Party, as well as with some Bantustans, the government refuses to allow elections for the Indian Council.

With the first so-called partly elected Council in November 1974 the government was not yet prepared to take the risk of throwing the election open to the community. The membership of the Council was increased to 30, 15 of whom were to be appointed by the Minister and 15 'elected' by a system of electoral colleges in Natal, the Cape and Transvaal. In 1973 a member of the Indian Council told the *Natal Daily News* that the electoral colleges meant that only about 400 out of a total of over 700 000 Indians would be able to vote for the first Council elections. Indeed even less than 400 in fact took part.

One of the matters considered by this body was the question of a fully elected Council. In January 1975 and again in July 1975 it resolved to ask the government to set up an elected council of 45 to hold office for five years. It also wants a fully elected Executive of seven and an elected chairman. All Indians over the age of 18 should be allowed to vote.

In all probability the government will be obliged to grant this request. But after having reached this stage, what then? Let Vorster answer. For he has got it all worked out already. He told members of the South African Indian Council: 'I am aware of the fact that the composition of the Council and the manner in which half its members have been elected has come up for criticism ... This should not worry you unduly because of the fact that this step in the development of an Indian constitutional authority is not the final word but just another phase ... It is not the ultimate goal but another stepping stone from which we can set out to chart the future ... The government envisages that constitutionally the Indian community will develop along the same lines as the Coloured people ... The main population groups which constitute the South African society must as far as practically possible be placed on the road to self-determination so that each and every one of these groups can determine in accordance with its own tradition and ideals and with due regard to the equivalent aspirations of other groups, its own destination.'

Lest the optimistic and credulous Indian councillors mistake their 'own destination' and begin to harbour illusions, Vorster, in all fairness, made clear their place in his scheme of things. In no uncertain terms he reiterated that the white man will remain boss. He said that 'sight should not be lost of the fact that the white population group, by virtue of certain cultural and historical circumstances has played and will in the future continue to play the leading role in the constitutional developments of the country'.

Nat policy could not have been more clearly pronounced, and the allegation should not be made that the Indian and Coloured people were misled. From Vorster's own mouth we have it that the existing machinery and institutions such as Parliament, the cabinet, and provincial and local authorities are to remain the preserves of the whites. What the Nats envisaged for the Indians as the ultimate in constitutional development is really little more than a change of nomenclature for the existing institutions. As far as its functions are concerned, it will confine itself to the same matters that have occupied the attention of the Indian Council since 1964, such as education, social welfare, sports and cultural affairs. Within the strict limitations imposed by the prophets of separate development the Indian councillors will be given a more or less free rein. One thing from which there would, however, be no departure, is that it must for all times remain a subordinate body. Laws will still be made for it, which it will merely be expected to implement. The final authority will continue to be vested in the white Parliament and whatever the Indians do they will have to act out within the room allowed by this mother and father of the whole conglomeration of Nat-style 'democratic institutions' catering at different levels for the different ethnic groups.

In spite of categorical pronouncements it appears that members of the Indian Council persisted in asking the Prime Minister to spell out the highest position that an Indian citizen could aspire to attain. Vorster obliged in clear and unequivocal terms: there was no question of Indians and Coloureds ever being represented in the white Parliament. It was neither his nor his party's policy that this should ever happen. But once the Indians reached 'cabinet status' he envisaged the creation of a 'cabinet council', 'which would serve the purpose of liaison between their Council on the one hand and Parliament and the government on the other'.

Further it had been agreed that Indians would be appointed as fully fledged members of the majority of statutory bodies dealing with matters also affecting Indians, for example, wage boards, transportation boards, etc. In pursuance of this, S.E. Bhan was appointed to Vorster's Economic Advisory Council during the latter half of 1975. It is in accordance with this line of thinking that the government included M.B. Naidoo in the UN delegation of 1974 to represent the Indians, together with K.D. Matanzima and D. Ulster to represent Africans and Coloureds.

Taken together with the conditions obtaining in the fields of education, housing, and economic life in general, as outlined above, it is obvious that the Indian South Africans are condemned in Nat thinking and policy never to rise above the level of second-class citizens in the land of their birth.

Under the circumstances what are the prospects of a movement among the Nats for the whites, Coloureds and Indians to stand together against the 'African danger'? There can be little doubt that this has rapidly become the desire not only of Nats but also of a considerable number of non-Nat whites in the Republic. At the same time it is clear that the members of the ruling party remain steadfast in their purpose to perpetuate the inferior status of the Coloured and Indian people. This was confirmed when the former Minister of Interior Theo Gerdner put the matter to the test within the National Party and among the white electorate. He had been outspoken in his belief that in the search for a solution to South Africa's problems top priority must be given to the complete integration of whites, Coloureds and Indians. This was totally rejected by the National Party. Gerdner then formed his own party and propagated his views among the whites. For holding such sacrilegious and almost criminal views Gerdner was unceremoniously flung into the political wilderness.

From the side of the Indian community it could hardly be expected that such a shoddy manoeuvre would meet with success. Ever since the emergence of the Naicker–Dadoo leadership in Indian politics in the late 1930s and early 1940s the community became increasingly committed to the view that its struggle for freedom was inextricably linked with that of the African and Coloured people. Prior to 1945 the policy of the Indian Congress had been to try to secure separate concessions and reforms in the conditions of the Indian people. In the mid-1940s Dr Monty Naicker and Dr Yusuf Dadoo, with the organised support of the overwhelming majority of the Indian people, gained control of the Indian Congress on the fundamental platform of unity with the other black groups, and for a militant struggle for a free and democratic South Africa for all its people. Referring to this event Premier General Smuts said in a letter to Lord Wavell (one-time Viceroy of India): 'The Indians have moved more to the left and have emphasised their standpoint more forcibly ... The Indian Congress has elected a new executive of a more uncompromising character who have pressed for their maximum programme – equal rights, equal franchise on a common roll, and other economic items of their programme.'

This policy has gained universal support among the people despite Nat attempts at separation. Events such as the African–Indian riots in Natal in 1949, and the blatantly anti-Indian policies of the Pan-Africanist Congress (PAC) since its foundation and until the mid-1960s at least, did not deter the Indians from following the policy of unity. Further, in spite of the setbacks suffered by the Indian Congress in the 1960s as a result of Nat repression the Indian people have not wavered from this path. Indeed, it must certainly be the continued strength of this feeling that obliges even leaders of the apartheid Indian Council to make statements such as the one made by its Chairman, J.N. Reddy, when he said: 'The leaders of the Indian community have on numerous occasions indicated very clearly that we stand for a South African society where all the inhabitants of the land will have equal opportunity.' On a more recent occasion he again expressed the hope for the complete 'disappearance of out-dated practices and unnecessary irritations ... which affect the lives of a large section of our population'.

When we examine the situation as a whole it cannot be denied that there have been improvements in the position of the Indian people. But this must most certainly not be ascribed to any desire on the part of the Nats to promote racial equality. It is essentially a phenomenon brought about by the economic upsurge that South Africa is experiencing. What the Nats want is a docile community, voteless and inferior, but at the same time performing all the tasks that the economy demands. There must be no doubt that at the first signs of a recession the main sufferers will again be the Indian people together with the Coloureds and Africans.

When looking at their prospects for the future Indians cannot be expected to find the slightest consolation in attempts at *'toenadering'* (rapprochement) with the ruling party and its policies. The Indians' path remains the continued and closer identification with the struggle of the oppressed people as a whole.

In 1962 the South African Communist Party (SACP) adopted its policy programme, which contained a careful analysis of the situation in South Africa and described the relations between black and white, between oppressed and oppressor, as colonialism of a special type. Here within the boundaries of the same country a situation had emerged in which the status of the white oppressor and the black oppressed was in many ways akin to that of the relations that obtain between the imperialists on the one hand and the colonial people on the other. The programme observed that before Union the provinces of South Africa had been, at one time or another, colonies of Great Britain. Thereafter, although there was a political withdrawal, massive British economic interest not only remained, but also increased manifold. Later this was supplemented by American and continental investments. In the meantime there came into being an indigenous white capitalist class which independently, as agents of, and in close collaboration with international interests, maintained a stranglehold on the economic life of the masses of the black people. In effect, beginning with the years of British rule, and subsequently throughout the entire period that followed right up to the present, the black people in South Africa live and suffer under conditions of colonial exploitation.

The programme, taking into account these conditions, set out its short-term aims for immediate attainment, and long-term aims towards which the SACP eventually hoped to lead the people. The demands and objectives contained in its short-term programme coincide to a large extent with the objectives set out in the Freedom Charter. The long-term objective is establishing a socialist South Africa.

Nothing of a fundamental nature seems to have occurred in the years since 1962 to warrant a departure from the basic analysis contained in the SACP's policy programme or from the objectives set out in the policies of the Congresses. Because of circumstances the views expressed in an essay of this nature relating to the tasks ahead must of necessity be tentative. On the basis of what limited information is available it does appear that the impending developments in the

Transkei and other Bantustans confirm the prognosis outlined in the programme. The urgent and immediate tasks remain the national liberation of the oppressed black people from racial oppression and the establishment of a free and democratic South Africa for all its people as envisaged in the Freedom Charter.

Opinions are increasingly being voiced to the effect that the political situation existing today necessitates a radical shift in the policies propagated by the freedom organisations. It is held that the character of the struggle has changed from one of national liberation to a class struggle for the elimination of capitalism and for the establishment of a socialist society. Such viewpoints have been greatly encouraged by the dramatic developments across our borders in Mozambique and Angola.

Meanwhile, it is essential that one should not allow oneself to be swept away alone by feelings of impatience or enthusiasm. The situation and developments in other countries, no matter how close in proximity, cannot just be transposed to our own. One cannot, however, escape the overpowering effects of the prospects of socialist states right on our doorsteps on the people of our country. Closely related is the fact that in South Africa we can boast of having not only one of the oldest communist parties in the world, but also one of the handful existing on the entire African continent. Through the years of its existence the SACP has consistently propagated the ideas of socialism and carried them to the distant corners of the land. Not only are our people today no strangers to the virtues of socialism, but despite the outlawing of the CPSA and concomitant repression and persecution, the government has dismally failed in its efforts to annihilate socialist thought and activity.

These facts notwithstanding, an objective analysis and approach to developments is indispensable. The historical development of our country, the economic conditions obtaining today, the social composition of our people, the 325 years of racial oppression and all it entails, are some of the factors that single out South Africa from the rest of the continent. Programmes and policies that seem clear-cut in other parts of our continent are not in ours.

The 1962 programme of the SACP is still substantially valid in today's conditions. The short-term objectives coinciding with the Freedom Charter still appear to be the immediate minimum goal to work for. The task of overthrowing white domination and *herrenvolkism*, and the attainment of national liberation for the black people seem as applicable in today's situation as they did in 1955, when the Freedom Charter was adopted. Freeing the black man spiritually and physically from oppression based on colour, ridding him completely of any vestiges of a 'slave mentality' and opening up to him full and equal opportunities in every walk of life is still the prerequisite of political and social advancement.

The remaining question then is an assessment of the forces that comprise the national liberation movement, the organisations that lead it and the methods to be utilised for the attainment of the objectives.

The burden of carrying the struggle remains the responsibility of the masses of African, Coloured and Indian people. It is an elementary lesson of history that benevolent rulers do not just arise out of the blue in order to confer freedom upon oppressed people. Those who are deprived of freedom have to fight for it every inch of the way.

Based on the data and facts relating to the condition of the Indian people provided earlier it is clear that no fundamental changes have taken place in their economic well-being. They remain part of the oppressed and exploited black people.

There is an aspect, however, that requires some elaboration. Arguments have periodically been advanced for the exclusion from the struggle of what is variously described as the 'Indian middle class' or 'Indian bourgeoisie' or 'Indian capitalist class'. So extreme have been some of the attacks as to place the said class of Indians in the camp of the enemy. This is an erroneous approach and serves only to dissipate the liberation forces. It is politically incorrect and does not take into account precedents and historical experience from the struggles of other peoples.

It is true that there is a more developed middle class among the Indians than among the Coloureds and Africans. In addition, there has come into being among the Indians the rudiments of a capitalist class in the Marxist sense of the term.[10] It follows that by virtue of their relative affluence the middle class and capitalists enjoy a higher standard of living. But there is no evidence that these people have been exempted as a class from the racial laws. It may be that these laws apply at different levels. But they, too, suffer humiliations and frustrations on account of the colour of their skin.

Racism and racial laws do not distinguish between classes. Even in their advanced economic status these people come up against laws which set a definite limit beyond which they may not progress. A number of individuals may have betrayed the struggle and, by accepting separate development, gone over to the side of the enemy. The majority may be conspicuous by their absence from the rough and tumble of the political struggle. As employers and landlords they may be no better and, in some cases, even worse than their white counterparts. In spite of this it will be a mistake to lump them together and discard the whole class as enemies of the people.

Not for a moment do I contend that as a class they can be expected to play a leading role in the struggle. The leading role must be taken by the working class, as has already been the position in the SAIC on this matter. At the same time the Indian merchant class is part and parcel of the people suffering from racial discrimination and they can play a positive role in the struggle.

In this regard one can do no better than to take a leaf out of the experience of the great Chinese Revolution. In an article in 1957 entitled 'On the Correct Handling of Contradictions among the People', Mao Tse Tung deals very clearly with the question of who constitutes 'the people'. He says that the term 'people' has different meanings in different countries and in different historical periods. In China during the Japanese aggression, all those classes, strata and social groups that opposed aggression belonged to the category of 'the people', while the Japanese imperialists, the Chinese traitors and pro-Japanese elements belonged to the category of the enemies of the people. During the war of liberation, the US imperialists and their henchmen, the bureaucratic capitalist and landlord classes, were the enemies, while all the other classes, strata and social groups who opposed these enemies belonged to the category of 'the people'. At this stage of the building of socialism, all classes, strata and social groups that approve, support or work for the cause of socialist construction, belong to the category of 'the people'.

Mao Tse Tung distinguished between antagonistic and non-antagonistic contradictions. He analysed contradictions among the people and contradictions between the working class and the national bourgeoisie. In the period of the bourgeois democratic revolution there was a revolutionary side to the character of the national bourgeoisie as well as a tendency to compromise with the enemy. But he went on to explain that the national bourgeoisie differed from the imperialists, landlords and bureaucratic capitalists. He also noted the contradictions among the intellectuals, and made an observation that must always be remembered: since the contradictions between ourselves and the enemy and those among the people differ in nature they must be solved in different ways. The former was a matter of drawing a line between ourselves and our enemies, while the latter was a matter of distinguishing between right and wrong.

In South Africa there are apparent contradictions between the interests of the masses and the more affluent minority. But as in China, if these contradictions are handled properly, they can be resolved. In the meantime it will be correct to regard them as contradictions among the people. Based on Mao's writings, it remains the primary task of the national liberation movement in South Africa to guard against any tendency towards sectarianism, and to work to unite the broadest sections of the people. Once convinced of the correctness of the policies and objectives of the movement the main aim should be winning friends and adherents and to avoid dissipating energy on seeking, creating and increasing the number of enemies. In the final analysis it will be the policies and activities of the liberation organisations that will be decisive.

Then there is the question of the whites, more especially the role of white progressives. Just as it is wrong to lump together the entire Indian middle class as enemies of the struggle, so it will be equally incorrect to dismiss all whites. In spite of their bloody history of aggression, of dispossessing the African people of their land, of conquest, of enslavement and domination over all black people, the whites in South Africa are here to stay and they form part of the permanent population. Unlike in other African states, the whites in South Africa cannot be regarded as a settler population. It is unfortunately true that the overwhelming majority of them still cling to the racist policies of the National Party, the UP and the Herstigte Nasionale Party (HNP) and would like to see the perpetuation of racial discrimination and exploitation.

Over the years, a crack has appeared in the monolithic attitudes of the whites and gradually this crack is widening. The gallant band that followed the footsteps of Bram Fischer and the communists, and Helen Joseph of the COD, have identified themselves fully with the Congress movement. By their bravery and sacrifice they have established for themselves a position second to none.

There are a variety of white anti-Nat attitudes represented in organisations like the Christian Institute, the Liberal Party, the ARM, the Christian churches, NUSAS, the South African Institute of Race Relations, the Progressive Reform Party, TUCSA and others. In so far as they represent a departure from the brazen racism of the two major parties they must be welcomed. There remains, of course, the uphill of persuading them and winning them over towards the goals outlined in the Freedom Charter.

There should be no illusion about the possibility of winning the majority of the whites over. At best one can hope to neutralise very small portions of them. They have a great deal of vested interest in maintaining the dominant position they occupy and must be expected to vehemently resist any moves that threaten to shift them from their position in any way.

After 28 years of Nat rule, the government remains an Afrikaner government. In spite of the social transformation it is rapidly undergoing, the bulk of the Afrikaners are still the most narrow, prejudiced, parochial and bigoted of the white groups. Although somewhat hidden by the 'sophistication' of a new leadership, anti-Semitism and anti-English feelings are still rife among them. One must be careful not to attach too much importance to this divisive tendency. On the question of racial discrimination the English and the Afrikaners stand solidly united and should be expected to do all in their power to defend the status quo.

Thus an assessment of the forces pitched against each other in South Africa reveals broadly the following position: on the one hand there is the overwhelming mass of black people – African, Indian and Coloured – from all walks of life; workers, peasants, students, intellectuals and merchants. To this must be added the small number of whites represented by such people as Bram Fischer and Helen Joseph. This side stands uncompromisingly against the racist policies of the Nats and for full freedom and equality of opportunity for all. On the other hand there is the overwhelming majority of whites who are committed to the perpetuation of racial discrimination and white domination. To them must be added a small minority of blacks who have openly accepted the ideology of apartheid and separate development and who have ranged themselves on the side of the oppressor. Then there are the whites represented by the Liberal Party, the Progressive Reform Party (PRP) and others who have firmly come out against the Nats but at the same time refuse to throw their lot in with the aims and aspirations of the liberation movement, and remain a wavering element.

We come next to the organisations that make up the freedom movement. These include the African, Coloured and Indian Congresses and the COD, the PAC, the NEUM, the SACP, the BPC (including SASO) and the various bodies represented by the Black Consciousness Movement. Of all these organisations, only the SACP and the Congress movement have evolved a programme and policy that can realistically be put forward for acceptance by all the people of South Africa, black as well as white.

It should be clarified that the BPC, SASO and allied bodies have not been set up as rivals to the existing bodies and, apart from fulfilling an *ad hoc* role in the political vacuum created by the banning of the ANC and PAC, have never claimed to usurp the role of the old established organisations. The emergence of the Black Consciousness Movement is an understandable reaction to the racist policies of the Nats. The commendable and inspiring activities and the display of political awareness especially by SASO and the black students have greatly boosted the national liberation movement. The fact that they have, in the face of great odds and extreme provocation, preserved a balance and refused to succumb to racism is a display of their maturity.

It is to be hoped that the feeling already existing will gain ground and give a broader connotation to the term 'black' so as to embrace all South Africans, regardless of colour who suffer persecution and are hounded, jailed, banned and outlawed as a result of their opposition to the pernicious doctrines of racism. In a word, to make the term 'black' include the Bram Fischers, the Helen Josephs and others who have by their courage and sacrifice earned nothing less than a glorious niche in the history and hearts of all South Africans who struggle against racism. Indeed, could it be disputed that if Bram Fischer in his lifetime were to have contested elections against K.D. Matanzima in Soweto or against J.N. Reddy in Durban or Tom Schwartz in Cape Town, the black people would have given a resounding 'Yes' to Bram Fischer?

While it is not for a moment asserted that the tenets of the Freedom Charter and the Congress movement and of the 1962 policy programme of the SACP should remain unalterable, it is maintained that these two documents remain the only ones that offer substantial guidance for the solution of the problems of this country. The 1946 Passive Resistance Campaign, the Xuma–Dadoo–Naicker Pact of Unity of 1947, the ANC Programme of Action of 1949, the national strike of 26 June 1950, the Defiance Campaign of 1952, the Congress of the People of 1955, the birth of MK in 1961, and the activities of the ANC External Mission are some of the outstanding landmarks in a process that has found increasing support among the people of South Africa and has helped entrench the ANC and its allies as the undisputed leaders of the freedom struggle.

As a result of the repression let loose by the Nats in the early 1960s the Congress organisations have been severely handicapped in their public activities. Nevertheless, the results of their pioneering work among the masses of the people have never ceased to make themselves felt in many spheres of life. Directly or indirectly the grinding spadework of individual Congressites, assisted by the consistent campaigns of politicisation and education of the masses led, for instance, to the earlier doctrine in the field of sport of an uncompromising policy of non-racism. In this regard, special mention should be made of bodies such as the South African Soccer Federation, the South African Cricket Board of Control, the South African Sports Association (which preceded SANROC), SANROC and other bodies. Their activities led to the isolation of white racist sports bodies from the arena of international sports. The leadership and example set by Congressites such as George Singh, Dennis Brutus and many others in the field of sport led to banning and persecution. But instead of thwarting their efforts the ideology of non-racism gained increasing ground. Sports leaders among the whites and blacks who were the principal opponents of non-racial sports are today becoming its main proponents.

In all aspects of South African life one sees the impact of the policy and activities of the Congresses. If one were to trace the historical origin of the courageous activities of the students in the 1970s and their united stand in the face of Nat attempts at racial separation, one will find that this can in no small measure be regarded as the fruits of the early efforts of the Congresses.

The white students too have not remained unaffected by this influence. Similarly, in the trade unions, in the churches, in women's organisations, in cultural bodies, in business and professional organisations, in every field, the cry is being raised for the abolition of racism and by word and deed stamping their approval on the ideals symbolised by the policies of the Congress movement.

These remarks should not be understood as claiming that the other organisations of the liberation movement were without influence. This is certainly not so. For example, the NEUM has made its influence felt among the Coloured people in the Western Cape, especially among the teaching profession and students. The impact of the PAC has been more widespread among the African people. Its campaigns of 1960 and 1963, with all the reservations and criticisms one may have about them, made a significant impact, particularly on the minds of African students and youth and on sections of the African intelligentsia. In today's context of rising African Nationalism it would be unrealistic to ignore its future role and influence. The Freedom Charter provides an adequate basis for the broadest unity among the people of South Africa. At the same time it should not be ruled out that circumstances might necessitate a flexible approach. While insisting on the spirit embodied in that document the Congress organisations may be called upon in the interests of unity to make concessions to the letter. It is certain that the ANC and its allies appreciate the vital importance of unity and can be confidently relied upon to display their usual mature and non-dogmatic approach.

Being a national movement that claims to offer to the people of South Africa an alternative to the policies of *herrenvolkism* perpetuated by successive regimes, the Congresses are repeatedly called upon to expand on aspects of their policy, to clarify problems, to answer accusations, to give assurances. The experiences in several African states, in the post-independence era in particular, added to doubts, reservations, criticisms, fears and antagonisms among sections of the public. By and large these attitudes are the result of deliberate and systematic propaganda by the enemies of the freedom struggle and therefore it is often the best approach to ignore them. But unfortunately such allegations do succeed in pervading the minds of ordinary, well-meaning people and can cause disquiet. Moreover, they tend to inhibit some partisans of the movement and place them on the defensive. The type of things said include:

- blacks are incapable of exercising the vote intelligently and of utilising state institutions in a responsible manner;
- black majority rule means the swamping of whites, the perpetration of cruelties against them, and eventually driving them into the sea;
- the activities and demands of the liberation organisations are 'communistic';
- by seeking aid from outside countries, especially the communist countries, the liberation organisations have shown disloyalty to South Africa and are guilty of treason;
- multi-racial societies have not succeeded anywhere;
- there would be no safety under black rule for minority groups such as Indians and Coloureds.

We do not intend a detailed refutation of these and similar allegations, but only to offer a few comments. The oft-quoted examples of the Congo, Uganda, etc., as models of 'inefficiency', 'instability' and 'irresponsibility' should not be allowed to undermine confidence in our own organisations and struggle. While one cannot condone the unfortunate excesses that have taken place in these and other countries, these happenings must be placed in their proper perspective. It is true that a handful of white nuns cruelly lost their lives in the Congo disturbances in 1960. It is also true that the Indian communities in Uganda, and to a lesser extent in Kenya and Malawi, experienced unnecessary hardships, and it cannot be denied that a number of newly independent states experienced instability and even chaos. But having said this, the question must be posed: can these, and even more serious events such as Biafra, Rwanda and Burundi, be placed higher than the teething troubles of emergent nationalism?

Comparisons are not always apt, but one should also recall the warfare, the bloodshed and dislocation that accompanied the rise of nationalism in Europe and of Afrikaner nationalism in South Africa. One should also note that while constant references are made to half a dozen or so countries, many African states underwent such momentous transformations in relative peace. And when it comes to cruelty, violence, plundering and rape, would it not be better if Christian European accusers paused for a moment to examine the biblical beam in their own eyes? In case the reprehensible slavery activities and the rape of black colonial lands are deemed to have taken place long ago, one needs to point to the Second World War in our lifetime, which was the cruellest in all history. It was the Germans, with their thousand-year-old civilisation, who conceived of the Auschwitz and Buchenwald concentration camps, where the most unbelievable brutalities were committed. It was the Germans who wiped out six million defenceless, non-combatant Jews. Then, at the tail end of the war, when Allied victory was only a few weeks away, it was the civilised Americans who wantonly thought it necessary to drop atom bombs on Hiroshima and Nagasaki. When peace was declared in Europe, the British, French and Dutch imperialists continued to fight viciously to maintain their stranglehold on the black colonies. In 1950 the Americans used the ghastly napalm and germ bombs against the people of Korea; in the 1950s the British bombed villages in Kenya and Malaya. In Vietnam, the American atrocities of Mai Lai and countless others are still fresh in our minds. And, when South African whites point self-righteously to the unfortunate nuns in the Congo, they seem to forget that nowhere amidst the turbulence and turmoil of emergent Africa have whites been subjected to anything reminiscent of the Sharpeville massacre of 1960. The 70 Africans cold-bloodedly shot at Sharpeville were by no means the first or the largest number to be killed that way. The history of white oppression is studded with numerous such tragic incidents.

Soliciting aid from foreign lands for freedom struggles has a long history and is not without precedent, even in our own country. In 1946 the SAIC persuaded the government of India to break off diplomatic relations with South Africa, to impose trade sanctions and to raise the question of South African racism at the UN. India took the lead in opposing the incorporation of Namibia into South Africa. Since then, these issues have been increasingly internationalised.

Today the Republic stands alone in the forums of world opinion. This isolation of South Africa and the universal condemnation of its policies are in keeping with the policy of the Congress movement. The External Mission of the ANC must to a great measure be credited with the mobilisation and consolidation of this international solidarity. Apart from support by the UN and the OAU, the ANC has received most consistent and unselfish material and moral aid from the socialist countries, aptly described by President Samora Machel as the natural allies of the liberation struggle. In Angola, where socialist Cuba and the Soviet Union rendered such massive practical and material aid to the MPLA government in its victorious fight against the South Africans, imperialist-backed FNLA and UNITA have evoked a chorus of protest from the Nats and other oppressors. Not only do they conveniently forget the blatant aggression committed by South Africa in Angola, but they also seem to take no notice of an analogous position in their own history. During the Anglo-Boer War a foreign legion was organised by a Frenchman, General De Villebois-Marevil, at the behest of presidents Kruger and Steyn to fight on the side of the Boer republics. The legion was made up of French, German, Dutch, Irish and Scandinavian soldiers. Boer generals Botha, De Wet and De la Rey were sent to Europe to organise the aid.

Let us consider the question of communism and the freedom struggle. For many years the Nats and UP have been busy whipping up a communist bogey. The Nats see the ghost of communism in every activity, in every organisation and every individual who does not subscribe to the policy of white domination. The axe first fell on the CPSA in 1950 and thereafter, as predicted, more and more organisations and individuals fell victim to the persecution conducted under the guise of combating communism. From the outset the Congress movement exposed the real aim of the witch-hunt, which was to destroy all effective opposition. In the SAIC Indian trade unionists, led by well-known communists, helped the Naicker leadership gain control of the Natal Indian Congress in 1945. In 1946, the Transvaal Indian Congress elected Dr Yusuf Dadoo, a known communist, as its president. Communists like Debi Singh, Dawood Seedat, S.V. Reddy, George Poonen, M.D. Naidoo, M.P. Naicker, M. Thandray, T.N. Naidoo, Cassim Amra and many others have been in the forefront of the activities of Congress. They worked in close harmony with nationalists like Monty Naicker and Moulvi Cachalia, with devout Muslims like Moulvi Saloojee, with ardent Gandhiists like Nana Sita, and never has there been the slightest conflict as a result of their differing ideological beliefs. Never has the Indian Congress been faced with demands by its members to exclude communists. Even in the face of severe persecution of communists by the government the Indian people, through the Indian Congress, consistently expressed their fullest confidence in the leadership, communist and non-communist alike.

A similar position obtained in the ANC. In their attitudes, the Congresses displayed great foresight and maturity. They refused to allow themselves to be deflected from the main issues facing the oppressed people, namely the building of the broadest unity among the people in order to bring about the defeat of white domination and racism. The Congresses also never allowed the class issue to cause divisiveness in their ranks. Within their leadership and rank and file are to be found workers, intellectuals, businessmen and religious leaders – men and women from all strata of the population. The Congresses brought them all together against the common enemy. This correct attitude has stood the test of time.

Finally the propaganda about the failure of multi-racial societies and the danger to and insecurity of minority groups under black majority rule calls for a few comments. One has but to look at the countries of Latin America and the Caribbean Islands. Whatever criticisms one may have about the conditions of the people there, whatever conflicts one may perceive between rulers and ruled, the outstanding thing is the absence of conflicts arising out of race and colour. In Cuba, Brazil and in the West Indian Islands, black and white live and go forward together without a consciousness of or concern with skin colour. The greatest living example of harmonious existence of different nationalities and people of varying backgrounds can be found in the USSR.

As to the question of minority groups in South Africa, the SAIC has long examined this matter, especially relating to the future of the Indian minority here. It sees in the path and policies pursued by the Congress movement, in the successful realisation of the ideals contained in the Freedom Charter the greatest guarantee of a harmonious future for all the peoples of this land. However, it must be admitted that owing to several reasons the prospect of black rule in South Africa does give rise to misgivings, feelings of doubt, insecurities and disquiet among Indian people. In an atmosphere where racial thinking is deliberately kept to the fore by the powers-that-be, this is understandable and not untypical of minority groups in other countries. Even if it exists among a small number the matter cannot simply be brushed aside. However, even their experiences under white rule will not automatically make them votaries of black rule. It remains the responsibility of the ANC and the SAIC and their allies to continue to do all in their power to educate and win the confidence of all the people. Their record in this respect already stands them in good stead. The task remains to extricate the people's attention and thinking from the racial groove in which they move.

Although for historical reasons the establishment of majority rule in South Africa will invariably mean the rule of the African majority (at least for the immediate future) the ANC and its allies have consistently refrained from giving emphasis to the factor of colour or race. When racist thinking is done away with, the colour of the legislators will be of no importance. The fundamental requirement is the adherence to policies and principles aimed at bringing about maximum security and peace to all the peoples of the country, irrespective of their colour.

The starting point of this essay was the promise made at the UN by white South Africa's ambassador Pik Botha that South Africa was to end racial discrimination, and the feverish diplomatic activities that followed. An examination was attempted of the educational, social, economic and political position of Indian South Africans in the light of these developments, more particularly against the background of speculation about the integration of the Indians, Coloureds and whites. I maintained that both from the point of view of the white ruling class and the Indians there would be no integration as envisaged by some Nats. Under the circumstances, the task of the Indian community, in close collaboration with all the oppressed people of South Africa, is to continue to strive for the achievement of a radical change in South Africa – the establishment of a non-racial society based on the Freedom Charter. Finally some of the problems that confronted the liberation movement in the struggle to realise these aims were touched upon. Having set our sights on the achievement of a minimum programme, some expression of ideas is desirable on matters such as the methods available to the oppressed people for the realisation of these aims. Ever since they were established – the Natal Indian Congress in 1894, the African People's Organisation in 1902, the African National Congress in 1912 – the liberation organisations have consistently striven for better conditions for black people by methods that caused the least friction. Only when all else failed have they found themselves obliged to seek recourse to methods that the authorities describe as 'confrontational'. The passive resistance movements and general strike of Indian workers in Natal in the early part of the century under the leadership of Mahatma Gandhi and the Congress were proceeded by numerous resolutions, appeals, mass meetings, petitions, deputations and lengthy negotiations. An ANC delegation even proceeded to Versailles at the Peace Congress in the hope of making heard the black voices whose requests had fallen on deaf ears at home. And when the white legislators did consent to lend them their reluctant ears they were willing to open the doors only very slightly – and insultingly. They said that they would allow three white men to represent each of the black groups in order to convey to the 150 parliamentarians the feelings and frustrations, the desires and dislikes of the black millions. Humiliating, totally inadequate and ineffective as it was, even this mock representation was deemed by the Nats as conceding too much. And in due course it was withdrawn. Instead, the *herrenvolk* mind conceived of formulas for representations even more unjust, farcical and humiliating. The millions of Africans, regardless of where they were born and bred, regardless of where they worked or where they desired to spend their lives, were assigned to one or other of nine tribal areas. Instead of one they are to be given nine parliaments, nine speakers, nine maces, nine prime ministers and cabinets, nine sets of laws in nine languages. Nine enormous pieces of humbug – fraudulent, futile and ludicrous – which could all be dismissed as comical were it not for the fact that they contained the seeds of inevitable tragedy.

The Coloureds and Indians, who have no homeland of their own are not to suffer the slightest deprivation as a result of this difficulty, we are told. They, too, will be able to exercise the vote – in the South African Indian Council and the Coloured Representative Council – where they, too, will be able to play the parliamentary game to their heart's content. With mock maces, sergeants-at-arms, speakers and all the parliamentary paraphernalia, these legislators will be able to gather together every year to give free rein to their eloquence, but not to legislate. This worrisome burden would be borne by the parent parliament. In other words, the Indians and Coloureds are to be given all the tinsel and trappings of parliamentary democracy, but not the substance.

The prospects of securing democratic rights and equality of opportunity cannot and do not lie along this path. The Coloured and Indian people will have to turn elsewhere and seek other methods. Reference has been made to extra-parliamentary forms of struggle employed in the past, such as the Passive Resistance Campaign and Defiance Campaign, the political strikes, boycotts, meetings and demonstrations. These have been the methods par excellence of oppressed people everywhere. One or other, or combinations of them have been used with great success in Russia, China, India, Latin America, Europe and Africa. In South Africa, too, all these well-tried methods have been used and have come under heavy attack from the oppressor. Anything that is not in conformity with separate development has been condemned as communism and has frequently provided an excuse to let loose a reign of terror, of detention without trial, torture, bannings and house arrest, heavy jail sentences, prohibition of literature and cold-blooded killings.

After the wanton massacre of defenceless demonstrators at Sharpeville in 1960, which was followed by the declaration of martial law and the banning of the ANC and PAC, the crushing of the peaceful political general strike of 1961, a new phenomenon made its appearance on the South African scene – the decision by blacks to meet violence with violence in an organised manner. On 16 December 1961 Umkhonto weSizwe, under the aegis of the ANC, announced this to the people of South Africa to the accompaniment of bomb attacks against the hated symbols of oppression. In the following year the ANC sent the first batches of young men out of South Africa for training in methods of guerrilla warfare. In the course of 1962 members of the PAC also engaged in forms of violent activity. Instead of reading the writing on the wall and taking appropriate action, the Nats responded with wholesale terror and repression on a scale unprecedented in South African history. And for a short while they vaunted that all 'subversive' activity had been effectively subdued.

But freedom movements have a certain resilience and even the worst forms of persecution have not succeeded in obliterating them. So it has been with the ANC. Now signs are increasing that ANC freedom fighters abroad are making active preparations to launch guerrilla activities. This follows the breathtaking events of the last year, which witnessed the birth of Frelimo and MPLA governments in Mozambique and Angola. Attention is at present focused on Rhodesia, where the struggle is fast gaining ground. To underline the gravity of developments Fidel Castro issued the timeous warning that continued South African aggression in Angola could very well lead to full-scale war, which was likely to overflow not only into Namibia but into South Africa itself.

About a decade ago an Afrikaner author writing of developments in southern Africa gave his book the title *Die Vuur Brand Nader* (The Flames Come Closer). Not only have we begun to feel the heat of the flames but front-line defenders of apartheid have already been locked in actual combat and a number have fallen. Vorster showed a proper appreciation of the situation when he said that the alternatives to a peaceful solution in southern Africa were too ghastly to contemplate. Yet he and his government stubbornly go about finding the answers in the wrong way. They offer not a morsel that can be regarded as a significant departure from the policies that condemn in perpetuity the African people to 13 per cent of the land and the Coloured and Indian people to an everlasting status of inferiority. There is no indication that South Africa is willing to forgo her imperialist domination of Namibia. Surely even the most naive Nats cannot seriously expect that their insincere utterances and outdated policies will appease the intense hunger of the black millions for freedom.

In this state of affairs what is to be the role of the oppressed people, especially of Indian South Africans? There is no room for doubt that, being part and parcel of the oppressed and exploited people, their future is indissolubly linked with them. Their only way forward is by way of relentless struggle to which they have made a consistent and honourable contribution.

One thing is clear: the only effective weapons at the hands of the oppressed people are the weapons of extra-parliamentary action – meetings, demonstrations, boycotts, campaigns of defiance, political strikes and organised violence, including sabotage and guerrilla warfare. The oppressors have brought about a situation that leaves the oppressed people with no alternative.

Recent events in southern Africa have increased speculation about the imminence of guerrilla activities at home. It is evident that this is going to be the primary form of struggle and the resources of the movement will have to be harnessed more and more towards it. While the armed struggle takes precedence, this does not mean that other forms of political activity and methods of struggle are to be abandoned. Indeed, a successful armed struggle is dependent on building and consolidating political activity. In the meantime the day-to-day political work must not be neglected. Continued attention must be given to building and strengthening the organisations of the people within the country. The SACP, ANC, SAIC, CPC, COD, SACTU and others are the most experienced and mature organisations of the struggle and there can be absolutely no substitute for them. Under their leadership the systematic and large-scale politicisation of the masses must continue. The message of the struggle must reach every nook and cranny of the country and all available means must be utilised for the purpose.

Congress members will have to search continuously for new platforms and means of reaching the masses of the people. Individual Congress members must be active in trade unions, ratepayers' associations, vigilante and tenants' associations, student and professional bodies, churches, women's organisations, sports and cultural groups – in fact, in every organisation catering in one way or another for the needs of the people. No body of organised people must be deemed too small or unimportant. Indeed, if the Congress organisations should deem it necessary, then the very dummy institutions and creations of separate development might have to be utilised. The history of freedom struggles is full of examples where similar institutions were used to good effect. The activities of the Bolshevik deputies in the Tsarist Duma and the capture of state governments by the All India Congress are but two outstanding instances. They emphasise the point that the utilisation of such bodies by the freedom movement is not a matter of principle but a tactic that can be resorted to if necessary. However, great care must be taken to ensure that in the process the attention of the membership and of the people at large is not in any way diverted from the main struggle. At their very best these are secondary methods that can only be used for very limited objectives. And if it is found that the limited objectives can be attained without recourse to this method, so much the better.

The main tasks are the building of the existing organisations and the mobilisation of the masses to bring them into a constant state of preparedness for the struggle ahead. This is an absolute prerequisite for any advance we are to make. With this aim we enter the second half of the decade. The eyes of the world are increasingly focused on the southern part of our continent as they witness the unfolding of the dramatic battle against the last bastion of racism. It is evident that the white supremacists are determined to plunge the country into a bloodbath rather than make efforts at a peaceful solution. South Africa can do this by withdrawing from Namibia and by extending full democratic rights and equality of opportunity to all the people, regardless of race, colour or creed. It is saddening to contemplate the chaos, disorder, bloodshed, death and destruction that are the concomitants of violent struggle. For their irresponsibility and disregard of the consequences and their stubbornness history will hold the Nat regime criminally responsible.

It is five minutes to midnight. At this late hour the hope still lingers that somehow the white racists will come to their senses and avert disaster. Let the responsible and oft-repeated message of the ANC and its allies ring louder, and let it be drummed into the hard racist heads. It is not in the policies of the National Party or the United Party, but only under the banner of the ANC that there is a guarantee for the safety and bright future for whites. It has never been in the past nor is it now the desire of the ANC to substitute white racism with black racism, to subjugate the whites and drive them into the sea. All we wish is to win and enjoy full rights to work and live our lives in the land of our birth in full dignity and respect, shoulder life's challenges, and together partake of its joys. Instead of fragmentation let there be one united, indivisible country; instead of a dozen divided ethnic groups let there be one powerful people; instead of 4 million let there be 24 million South Africans speaking with one voice. Once and for all let the humiliation and hardship of colour be done away with. Let there be raised in its place and to its full height the majesty and greatness of human worth.

GOVAN MBEKI

Govan Archibald Mbeki was born on 8 July 1910 in Mpukane Location in the Nqamakwe district of the Transkei. He obtained a BA degree and a Diploma in Education from the University of Fort Hare in 1936. In 1941 he became Secretary of the African Voters' Association and served in the Bunga. In the 1950s, while teaching in Northern Natal, he was fired for organising coal workers. He went into full-time journalism in 1954 and was appointed Eastern Cape manager of *New Age* and *Spark* and their banned predecessors. He was a member of the team of African intellectuals who drafted the *African Claims* in 1943. He was served with his banning order in 1962, after which he went underground. At the time of his arrest in 1963 at Rivonia he was a member of the National Executive Committee of the ANC, of the Central Committee of the SACP, and a member of the High Command of Umkhonto weSizwe. In the late 1950s he often chaired conferences of the ANC.

He obtained a BA Hons. degree in Economics in prison.

He was released in 1987. In 1994, he was elected to Parliament and became Deputy President of the Senate.

He has written several books and pamphlets, including *The Transkei in the Making* (1938); a booklet on co-operatives titled *Let's Do it Together*; *The Peasant's Revolt*, published in 1964 by Penguin Africa Library, London; *Learning from Robben Island – the Prison Writings of Govan Mbeki*, published in 1991 by David Philip, Cape Town.

GOVAN MBEKI
BY SAM NHLENGETHWA

PROFILE

His quiet smile is accompanied by a deep, warm chuckle. His turn of phrase often bears a tone that suggests how much he relishes the spoken word.

Though he has served in many capacities and various jobs, he was once a teacher. There remains in him and his mannerisms something of the schoolmaster.

Before the Rivonia arrests he often chaired conferences of the ANC. I have an image of Govan opening such a conference, with his arms spread open like the horns of a bull, and a deep voice sombrely intoning, 'Comrades, fellow delegates, I take you in my charge …'

Many have described Govan as a person with ruthless determination. The iron will, the firmness of resolve, shines through at all times. Govan would have responded immediately to Mandela's proposal that the Rivonia trialists should not appeal against a sentence of death if it were imposed in their trial. The issue would have been clear-cut, personal. Sisulu would have deliberated the issue and considered its implications for the struggle.

Over the years his ruthlessness became separated from his determination. The perception grew that Govan was just ruthless. I have puzzled over this. Ruthlessness bears a connotation of having no pity or compassion. This image does not sit comfortably with his soft-spoken calm and gentleness.

Perhaps the answer lies in recognising the teacher, the pedagogue, in him, and therefore the way in which he tends to fashion his behaviour to what he perceives to be required by the objectives that have been set. How many teachers mask their warmth and gentleness with a ram-rod posture and a firmness which often appears as strictness?

There is nothing incompatible between a firmness of resolve and a warmth that exudes from the heart. The heart and head belong together. The demands of the struggle and the way in which one responds can quite easily make them seem incompatible.

A lifetime in the struggle has not rubbed out the pedagogue in Govan.

THE ANATOMY OF THE PROBLEMS OF THE NATIONAL LIBERATION STRUGGLE IN SOUTH AFRICA

GOVAN MBEKI

The various phases of the development of social changes do not lend themselves to fixing a precise date as to when they begin or end.

From the tiny enclave in the Cape the white settlers moved to occupy the entire country. The land grabbing resulted in military conflicts between the indigenous black people and the whites who had advanced northwards from the Cape of Good Hope. For a period stretching over one hundred years from 1779, when the first clash between the amaXhosa and British imperial troops took place in the Eastern Cape, to the last of the Wars of Dispossession in 1889/1890, the process of dispossessing Africans of their land has been met with resistance all along the line.

The last War of Dispossession had been preceded by an event that marked a qualitative change in the form the struggle was to take. In 1853 the British government granted responsible government to the Cape Colony. The right to the franchise was granted to all males, irrespective of their colour or race, who were in possession of certain qualifications. The granting of responsible government and of the right to the franchise pointed irrevocably to two courses – first, that the white man was going to remain permanently in South Africa; and secondly, that the African was not to engage in a long, drawn-out constitutional struggle for the attainment of equal political rights with the white man. The registered black voters sought to increase their numbers with a view to influencing legislation in their favour in Parliament, while white political parties by 1887, notably the Afrikaner Bond under the leadership of Jan Hofmeyr, sought to make the African vote ineffective by checking the increase in numbers of African and Coloured voters by introducing legislation to tamper with the existing qualifications. For example, land occupied under traditional African tenure was no longer to be regarded as a qualification for the franchise.

Towards the end of the nineteenth century the struggle for political rights in the Cape had become so intense that white political parties claimed that the dominant position of the whites was threatened by increasing numbers of black voters. Towards the end of the Wars of Dispossession the national liberation struggle of the blacks against oppression by the whites had already begun. These efforts were not co-ordinated, primarily because there was no unitary administration covering the region that later came to be known as South Africa. But the confrontation that built up over the years was not that simple.

It is to the brief study of the anatomy of the problems in all its interlocking complexity that we must turn to in the subsequent pages of this essay.

THE POPULATION STRUCTURE

The discovery and exploitation of diamonds in 1867 and gold in 1887 brought an influx of capital from Europe to South Africa. Where capital flows from a more developed capitalist economy to a less developed area it is accompanied by its stablemate, namely labour that has already acquired the technological skills of the former. Thus the development of the mining industry brought investment capital as well as skilled labour largely from Europe. Such imported labour would only form a small nucleus of the labour force required for mining and related operations and the development of the industries.

Large numbers of Afrikaners from the rural areas and Africans from the 'Native Reserves' flowed into the mining areas. It has been estimated that between 1871 and 1895 for every white man who came to the mining fields two or three Africans came.[1] In the agricultural sector the developing sugar industry had from its early days experienced a shortage of labour. The owners of the sugar plantations made up the leeway in the demand for labour by importing indentured labour from India.[2] Their descendants, who were not bound by the conditions under which their fathers had come, decided to make South Africa their home and their numbers have increased considerably over the last hundred years.

Economic necessity imposed co-existence on black aboriginal groups (Africans and Khoi-khoi especially) as well as slaves in the early days of the white settlement, leading to the emergence of the Coloureds as yet another racial group. At the turn of the century South Africa therefore rested on four distinct racial pillars – the Africans, Coloureds, Europeans and Indians.

Let us briefly look at the social structure of each racial group with a view to obtaining a clear understanding of the problems of the national liberation struggle that flow from such group social structures.

THE MARRIAGE OF WHITE CAPITAL AND WHITE LABOUR

The opening of the diamond and gold mines introduced a money economy as opposed to African subsistence economy. This dichotomy in the economic field was followed by a social and political dichotomy, which was drawn along the colour line. As in all capitalist societies the white group had differences and sometimes even class clashes such as the Rand Rebellion in 1922.[3] But over the years the paramount consideration was the question of colour, to such an extent that all political activities among white political parties concentrated on inculcating in the minds of whites the view that their existence was threatened by the black group, more particularly the Africans.

The drift of unskilled Afrikaners from the farms made the situation worse. If whites were not protected in the labour market they would have to compete with Africans in a market that was progressively becoming over-supplied. The unskilled white labourer sought shelter behind his skin colour, setting the pattern for the economic-political development of the country. This attitude found expression in the agreement between Jan Hofmeyr and Cecil Rhodes, even though they belonged to political parties that purported to hold differing viewpoints. The two argued that 'the African tribesmen [were] barbarous people who should be prevented from obtaining a foothold in the political systems of the colonies and the Republics'.[4]

The pattern that took shape during the early stages of the mining operation crystallised and hardened over the years. After Union in 1910 the various governments systematically passed legislation that provided for the existence of two opposing camps facing each other across the colour line. Although the white working class was in theory willing to advance the interests of the African workers, in practice it was only willing up to a point. The representatives of capital, by contrast, would resist the demands of white workers to a point short of a clash between the two white classes. In practice the two white classes observed the maintenance of a certain equilibrium, which ensured that whites stood and acted as a group *vis-à-vis* the blacks, especially the Africans.

All legislation since 1910 has been passed to entrench the position of whites as a group, and to undermine the position of blacks as a group. A year after the formation of the Union, Parliament passed two Acts – the Native Labour Regulations Act (No. 15 of 1911), which imposed restraints on the movement of Africans, and the Mines and Works Act (No. 12 of 1911), which entrenched the principle of the colour bar in industry and had already been used by a Transvaal Ordinance (No. 17 of 1907). This Act prescribed two elements, which were to be crucial to maintaining a privileged position and high salaries for the white mineworkers. The first element prohibited Africans from performing certain categories of work, for example, blasting – a crude colour bar provision. The second element specified a ratio of African mineworkers to white workers of 2:1. These two Acts laid the foundation not only for similar legislation in subsequent years, but also for an attitude of superiority on the part of the whites towards Africans. This government-sponsored superiority of the white man over the black man became encased in tradition and expressed itself in all walks of life, in insulting acts, in a belittling of his mentality and in humiliating practices towards Africans. Every white child, every African child, is nurtured in this atmosphere. Willingly he is expected to take his stand on his side of the colour line and play his role in the black–white group relationship over which he has had no more choice than characters in a Greek tragedy. The race-god as represented by the government carves his fate.

Two years later the Union government passed the notorious Land Act of 1913. In terms of the Act the confined areas to which Africans had been driven by the end of the Wars of Dispossession were regarded as scheduled areas outside of which Africans could not own land. The Native Trust and Land Act of 1936 vested land in scheduled and leased areas in a Native Trust administered by the government. This put an end to freehold ownership of landed property. The land area set aside for the occupation of 15 669 498 Africans compared with 3 750 655 whites[5] was 37 500 000 acres after all released areas would have been made available[6] – this out of the total area for South Africa of 302 000 000 acres.[7] It is a matter of no consequence to the government whether Africans have lived together with their families in the areas claimed to be the home of the whites. Legally they are foreigners in that area in South Africa outside the 'Native Reserves'.

In 1922 the government passed the Natives (Urban Areas) Act, which consolidated the various forms of pass laws, the implementation of which has subjected the Africans to some of the worst forms of degradation and humiliation. Since then there have been several amendments to the Act aimed at tightening the restrictions on the movement of Africans. The crowning refinement was the passing of influx control regulations, which regulate the entry of Africans into urban areas and the use of the Labour Bureau to distribute African labour amongst the various sectors of the economy. The recent setting up of Regional Boards to control employment of Africans in each region is a crude and naked method of oppression and exploitation of Africans in the interests of whites.

The first piece of industrial legislation providing machinery for consultation between employers and employees deliberately left out the African worker. This was the Industrial Conciliation Act (No. 11 of 1924), as amended. The fact that liberal white trade unions took up the case of African workers at meetings of the Industrial Councils made the African worker feel that he had to show gratitude, with bent knees and cupped hands, to his white fellow workers for any small gains, while the white worker felt that he had done the African worker a good turn, for which appreciation was to be expected. Instead of allowing African workers to participate in the machinery of collective bargaining, the government passed the Native Labour (Settlement of Disputes) Act (No. 48 of 1953). This Act provides for works committees administered by government officials. This arrangement was intended to divorce the African worker from the mainstream of the labour movement. In the meantime a new Industrial Conciliation Act was passed in 1956. In addition to the discriminatory provisions of previous legislation it included the principle of job reservation, that is, special jobs reserved for whites.[8] It also introduced the principle of compulsory racial segregation in trade unions. This also affected Coloured and Indian workers.

Francis Wilson sums up the effect of the two elements incorporated in the 1956 Industrial Conciliation Act thus: 'The effect of reservation is to prevent blacks moving into the skilled labour pool which is kept small … causing skilled (white) wages to be higher than they would otherwise be; the effect of the ratio is to create a joint demand where the demand for blacks creates demands on the supply of whites'.[9]

An illustration of the wide gap between the salaries of whites and blacks (mainly Africans) on the mines is reflected in the figures:[10]

	Whites	Non-whites
Average number in service during Dec. 1974:	37 255	318 243
Total salaries/wages earned during 1974:	R257 331 000	R202 875 000
Dividends declared:	R565 830 000	

The figures speak for themselves.

Furthermore, the government passed the Mines and Works Amendment Act (No. 25 of 1926), popularly known as the Colour Bar Act. In 1925 the Wage Act was passed, which provided for setting up a Wage Board to make recommendations on minimum wages for unskilled workers who fell outside the scope of the Industrial Conciliation Act, and this virtually meant African workers only. In practice the Wage Board has been more concerned with protecting margins of profit than with effecting increases in the wages of unskilled workers.

In addition, the government adopted the Civilised Labour Policy. In 1925 the government passed the Protective Tariffs Act for the establishment of the manufacturing industry. The Civilised Labour Policy fitted in well with this development as it required that no job in a protected industry should be given to blacks as long as there were unemployed white workers. This policy helped to wipe out the poor white problem within a decade. In doing so it created a poor black problem which is still with us today.

The path towards enfranchisement of Africans had been strewn with obstacles throughout the years of 'responsible' government in the Cape. After the formation of Union the franchise right was not extended to the other three provinces. It existed in an extremely attenuated form in Natal, and could be withdrawn by a vote of two-thirds of the two Houses of Parliament sitting together. The Natives Representation Act, passed in 1936, removed the African voters from the common voters' roll. Under this Act the Africans were represented in the two Houses as a group. When the National Party came to power in 1948 it lost no time in preparing the ground for a complete denial to Africans of a say in Parliament. In 1950 it passed the Bantu Authorities Act, which provided for the setting up of nine ethnic areas in the reserves. These came to be called Bantustans, and government policy laid down that Africans would satisfy their political aspirations in local government activities in the separate ethnic Bantu Authorities. Thus, by 1959, even the limited representation Africans had was discontinued with the repeal of the Natives Representation Act.

Without dealing with the multitude of other special legislation affecting Africans as a group we have traced the course of legislation sufficiently to illustrate, first, how Africans as a group have been denied political rights; secondly, how as a group they are placed at a disadvantage in comparison with the whites; thirdly, how as a group they are denied the right of ownership of land on a freehold tenure basis outside the reserves, and that even there ownership is extremely limited, as such land is vested in the Native Trust.

In the face of such all-embracing denial of rights to all Africans it would appear that every African would without much persuasion join the forces that fight for his rights. However, experience has taught us that to expect this would be over-simplifying matters.

Whatever reasons may be given to explain away this marriage of capital and white labour against members of their class who happen not to be white, the fact is that the white working class has sacrificed an overwhelming section of the working class at the altar of the race-god. They have created a situation in which black and white must stand at daggers drawn, facing each other across the colour line.

NON-CONFORMING WHITE MINORITY GROUPS

A small minority of whites have not lined up with either the Nat or United Party (UP) policy on blacks. Such individuals have found a home in small political parties or semi-political organisations. The largest of these is the Progressive Party, whose membership was originally open to everyone irrespective of race until the government put an end to racially mixed political parties. Although it is critical of apartheid policies it appears to insist on white leadership and is only prepared to concede political rights and franchise to Africans on a qualification basis. Other white minorities found a home in the Liberal Party, which disbanded after the government passed legislation against racially mixed political parties. The Congress of Democrats (COD), which had without qualification accepted the policy of the Congress movement, as embodied in the Freedom Charter, was banned.[11]

Then there is the small band of brave women who are members of the Black Sash. It is not a political party. It focuses attention on grave injustices perpetrated in the name of law against Africans. In recent years it has concentrated on taking up individual cases of suffering, especially under the Pass Laws.

Finally there are those whites who are members of the banned South African Communist Party (SACP), which operates illegally. They are not only unreservedly committed to the struggle towards attaining as a long-term aim a classless society in South Africa, but in the short term fighting side by side with the liberation forces to achieve the goals set out in the Freedom Charter.

The upshot was that a very small minority of whites are prepared to support equal rights for all in South Africa, irrespective of race of colour.

THE COLOUREDS

The Coloureds, numbering 2 018 262, form the third racial group after the whites, who number 3 750 655.[12] The Indians are the smallest group, constituting 620 422.

The Coloureds as a group have not yet reached a high level of class stratification. For decades they have provided labour in the manufacturing industry, the building industry and agriculture in the Cape. It is only recently that a merchant class nucleus has begun to emerge through encouragement by the government-sponsored Coloured Investment Corporation. Except for teaching and nursing, the numbers are still small in other professions, for example, law and medicine.

Like the Africans they enjoyed the right to vote until recently when they were forced to look to the Coloured Representative Council (CRC) for satisfying their political aspirations.

They have been uprooted from town areas proclaimed as white areas under the Group Areas Act. They have been thrown into locations away from the white areas. The difference between them and the Africans is that in the long run they will own property in these townships. Most workers belong to the trade unions, but as noted above, since 1953 they have been forced to belong to separate trade unions, that is, not mixed with white workers. In certain industries like the textile union, where they constitute the main membership of the union, they look after the interests of the Africans at Industrial Council negotiations.

Before the introduction of the CRC there were two main anti-government policy organisations that catered for Coloured interests. One was the Coloured People's Congress (CPC), a member of the Congress Alliance. It suffered serious setbacks in the late 1950s and the early 1960s as some of its leading members were banned and left the country. The other was the Anti-Coloured Affairs Department (Anti-CAD), an affiliate of NEUM, which disbanded as a result of internal differences. Some of its remnants have found a new home in the African People's Democratic Union of South Africa (APDUSA).

Two main political parties operate the government machinery. As such, despite protestations to the contrary, they support the government policy in practice. They are the Federal Party and the Labour Party, which vie with each other for the leading position in implementing government policy. While the Labour Party was in opposition, it promised that if it were returned to power it would destroy the CRC from within. When they were returned as the majority party in the last election, like the proverbial atheist, they remained within to enjoy the fruits of office.

THE INDIANS

Of the three black groups, the Indian community has reached the highest degree of class stratification. A clearly defined capitalist class, if still small, has taken shape. By the end of 1973 no less than 800 factories were reported to be owned by Indians.[13] The middle class, consisting of 9 per cent professional and executive elements plus the merchant class, is already established as a class distinct from the working class. Those who do not own property constitute 80 per cent of the Indian population.[14]

Property owners fall into two categories: first, the big property owners who have invested in a number of properties varying from rented houses to blocks of flats and offices. According to information from independent sources this section has not been affected unfavourably by the Groups Areas Act; secondly, small property owners, largely consisting of those who sank years and years of hard-earned savings into building a family home, are reported to have suffered heavily as a result of the Group Areas Act. We have no idea what proportion of the property-owning class belong to the latter category.

A large majority of the economically active population fall into the working class; reportedly, 44 per cent of the population are employed,[15] while only 0,6 per cent are unemployed.[16]

As with other black racial groups, the Indians as a group are denied political rights. The government has created a Department of Indian Affairs headed by a cabinet minister. This is the only platform the government has provided for them to air their grievances. Indian workers can belong only to racially separate trade unions if their workers' organisations receive government recognition.

Only one political organisation – the South African Indian Congress, a member of the Congress Alliance, specialises in organising Indians for their liberation as a group. Two other political organisations, which absorbed them as members, are the Communist Party (CP) and APDUSA.

It is mainly the capitalist and merchant class that co-operate with the government in making the Indian Council workable. No political party has been set up to implement government policy through the Council. In this respect the Indians have reacted differently from Africans and Coloureds.

With regard to the Indians and Coloureds there is an open and considerable amount of rethinking on the part of the whites as to what their position should be in the face of a widening gap in relations between whites and Africans. From various white quarters there is a growing demand that these two groups be allowed to enjoy political rights with the whites. Edgar H. Brookes and Colin de B. Webb go on to say: 'Natalians of Indian descent are in general strongly in favour of integration from which they have much to gain and little to lose; and the same may be said of the small, depressed and divided Coloured community, which contains many good citizens but lacks acceptable leadership.'[17]

Even from unexpected sources an alarm is being sounded. Delivering his presidential address to the annual conference of the Natal Agricultural Union, Mr D.C. Sinclair expressed anxiety that an independent black state may be established within the borders of Natal.[18] He said: 'The reality of the situation can only be visualised if it is believed that the relations between white and black areas will remain of the highest order. At the other end of the scale they are unimaginable.' To secure the position of the whites Sinclair posed the question: 'Should we not now consider ways and means of involving Indian and Coloured farmers in the province in organised agriculture?' In other words, he is posing the question of integration which, if it applies to Natal, should apply to farmers in all four provinces.

THE AFRICANS

The Africans constitute the largest racial group, numbering 15 069 498 out of a total population of 21 458 837. There is no capitalist class. The reasons for its absence are largely traceable to the conditions that have necessitated the existence of the national liberation forces, not against foreign oppression, not against class exploitation, but against national oppression by a group of their countrymen who claim superiority on the grounds of race and colour.

The middle class is in the early stages of development, more particularly if we think in terms of the trading class, the medical and the legal profession. The demand to foster the development of a middle class was brought to the fore by the orthodox white liberal thinkers as the struggle for liberation took extra-constitutional forms initiated by the Campaign for the Defiance of Unjust Laws in 1952. The Nat government, nurtured in the Boer tradition of *Die kaffer moet sy plek hou* (the kaffir must keep his place), gradually came to realise the need to use more sophisticated means to maintain the dominant position of the white man. As stated by the late Dr J.G. Strydom: *Die witman moet altyd die baas bly* (the white man must always remain boss).[19]

The government set up the Bantu Investment Corporation (BIC) and its subsidiaries like the

Xhosa Development Corporation that operate at the ethnic or Bantustan level. If we use the monthly turnover as a gauge, the sizes of these businesses may be classified as follows:[20]

		Turnover	Average
I	One-man-show	R100–800	R320
II	Relatively small enterprise	RI 000–2 000	R1 540
III	Medium-sized	R2 500–5 000	R4 040
IV	Large	R6 000–30 000	R10 400

The overwhelming majority of those engaged in trading activities operate on a small scale. Even in the case of those who fall into the fourth category, only a small number operate at a higher turnover than the average.

In general, the African entrepreneur is isolated from the community. He does not participate in politics and Gillian Hart states the reasons thus: 'Entrepreneurs, particularly those in urban locations, are in an extremely vulnerable position. The intricate maze of legislation provides for the political domestication of the entrepreneur. He dare not be openly militant save within the framework of the apartheid policy.'[21]

This observation applies equally to medical practitioners and lawyers who live and practise in the urban locations. The plight of the African middle class in particular and the African generally is summed up by Dr D.G.S. Mtimkulu: 'One feels that the urban African is a little too bewildered. He makes every effort to adjust himself to urban living … But he finds a strong authoritative pressure to obstruct such a change. For instance, in a property owning society he cannot own property; in a society that has grown and prospered by workers organising themselves, his own organisations are restricted.'[22]

THE CHIEFS

The position of the chiefs in the earlier days before Africans were brought completely under white rule was similar to that of the feudal aristocracy. Each chief ruled over a given area, which he sought to extend or defend, if there was a threat from outside, as happened in the years of the Wars of Dispossession. Their power began to crack under the military pressure of the British and the Boer forces that were armed with better weapons. Sir Harry Smith illustrated what the imperial forces intended to do with the chiefs in the Eastern Cape.[23] He gathered the chiefs at the site of the present King William's Town and ordered a charge of dynamite to be set off under an ox wagon. The wagon was blown to pieces that flew into all directions. Pointing at the scene, he warned them that this was what he would do to them if they persisted in resisting British rule. As subsequent events showed, the advancing whites did not stop short of crushing the power of the chiefs.

In Natal, Sir Arthur Havelock, Governor of Natal in 1887 when Zululand was annexed, said: 'The House of Shaka is a thing of the past, like water that has been spilt.'[24] To emphasise the fact that the chiefs had lost all power, Harry Escombe, speaking in support of the Zululand Annexation Bill, added: 'The ruling power of South Africa is the power of the Anglo-Saxon race.'[25]

This set the tone for what was to happen later. South Africa was to break free of Britain and all power was to be in the hands of the whites. On his return after a period of imprisonment at St Helena, Dinizulu was employed as a government induna at a salary. Throughout the country chiefs became employees of the government and were used to implement government policy. Dr Vilakazi points out that the Zulus regard their chiefs as 'police boys'. In fact, they also partly serve the functions of a police force and partly the role of a propaganda wing of the Department of Native Affairs.

THE PEASANTS

Although it is known that in every one of the 'Native Reserves' a number of heads of family units hold certificates or, in the case of a few districts in the Transkei and the Ciskei, title deeds issued on pain of paying quit rent, not much information is available. We do not know how many heads of families there are in the reserves, and how many own an arable piece of land as distinct from a residential site. The nearest estimate is that given in the Tomlinson Commission Report, which recommended that 300 000 families in the reserves should be removed in order to give those who remain the opportunity of making a living out of the land without resorting to periodic spells of work elsewhere.[26] If we take a family unit to consist, on average, of 6 persons, this amounts to 1 800 000 people. This means that about half the population of the reserves should be removed because there is no arable land available to be allocated to them. For those who remained the report recommended that stabilisation of land must embrace 'dividing the prescribed residential areas into residential plots of fixed size, and the arable land into plough land units of one morgen each'.[27] How much of a living can be eked out of farming one morgen[28] of dry land in South African climatic conditions? In practice, however, rather than remove people from the reserves to reduce the pressure on the land, the apartheid policy has operated in the opposite direction. People from the urban areas as well as redundant people from the farms have been moved into the reserves. There are more landless people in the reserves than peasants who own some piece of arable land. It is partly from this reserve of labour and partly from the peasants that contract labour is distributed to all sectors of the economy outside the 'Native Reserves'.

It is estimated that at any time of the year, 233 000 migrant labourers are away from the Transkei.[29] Yet, in spite of the fact that this labour force voluntarily leaves to find work in areas outside the Transkei, E. Kramer, one of the advisors on economic development of the Transkei, implies that poverty in the area is a result of the laziness of the people and suggests that the government take a leaf from Hitler's methods in Nazi Germany. 'Conscripted agricultural service, conscripted land service, was used with practical and very good results by Adolph Hitler in Germany.'[30] Yet another of the advisors on economic development of the Transkei, Dr J. Venter, argues that '[t]he Transkei has an abundance of land'.[31] This statement conflicts with the findings of the Tomlinson Commission and with statistics cited by another contributor, Hobart Houghton, who points out that of the Transkei's 4,5 million morgen 'less than one million is suitable for arable farming'.

We have already referred to the conditions to which the African worker is exposed. One of the main incentives to attract entrepreneurs to the Bantustans and the border areas is the availability of trained black labour at lower wages than those paid to unskilled labour in the urban areas.

WHO IS AGAINST WHOM?

From the preceding sections we can draw a number of inferences that enable us to get a clear picture of the problem in the national liberation struggle. First, we must emphasise that the struggle in which the people of this country through their respective organisations are engaged is not one for independence. It is not a struggle of a colonial people seeking to break free of ties that have bound them to the metropolitan power. It is not a struggle against people who have a home to run to when things get hot. It is therefore not a struggle to push the white man out of the country. Rather it is a struggle of the blacks to liberate themselves from the oppression of the white man. It is a struggle which aims at uprooting the race superiority of the whites and putting in its place a philosophy whose basic tenet is equal rights for all who live in and regard the country as their home, irrespective of race or colour. This is the basic premise.

The overwhelming majority of the whites of all classes and shades of opinion have drawn themselves together and lined themselves up against any advancement of the blacks, especially Africans, to a position that may threaten the superiority of the whites. This creates a serious problem in that the large majority of blacks see all whites as a group as the oppressor, and whites see themselves threatened by blacks. Looked at in this way it becomes a race confrontation in which the extreme poles are the Afrikaners on the side of the whites and the Africans on the side of the blacks.

The task is to get more and more whites to realise that the liberation movement is not against whites as a race, but against oppression by them. The liberation movement needs to devise ways and means that will assure both blacks and whites across the colour line that the conflict is not a racial one.

A factor that dissipates the energy of the liberation forces is the number of black anti-apartheid organisations. In such a situation a spirit of competition must prevail and, as sometimes happens, one organisation directs its criticism at another organisation and less at the common enemy. Such an exercise detracts the attention of the masses from the common enemy. The liberation struggle would be strengthened by the concerted action of organisations committed to a struggle to destroy all forms of racism. Jail conditions have forced political prisoners who are members of rival organisations to realise the need to act together.

The Nat government has become adept at implementing its racial policies. First it drives wedges between the different racial groups in the country by focusing the attention of each group on what is made out to be of interest to that group. In all its propaganda it bombards the minds of each group with the idea of the uniqueness of the interests of each group as distinct from the overall population of South Africa. Certain sections of each of the three black racial groups have fallen for this. These are the people who co-operate with the government to implement its policy through their respective councils and Bantu Authorities. The excuse such co-operators put forward is that there is nothing they can do in the absence of anything better. As if what they would like to see happen must do so on its own, without any effort and sacrifice on their part. Any course other than co-operation would lead to bloodshed and this they must avoid! Secondly, it drives wedges between the social groups within each racial group by directing the attention of each social group or class to its special interest as distinct from those of the racial group as a whole. The effort of such tactics is to get each social group to disregard the disabilities of the racial group to which it belongs, to say nothing of the other similarly oppressed racial groups. Thus a situation is created in which the upper social groups or classes grasp at opportunities that always appear to be within reach, and if they appear to be receding the fault is not sought in the conditions that stem from the oppression, but in the fact that they do not apply themselves sufficiently.

These tactics have been successful to some extent. The setting up of finance corporations for the respective black racial groups is regarded by these classes as an indication of the sincere intentions of the government to help them along the road to economic success. The Nat government found ready co-operators among the upper strata. The capitalist and middle class among the Indians and Coloureds, consisting of a substantial number of merchants, are filling positions in the respective councils provided for under apartheid policies. The government relies largely upon them to make this apartheid machinery workable within each racial group.

Amongst the Africans the government has relied mainly on its servants – the chiefs – in the Bantustans and on merchants in the urban councils. As already indicated, the restrictions under which the merchant class trade acts as a bridle to any political activity, even where their own interests, such as denial of the right to diversify in urban areas, at least until very recently, are affected unfavourably. The inference appears to be that the liberatory forces may not count on them as a group for active support for the time being.

Compared to the total population of each of the three black racial groups the co-operating social groups and classes may be small, but they are articulate and generally occupy positions of importance in social and traditional life. The role they play in implementing government policy creates a real problem for the liberation struggle.

A significant factor is that the professionals from all three black racial groups have not come out actively as co-operators. Medical practitioners and lawyers in the three groups have kept out of the respective councils and the various levels of Bantu Authorities except for a very few individuals in the Transkei and Sekhukhuneland (Lebowa). The inference is that this important section of the middle class have up to now refused to be used by the Nat government to further the cause of white supremacy – a factor the liberation forces may do well to study carefully because these professional groups are highly respected in their respective racial groups.

When the Bantu Authorities Act was passed, there was no intention on the part of the ruling Nats that the Bantustans set-up in terms of the Act would one day – all in the short space of 25 years – have imposed upon them sovereign independence. The report of the Tomlinson Commission does not envisage this. Regarding the political responsibilities the government may give to Africans under the apartheid policy, the report states that the Bantustans' 'administrative responsibility can in time be increased to government on a regional basis. Thus they can eventually carry the functions of government in accordance with a system similar to the present system in each of the seven parts of the Bantu areas'.[32] There are nine today.

The Bantustans were set up as a form of local government intended to be a departure from the Bunga (Council) system, while the latter was still permitted to run side by side with the African representation in Parliament.[33] The Nat government sought to revive chieftainship and made it serve under its control and direction the traditional role which it had played before it was crushed towards the close of the nineteenth century. The Nat government wanted the Africans to divert their energies from a struggle for equal political rights. They wanted the Africans now to concentrate on reviving tribal institutions.

When the Bantu Authorities Act was put before the Transkei Bunga, the members of the Bunga saw the Act as giving them scope for increased administrative powers in local affairs and no more than that. This is borne out by the statements from some of the leading members of the Bunga. Harry A. Masebe said: 'I take it that the purpose of the Act is to encourage the black people to integrate themselves to control and administer their own affairs so that all matters concerning them will be handled exclusively by them.'[34] C.K. Sakwe added: 'The Bantu Authorities Act is not in opposition to the Bunga.'[35] C.B. Young, a member of the Tomlinson Commission and later secretary of Native Affairs, did not think that the Bantu Authorities Act was much different from the Bunga. In his words there is 'little difference between the functions and duties of a system based on the Bunga as under the Act'.[36]

Even by the middle of the 1950s J.G. Strydom, then Prime Minister of South Africa, did not think self-government was a matter 'for today's practical politician'.[37] He went further to say of self-government in the Bantustans: 'It will not crop up for generations to come, if you look at the backward state of the Natives. We are dealing with the actual problem as it faces us today. They must remain under the trusteeship of the whites, who are the dominant race. I am not philosophising about what will happen 100 years from now.'[38]

By the late 1950s statements from the highest government quarters, when pressed about whether they intended complete apartheid, showed significant uncertainty about plans in the future. In the late 1950s De Wet Nel, then Minister of Native Affairs, stated in Parliament: 'Total racial separation was never seriously considered. Apartheid would be implemented under the umbrella of a South African economy.'[39]

Even in the early 1960s the question of the independence of the Bantustans, as a policy of the Nat government, was dismissed. An illustration of this is J.B. Schoeman's answer to the question of whether separate development might evolve into independence. His reply was: 'How politically naive that question is! After all history has taught us that the road to independence in our case took more than a full century.'[40]

In the midst of the policy uncertainties that prevailed at the time, H.F. Verwoerd became Prime Minister and stated that apartheid was an ideal to aim at. Even to him it did not appear to be a matter for practical politics. He added that 'if it should happen that in the future they [the Bantustans] progress to a very advanced level, people of those future times will have to consider in what further way their relationships must be organised'.[41]

Dr W.W.M. Eiselen, one of the main architects of the apartheid policy and for a period appointed Secretary for Native Affairs to implement it, had this to say in an article in *Optima*, March 1959: 'The utmost degree of autonomy in administrative matters which the Union is likely to be prepared to consider to those areas will stop short of actual surrender of sovereignty by the European trustee and there is therefore no prospect of a federal system with eventual equality among members.'[42]

Even Dr H.F. Verwoerd, who had held out total apartheid as an ideal, had hastened to lay down the conditions that Africans would be required to fulfil. They would only be granted such autonomy and independence if '[they] have within their power to develop sufficient maturity to assume ... the most responsible of functions'.[43] Even with this condition fulfilled, it did not follow that autonomy would be granted. No! Instead '[t]he white Parliament would be the final arbiter of what is development, ability and maturity'.[44] In other words, advancement in powers of the Bantustans would take place at the instance of the white Parliament, if and when it suited the interests of the whites.

Although Dr Verwoerd had in 1958 seen total apartheid as an ideal to pursue he was shortly thereafter to make a statement which was not in keeping with that ideal. On the question of the desirability of incorporating in the Union the three former British Territories bordering on South Africa, he stated in 1959 that the possibility of incorporating these territories was incompatible with the British policy of granting independence to African territories. As Wilson and Thompson point out, this 'clearly revealed his inability at that time to conceive of full independence for the Bantustans'.[45]

By 1962 the position had not been stated with any greater clarity. All that Verwoerd said was that '[s]eparate development introduces new institutions and revives fading ones. Because the Transkei has a relatively homogeneous population speaking one language it is natural that it should be the first area selected for the experiment providing semi-autonomy, a status that might be the first step towards ultimate independence.'[46]

The granting of self-government in 1963 was an experiment. In this way the Nat government placed itself in a position where it could meet criticism from friend and foe alike. To its foes there was the experiment, to its friends it signalled that the experiment might fail and, in any case, '[t]he white Parliament was the final arbiter' of African ability and maturity.

The Bantustans have created a problem in that they threaten to drive wedges between

Africans and would have retarded the struggle for liberation. But the new development whereby the Nat government imposes independence on Bantustans at such times as suits the programme of the National Party poses a much more serious problem to the liberation forces than the role the Bantustans were to play originally. The question that arises is: what has precipitated this step and in what respect is it intended to operate in the interests of white supremacy?

If we recall that the announcement to ask for independence within two to five years came from Kaiser Matanzima after the parliamentary session of 1974 and that independence was scheduled to take place within two years rather than five, then one might ask, notwithstanding the possibility that independence of the Bantustans might have been an item in the programme of the National Party: what was the immediate cause for the Nat government to impose independence on the Bantustans?

The decision came hard on the heels of the independence of the former Portuguese colonies in Africa. To the government, Mozambique, Angola and Zimbabwe had constituted a buffer partly against infiltration of units of the liberation forces trained abroad into South Africa, and partly against possible military attacks from the north. The collapse of Portuguese dictatorship and the armed action of the liberation forces in Zimbabwe have forced the Nat government to create a new buffer behind which race-inspired white South Africa hopes to take cover. The Bantustans must now be the new buffer. They must be given something that gives them a stake in apartheid in the name of defending their own territories. According to announcements by Kaiser Matanzima and spokesmen for the Nat government, the parties are to enter into agreements for mutual military assistance.

The problem facing the liberation forces takes on two forms. First, independent Bantustans will not tolerate the operation of liberation forces, whether those operations are to mount propaganda or to organise military activities against white South Africa. The Bantustans will join hands with the white supremacists against the liberation forces. The Bantustans will be indebted to the apartheid policies of the Nats for their new status.

Secondly, if one Bantustan after another is declared independent and a large number of Africans outside the Bantustans are forced to accept the citizenship of one or other of the Bantustans, then the liberation forces must accept the fact that the Coloured and Indian racial groups will be open to intensified wooing and promises by the white supremacists. We have referred to increasing demands by yet uncoordinated sections of white public opinion to draw the Indian and Coloured racial groups closer to the whites. The inference is clear: strengthen the whites in the event of a physical conflict between the whites and Africans. What the propagators of this idea have in mind is that political, economic and social rights should be extended to the Coloureds and Indians on an equal basis to the whites. This would give them a stake in the joint defence of a vested interest in race superiority.

In terms of relative population figures the propagators of the integration idea are seeking to obtain a balance between the proposed integrated group on the one hand and the Africans on the other. In 1970 the white population was 3 750 000 with an annual growth rate of 1,92 per cent. The whites would be expected to be 4 million in 1980. If the Coloureds and Indians were integrated this would increase the number of those who have a stake in apartheid by almost 4 million by 1980.

It may be expected that as the struggle for liberation intensifies the volume of white public opinion pressing for integration of Coloureds and Indians will increase considerably. In the South African situation it is easy to whip up fears of one racial group or another. The liberation forces must face the fact that certain sections of the minority black racial groups fear a rampant African Nationalism. A programmed campaign in which the aims of the liberation struggle are painstakingly explained seems to be called for to dispel this fear.

CONCLUSION

In our discussion we have dealt with the problems the government has created in order to obstruct the progress of the liberation forces. For instance, we do not refer to the activities of the Security Branch or to the fact that the major liberation organisations are banned. These are instruments the government uses to frustrate the liberation forces and make government policy unacceptable to the people. It is the function of the liberation forces to seek improved methods to circumvent these operational problems.

The serious problems are those which are inbuilt in the social and class structure of each oppressed racial group, whether these are of government making or a natural development of society that the government seeks to harness. There is a continuing struggle between the National Party government and the liberation forces to enlist the loyalty and support of all sections of the oppressed people. But a fact the liberatory forces have to face is that the struggle for liberation is still confined to words rather than action. In this regard, government propaganda, backed by financial inducements, will gain the support of a significant section of the upper social and class strata among blacks.

The government's decision to grant independence to the Bantustans, starting with the Transkei, is a problem that will exist as long as opposition to apartheid is confined to talking only. When the struggle against apartheid assumes sharper forms, when words are supported by physical action, most of the problems will be reduced and, in some cases, may be turned into problems for the oppressor. Only then will the force of the words of Marshall Campbell be appreciated: 'No country can prosper when the largest section of its people has no say in the government of its people'.[47] In the spirit of Karl Marx's famous slogan, the oppressed people of South Africa must unite, for they have nothing to lose but their chains of oppression. As such unity is forged in the day-to-day struggle against apartheid, the eyes of Africans, Coloureds and Indians will be turned to Parliament, where they are destined to have a say side by side with the whites.

BILLY NAIR

Billy Nair was born on 27 November 1929. After primary school he went to work to supplement the family's income. He attended night classes and obtained his Matriculation certificate and a Diploma in Accounting. He began his trade union career by organising the Natal Dairy Workers Union in 1951. After being fired from his job, he became full-time Secretary of the Union. He was appointed Secretary of the Natal Indian Youth Congress in 1951 and member of the executive of the Natal Indian Congress in 1954. He served on the National Executive and was the Natal Secretary of the South African Congress of Trade Unions (SACTU). He was one of the 156 leaders arrested and charged with high treason in 1956. After being detained for three months during the 1960 State of Emergency, he was served with a two-year banning order in 1961. He continued to work in the underground structures of the SACP and Umkhonto weSizwe. He was again detained on 6 July 1963 and sentenced to 20 years for sabotage.

In prison he obtained a BA and a B. Com. degree and was studying towards a B. Proc. degree at the time of his release. On his release from prison in 1984 he became active in the United Democratic Front. He served on the National Executive Committee of the UDF and was Deputy Chair for Natal of the UDF. He was again detained in 1984 and in 1985. On the eve of the 1986 State of Emergency, he went underground. He was arrested once more on 23 July 1990 and was charged with nine others in the 'Vula' trial.

Billy served as a member of the Central Committee of the SACP from 1990 to 1997, and of the National Executive Committee of the ANC from 1991 to 1994. He was elected to Parliament in 1994 and re-elected in the 1999 election.

PROFILE

In a freedom struggle every battle has to be fought as if it spells the end of the war. At the same time it is winning the war that counts.

Billy has that mettle, that stubborn streak, which is essential to the make-up of a freedom fighter. He engages in every battle as if it were the last.

He was detained in 1963, and experienced torture and brutality in detention while awaiting trial and again after sentence. It didn't end when he reached Robben Island in 1964. The warders would descend on the prisoners with batons and pickaxe handles without reason.

By the time Billy was brought to the isolation section he was in a fighting mood – better to die fighting than to subject oneself to such brutality was becoming his motto. At the time, the prisoners in the isolation section were seated on rows of concrete blocks, about a metre-and-a-half apart. No talking was allowed between prisoners. Equipped with four-pound hammers we were to break slabs of blue stone into tiny pebbles.

Billy's hackles would rise at the slightest provocation from a warder. Time and again such a flare-up would result in summary punishment for him. Mandela would send whispered messages down the work-line, passed from one prisoner to another and on to Billy, urging him not to react to the provocation. Billy was in no mood for such advice. Only after being urged repeatedly and reminded that we were in a protracted struggle for freedom, did he calm down, but not without accusing some of being faint-hearted.

That stubborn grit in Billy should never be mistaken for inflexibility. His life as a trade unionist had taught him that winning one battle does not spell victory in the war.

As a trade union leader he had learnt that organising workers in South Africa was an extremely difficult and hazardous task. At the beginning the workers at a factory would need repeated persuasion to come to a union meeting. Once convinced, they would respond with great enthusiasm. By the time they reached the point of formulating and submitting their grievances and demands, they would be itching for action. As a leader Billy was often confronted with the task of persuading them to prosecute their demands resolutely and methodically. Only after going through such procedures should they contemplate strike action. Often enough, by the time strike action was resorted to, there would be workers wanting to continue the strike indefinitely.

Almost every strike required a sense of timing on when to compromise, the key being to consolidate gains while maintaining the unity and cohesion of the workers to take issue in the next round.

A union leader learns fast that leadership is a somewhat lonely task requiring one to urge one's colleagues forward when they are hesitant, and urging them to take it easy, to accept settlement – even a compromise – when their unity in action is at its height. None of this comes easy. Such leadership requires strength of character, a sense of timing and an eschewing of demagoguery.

Never should Billy be judged by his temper at a given moment. His head and heart may appear to be disjunct, but he is always able to respond to the counsel and persuasion of his peers – because deep down he always has stamina. This he combines with an impish humour, marking him as a prankster among his comrades.

THROUGH THE EYES OF THE WORKERS

BILLY NAIR

This essay sketches, among other matters, the problem of trade union unity, the struggles of the workers and the trade union movement, and attempts to examine separate development from the workers' point of view.

The advent of capitalism in South Africa since the discovery of gold and diamonds in the 1860s brought with it the insatiable demand for labour. The central task of successive governments has been to ensure a smooth and steady flow of labour. To this end skilled labour was imported, while unskilled labour came from the blacks.

The Wars of Dispossession against the indigenous people that began in 1652 now took a more serious and desperate turn. The imperialists unleashed furious wars against the blacks, conquering, annexing their remaining lands, grabbing their cattle and other means of wealth, and converting the once proud owners of land into an industrial proletariat.

The skilled workers who arrived from Europe brought with them ideas of trade unionism. The first organised union, the Amalgamated Society of Woodworkers, formed in 1881, was a branch of its parent union in England. Soon unions were formed in the mines, railways, the printing and other industries.

From its inception, trade unionism in South Africa has been dogged by racism. The craft unions jealously preserved their positions and status by confining skills within a narrow group. They refused to train blacks or to agree to their apprenticeship under the pretext of maintaining a 'Civilised Labour Policy' in terms of which the 'rate for the job' and so-called 'civilised standards' were defended. The closed-shop policy[1] and legislation barred blacks from skilled work.

A storm of protest broke loose when the government was forced to import 50 000 Chinese workers in 1904 to work on the mines, which had remained closed during the Anglo-Boer War (1899–1902). The labour crisis was caused by the refusal of over a hundred thousand African workers to return to the mines, notwithstanding the increase in wages from 20 shillings to 30 shillings per month. India would not allow emigration of its citizens because of South Africa's discriminatory practices against Indians who had come to South Africa as indentured labourers. South Africa was at this point intent on repatriating the Indians. Almost all 50 000 Chinese workers were unceremoniously repatriated in 1910, by which time the mines had been put back on a profitable basis.

African labour supply to the mines improved only after stringent measures were taken by the authorities to break the last vestiges of independent livelihood of the Africans. Labour laws were tightened, a squatters' tax and poll tax were imposed. In addition, high rents were charged for those squatting on white-owned land and there were wholesale evictions of squatters. The poll tax was the last straw – it gave rise to the Bambata Rebellion in 1906. Twelve leaders were executed and many others were jailed.

The early twentieth century witnessed some of the most militant struggles of the workers. One of the earliest strikes was that of the white workers on the gold mines in 1897. Among those who went on strike were Bill Andrews and Percy Bunting. Both lost their jobs and as leaders they were ejected from their compounds on the mines. Rather than return to England, they stayed and helped to organise their fellow workers into trade unions. They also played a prominent part in the formation of the Labour Party in 1907. Both helped to form the Transvaal Federation of Trades in 1905, the forerunner of the South African Industrial Federation established in 1913. Trade union membership grew from 3 836 in 1900 to 11 941 in 1914.

In 1907, at the height of the Depression, thousands of workers went on strike on the mines. The government declared martial law. British regiments controlled the Rand. The strike was defeated because some of the English skilled workers, working with a large unskilled Afrikaner labour force, were prepared to work for a lower wage. The trade unions protested against the employment of cheap Afrikaner labour, but within the space of 20 years the Afrikaner workers flooded the mines and Afrikanerised the industry and thereby the labour movement.

A strike that erupted at the New Kleinfontein mines in 1913 on the issue of the recognition of the mine union, became a general strike for the recognition of trade unions. Troops were called in and violence erupted. The workers scored a resounding victory in winning recognition for their trade unions.

In 1914, after a strike by the coal miners of Natal against wage cuts, the railway workers joined it. The South African Federation of Trades called out the gold miners and soon a general strike for higher wages had the country in its grip. Martial law was declared and 60 000 troops were called out. Nine syndicalist leaders of the strike were summarily deported to Europe. A storm of protest forced the government to allow the men back into the country. Only a few returned. The workers won wage protection, a phthisis allowance and other improvements.[2]

The Labour Party, formed in 1907 by Bill Andrews, Percy Bunting, Ivor Jones, Robert Cresswell and others, was increasingly dominated by the Transvaal unions, which were very colour-conscious. Cresswell, who became its leader, had advocated a white labour policy when he was a mine manager. He suggested that the mines employ white labour only. Through its agitation, the Mines and Works Act, which shut out blacks from skilled jobs on the grounds of 'safety, health and discipline', was passed in 1911.

The membership of the trade unions and the Labour Party was confined to whites. Bill Andrews and Percy Bunting fought to get the unions of the Federation of Trades to throw open their doors to the blacks. They opposed the colour bar tooth and nail, to the extent that Bunting advocated the establishment of a black republic as a solution to South Africa's problems.

Andrews, Bunting, Jones and some of their colleagues constituted the socialist wing in the Labour Party, which later formed itself into the 'War-on-War' movement. They opposed participation in the imperialist war and advocated socialism. In 1915 they broke from the Labour Party, whose policies with regard to the First World War, and more particularly its colour policies, they found repugnant.[3] They then formed the International Socialist League (ISL) in 1915.

The ISL set about organising the black workers into trade unions. It formed the Industrial Workers of Africa in 1915 and actively co-operated with the ANC and other black organisations. Sanitary workers downed buckets in Johannesburg in 1916. The ANC and ISL leaders were charged with instigating the strike. Strikes broke out at the Cape Town docks and at the Kimberley municipality. The pass burning on the Rand conducted by the ANC was followed in 1920 by a massive strike of 71 000 African miners in Johannesburg. The miners were cordoned off to give the police freedom to shoot. An ANC meeting at Vrededorp called to support the miners was fired on. Many were killed.

In 1920, the white municipal workers went on strike in Durban and occupied the City Hall for several days. Owing to the militant struggles of the white workers and, more particularly of members of the ISL like Andrews and Bunting, black workers were inspired into trade union activity. The formation of the Industrial and Commercial Workers Union (ICU) under Clements Kadalie in 1917 was a unique approach to trade unionism. The ICU grew into a mammoth organisation embracing workers, peasants, professionals, businessmen, tradesmen, and others. It was not a co-ordinating body of trade unions and it recruited its members individually. Herein lay its chief weakness: it was unable to take up the issue of the workers on an industrial basis effectively. Nevertheless, its membership grew to over 150 000 by 1930.

From the beginning many communists like Jimmy La Guma (who was treasurer of the ICU) played an important part in organising the ICU. During the period of reaction in the 1920s when the state took action against the communists and other trade unionists and progressives, culminating in the promulgation of the Riotous Assemblies Act and the Native Administration Act of 1927, the ICU conducted its own witch-hunt against communists. The expulsions removed the most dedicated and upright members from the leadership. This weakened the ICU, which became inefficient, corrupt and bureaucratic and alienated itself from the general membership. Leadership troubles mingled with personality problems caused further splits. A.W.G. Champion broke away and formed a separate *ICU wase Natal* (ICU of Natal).

Both Smuts and Hertzog were prepared to meet the leaders of the ICU, but they were not prepared to accord it recognition. Under the pretext of the ICU 'causing hostility between blacks and whites' in terms of the Native Administration Act and of the Riotous Assemblies Act, the government banned the leaders and meetings of the union. Constant raids on the offices of the ICU, the use of police spies to bring false charges against the leaders, the use of force by the police and the physical smashing of the offices of the ICU seriously undermined its activities.

Mass unemployment, high prices, scarcity of goods, and mass starvation in the 1920s and 1930s were the main factors that set the workers on the revolutionary path. Black and white workers conducted some of the most militant battles. Unfortunately they conducted their struggles separately, although against a common enemy who was exploiting them both and had plunged the country into an imperialist war, for which the workers were being asked to make sacrifices in the form of higher productivity, lower wages and lower standards of living.

Andrews and Bunting led the workers towards socialism by founding the Communist Party in 1921. Their activities from the time of the formation of the Labour Party in 1907 show a conviction that the salvation of the workers lay in socialism. The formation of the Communist Party drew together the strands of the militant struggles waged throughout the preceding decade. Immediately after its founding it plunged itself into one of the most militant struggles of the workers.

Apologists of the bourgeoisie, and among these are many trade unionists, tend to write off the 1922 miners' rebellion as just another 'episode' in which workers made a foolish attempt to challenge authority. The truth is that it was an armed rebellion. The rebels took control of a large part of Johannesburg. The army failed the workers' cause by not joining it.

By that time the Soviet Union had emerged as the first Workers' Republic. The Soviets had just smashed the reactionary White Russians, who were backed by the imperialist powers. This inspired the workers the world over, including in South Africa. The Communist Party emerged as one of the largest single forces in Germany and in other European countries.

What began as a strike to defeat the attempts of the Chamber of Mines to increase the ratio of black to white workers culminated in an armed struggle. The mines maintained that they were faced with falling premiums from 42 shillings to 19 shillings per ounce and that if the fall continued, 24 out of the 39 mines would be forced to close. This would lead to the retrenchment of 10 000 white and 100 000 black miners. The mine management therefore proposed that the ratio of white to black be changed from 3,5:1 to 10,5:1. In other words, it wanted to employ more blacks per white skilled workers so as to cut costs. The mines also wanted to increase the number of black semi-skilled workers. The white miners wanted the reverse.

The Chamber of Mines, working in close collaboration with the state, decided to provoke the workers into action. The Chamber began by deliberately cutting the wages of the coal miners. Gold and other workers were similarly threatened. The South African Federation of Trade Unions called the miners out on a general strike embracing the railways, mines and industrial workers.

Both the Chamber of Mines and the government stalled negotiations. Prime Minister General Jan Smuts declared martial law. This was about the sixth time the country was under martial law as a result of strikes over the 15 years from 1907 to 1922. This time the country was virtually engaged in a full-scale war.

When soldiers and police started shooting in Boksburg, the Federation of Trade Unions began to waver. It failed to act in the face of army provocations. The workers decided to form an Action Committee, which began military drill and prepared the workers to handle arms. They established headquarters that were well fortified. Within a matter of weeks Johannesburg and its environs (the mining and industrial hub of South Africa) fell into revolutionary hands.

Smuts and the Chamber of Mines were in constant consultation at the Rand Club throughout the rebellion. A few men sitting at the Rand Club were able to defeat the working class masses. They did this by detaching the army from the workers and using it against them. This problem has always stood in the way of victory for workers the world over. The ruling class bribes the army with status, letters and ribbons. Unless the army and police are politicised, enlightened, trained and disciplined under a revolutionary code they always serve as the handmaidens of the ruling class.

In the rebellion 230 were killed, hundreds were injured. Smuts bombed and strafed the workers' headquarters from the air. Three of the leaders who were hanged sang the 'Red Flag' as they were marched to the gallows.

Smuts did a wonderful job for the mine owners. The 'status quo' agreement was scrapped and semi-skilled work was given to the blacks at low wage rates. The working costs were cut down by over 17 per cent in December 1922.

A more important factor was that the white workers displayed a strong indifference to their black brothers. Although basically the action was a class war, it was distorted by anti-blackism. The slogan 'Workers of the World unite for a White South Africa' does violence to the militancy and heroism displayed by the workers.

After the strike hundreds of English people and other Europeans left the country, and thousands of Afrikaner workers flocked to the mines and industry. The white population of the 1920s had a few wealthy and prosperous agriculturalists, industrialists and mine magnates and financiers at the apex; at the base were the poverty-stricken masses, especially Afrikaners. By 1923, 10 per cent (160 000) of the white population was poor. Poor blacks and poor whites were the direct result of the process of land consolidation that went on following the advent of capitalism. The rapid conversion of the once independent farmers into proletarians became a nightmarish experience. Slipshod methods of production and the easy and carefree life gave way to new demands of a largely impersonal industrial society. This society demanded efficiency, it wanted profits, and it was a force that reduced blacks and whites to a common denominator – a servile wage-labouring mass.

At first the landless Afrikaners squatted and sharecropped on large estates, but because of their antipathy for manual labour (the so-called 'kaffir' work), the Afrikaners became real squatters. Even in unskilled work in urban areas the blacks were in demand, and because industry and the mines preferred cheap black labour, the white workers' attitude to their black brothers became more hostile.

Changes in the composition of the white labour force brought about changes in the composition of the Labour Party and other political parties, especially the National Party. The development of the Afrikaner labour force and the anti-working class image that Smuts earned, welded the NP and the LP into a powerful coalition that defeated Smuts in the 1924 general election.

Both the LP and the NP stood for a white South Africa, the colour bar, and a white labour policy. Although both parties claimed to be anti-capitalist, and particularly against the Chamber of Mines, there was no basic antagonism between them and the bourgeoisie.

The Labour–Nat coalition set about enacting legislation that protected the unionists and the white workers. The ruling class did not want a recurrence of the militant struggles of the years from 1913 to 1922, which almost toppled the bourgeoisie from power. Although Labour coming to power on a joint ticket was a victory for the white workers, that power was used to advance the position of the white workers to the exclusion of the black workers.

While the Industrial Conciliation Act of 1924 accorded recognition to the trade unions of white, Coloured and Indian workers, it specifically barred African trade unions and prohibited strikes by African workers. Apprenticeship laws and the Mines and Works Act excluded blacks from skilled employment. The Native Administration Act and the Riotous Assemblies Act were used to cripple the ICU and the black trade union movement. Communist and progressive trade unionists were either banned or their movements restricted. Anybody fighting for freedom, democracy, equality, higher wages or trade union rights was charged with 'creating hostility' between blacks and whites.

The recognition of trade unions, social and job security, the colour bar and job reservation, rapid promotion to supervisory positions in the mines, industries and the civil service, and, in particular, higher wages (sometimes totally incommensurate with the type of work done or the productivity of the worker) inculcated in the white worker a class-collaborationist attitude. They identified themselves with the interests of the ruling class and were only antagonistic to it when their own interests were threatened. The government either quickly retracted anything against the white workers' interests or came to their aid, even if the best interests of the economy were not served, for instance in its refusal to admit blacks to skilled jobs although the pace of economic development demanded it.

The ruling class accordingly found a suitable vehicle in the white worker for the defence of the capitalist system. In turn, the white worker saw the ruling class as his protector. The white worker used his vote to return the National Party to power in successive elections since 1948. The white worker is conscious that his high standards and supremacy are dependent mainly on the super-exploitation of the blacks. Besides the normal disparity in wages between the rural and urban areas, the white artisans earn wages that raise them to the status of aristocrats of labour. As far back as 1914 the average white coal miner enjoyed the highest standards in the British Empire.

In 1969 five of the wealthiest mines, four of which belong to the Anglo American group, accounted for half of the 306 million pounds sterling earned by 48 mines. All the mines belong to the Chamber of Mines, which enjoys labour monopoly in that individual mine employers do not compete among themselves for labour. This naturally depresses the black workers' wages, which in any event cannot be raised through collective bargaining, because black trade unions are not permitted. White trade unions virtually dictate the labour policy of the mines. The result of this is:

Annual cash earnings	Whites	Blacks
1911	R666	R57
1969	R4 000	R199
Earnings ratio: white to black	20,1	1

Other forms of discrimination include: only white workers enjoy a cost of living allowance; whites enjoy 18 to 30 days paid annual leave, while there is none for African workers; blacks are excluded from provident pension funds; in the case of permanent disablement as a result of injury on duty, black workers receive a lump sum payment that is less than the amount whites receive annually for disability; in the case of the Phthisis Fund, two-thirds of the annual payment of R10 million goes to whites; there is no unemployment fund for the Africans; there are housing loans for whites, but none for blacks; with regard to recreational facilities, 37 cricket fields, 63 football fields, 20 golf courses, 255 tennis courts, 80 bowling greens, and 38 swimming baths are provided for 46 000 white miners; for the 291 000 blacks there are 'bar lounges' in each compound, a total of 101 playing fields, two cycle tracks and 55 dance arenas.

In 1946, 75 000 African miners led by the African Mine Workers Union went on strike. Thirteen mines were brought to a standstill. The workers were fired at, nine were killed and 1 200 injured. The Mine Workers Union, and ANC and CPSA leaders were arrested and charged with sedition.

The Chamber of Mines refused, and still refuses, to recognise the African Mine Workers Union, saying 'in their tribal state the Africans are not ready for trade unions'. Meetings of trade unions are banned on the mines and spies abound to report any 'subversive' trade union activity. The Chamber of Mines, however, is keen to employ blacks because it is alleged that 'blacks thrive on wages that mean starvation to whites'. Africans require a smaller phthisis allowance and no unemployment or sick funds. They can be housed in compounds and can be criminally arraigned for striking. They do not have the vote and are not allowed to have trade unions.

White workers enjoy high wages and therefore higher purchasing power and high standards of living only because of the low wages paid to black workers. This gives whites an aura of racial and cultural superiority and concomitantly psychological and intellectual advantages over blacks. The myth of white superiority, which evolved out of a superior economic position of the whites, is used by the ruling class to harness the white workers as defenders of the system of apartheid, thus making them aid and abet the exploitation of the blacks.

General Smuts, addressing a conference of the South African Institute of Race Relations in 1941 in the atmosphere of war, when black co-operation was needed, said that the African worker was 'carrying the country on his back'. Smuts again, after rioting in 1950, said that 'the government has squandered this country's greatest asset, the goodwill of her workers, by driving into those vast labour masses [the idea] … that they were a menace to Eurocivilisation'.

THE SOUTH AFRICAN TRADES AND LABOUR COUNCIL (1930)
Since its formation, the CPSA and progressive trade unionists plunged themselves into organising and leading the workers in militant struggles for higher wages, trade union rights, democracy, socialism and a society free from exploitation and oppression.

At the same time the white workers, under the leadership of the Nat–Labour Pact government began shifting to the right. Bribes and sops in the form of votes, trade union rights, skilled job monopoly, and thus protection against black employment in skilled jobs, made the white workers the aristocrats of labour.

The formation of the South African Trades and Labour Council (SAT&LC) in 1930 by Andrews and Bunting and others was a triumph for the progressive forces because the Council admitted bona fide trade unions irrespective of racial composition.

The valiant battles of communists and progressives during the 1920s and the 1930s in the face of state and state-inspired fascist opposition are a credit to their dedication to the cause of the working class. Trade unionists like Andrews, Bunting, Solly Sachs, Gana Makabeni, Benny Weinbren, H.A. Naidoo, Gladstone Tshume, Ray Alexander, Piet Huyser, George Poonen and S.B. Mungal are among the many who contributed to building the progressive trade union movement.

THE REACTION

Out of fear that the workers of their own country would create soviets similar to that of the Soviet Union, the ruling classes the world over aided and abetted the formation of fascist organisations to stem the tide of revolution. Side by side with Hitler, Mussolini, Franco and Salazar in Europe, other 'little Hitlers' and Pirow in South Africa were given a free hand to organise storm troopers who engaged in open acts of terrorism and violence against manifestations of change and progress.

The Broederbond, a secret Afrikaner organisation with '12 apostles' at the helm, took control of the NP. It infiltrated the fabric of Afrikaner life. Dr Albert Hertzog and Dr Nico Diedericks, founders of the Reform League, were sworn to freeing the Afrikaner workers from the 'Red menace'. The grey- and black-shirt fascists, swilling in anti-Semitism and anti-blackism, broke up workers' meetings in the 1930s and 1940s. They used force and terror to intimidate the workers. A relentless campaign was launched to detach the Afrikaner worker from the rest of the working class. To this end Diedericks and Hertzog infiltrated the mining, building, glass and other trade unions.

Pirow, the Minister of Justice, waged war on the trade unions. Meetings and leaders were banned, and offices raided. The police were incited by Pirow to use batons and fists freely. The dock workers of Durban were beaten up and shot at in 1929. In 1938 Pirow air-freighted teargas bombs to the Rhodesian government to quell strikes there. Pirow, the little Führer, was reaching out beyond the borders of South Africa.

The stance of the NP has always been anti-imperialist and anti-capitalist, but the party itself was undergoing changes. Initially a party of agricultural capitalists, it gradually became a spokesman for industrial, financial and banking interests. In the process it became enmeshed with the imperialists, serving their interests as well as advancing its own with imperialist aid.

When the NP came to power in 1948 it dedicated itself to implementing the programme of action of the Reform League adopted in the 1930s. It also carried out the task the Broederbond had set itself of establishing an Afrikaner-dominated Republic in which all other racial groups would be subordinate. The cornerstone of the programme was a war against communism. Under the pretext of fighting communism the government passed the Suppression of Communism Act in 1950, which defines communism and communist activity in such wide terms that even avowed anti-communists have fallen foul of that law.

Hundreds of people were subjected to bans, house arrest, deportations and imprisonment for offences designed to control the limited rights of the people. Seventy-five trade unionists were placed on the banned list by 1950 and they were forced to resign their trade union and other political positions. Twenty-three SACTU officials appeared on charges of High Treason in 1956. During 1963, 35 SACTU officials were held under the 90-day detention law and large numbers were sentenced to long terms for so-called 'sabotage' and 'terrorism'. Between 1963 and 1965, 200 political trials were held, involving, among others, trade unionists. Over 2 000 were brought before the courts. Altogether, 49 were sentenced to death, 15 to life imprisonment and about 1 300 to terms of imprisonment totalling 8 000 years.

The Nat government's onslaught against every vestige of opposition was a continuation and hardening of the process started by its predecessors. Legislative enactments and administrative measures apart, the Nats penetrated the trade unions, especially the larger ones. They captured the Mine Workers Union. After banning Piet Huyter, they successfully penetrated the Building Workers' Union. They formed the Blanke Beskermingbond in 1948. A splinter Clothing Workers' Union was a direct result of the process of white-anting. It was the forerunner of the fragmentation of the trade unions that the Nat government prescribed through law after it came to power in 1948.

The wholesale banning order and the removal of dedicated communists from office weakened the trade union movement to such an extent that it paved the way for the triumph of the right wing.

THE TRADE UNION MOVEMENT CRACKS UNDER THE WHIP

Six Pretoria unions with 13 000 members disaffiliated from the Trades and Labour Council in April 1947 on the issue of African trade union affiliation. They formed a separate co-ordinating body. In 1950, after the Suppression of Communism Act was passed, 23 trade unions with a membership of 100 000 disaffiliated on the same issue, leaving the Trades and Labour Council with only 83 000 members.

A final breach occurred in 1954 when the Trades and Labour Council itself was dissolved on the race question and a co-ordinating body, the Trade Union Council of South Africa (TUCSA), exclusively for registered trade unions of whites, Indians and Coloureds, was formed. The crux was again the question of African workers.

Before the Trades and Labour Council was dissolved a so-called 'Unity Conference' of registered trade unions was held in Cape Town in 1954. It was the biggest mass conference of its kind and represented over 400 000 white, Indian and Coloured workers, ranging from mines and railways to industry, commerce and fisheries. The trade unions from the extreme right and the left attended to fight the proposed Industrial Conciliation Bill, which sought to mangle the trade unions by splitting them on racial lines, to prescribe job reservation and to set up an Industrial Tribunal to be the final arbiter on disputes between employers and workers. This measure was carefully thought out by the Nats and was consistent with their declared aims and that of the Broederbond way back in the 1930s to cripple the trade union movement and make it impotent.

George McCormack, leader of the South African Federation of Trade Unions, explained the treachery and shameless collusion of a ministerial committee of trade unionists that had been created in 1953. This committee not only accepted most of the contents of the Bill in principle, but also had actually collaborated in formulating parts of the Bill. McCormack said that it was therefore senseless to make any representations to the government because the content of the Bill was virtually inspired by the (white) trade unionists. Among those who served on the ministerial committee were George McCormack himself, Tommy Rutherford (Typographical Union), Ben Caddy (Engine Drivers), J. Ellis (Mines), and Tom Murray (Boilermakers). All the trade unionists were from the right or centre, which accepted the tenets of apartheid in the trade union movement as long as control of the movement remained in the hands of the whites. The conference elected a delegation of about 20, made up mainly of those very ministerial committee members, to meet the Minister of Labour to effect certain changes to the Bill. As was expected, the Minister refused to make the changes.

The white trade unionists and the white-led unions of Coloureds and Indian workers rejected strikes or any form of action to pressure the government to withdraw aspects of the Bill. Instead, the conference decided to issue leaflets to 'educate' the workers. Nothing more was heard of this process of 'education'.

The left trade unionists who attended the conference fought hard to convince the delegates that it was incumbent on the white and black workers to unite to fight the drastic inroads the Nat government was making into the trade union movement. In 1953 the government passed the Native Labour (Settlement of Disputes) Act, which, according to the Minister of Labour, was intended to 'bleed the African trade unions to death'. But the trade union bureaucrats present at the conference, reared in the school of class collaboration and opportunism, would not hear of any fight. They shunned militant struggle and were ready to collaborate in meeting the wishes of the government to destroy trade union unity.

The Trades and Labour Council experienced a slow and agonising death at the hands of the right-wing trade unionists through several breakaways. In 1954 it faced final strangulation, not by the right, but by centrists like Dulcie Hartwell, Johanna Cornelius, Anna Scheepers, Carl Meyer and Louis Nelson. Amid crocodile tears from these hypocrites, the Trades and Labour Council was laid to rest by a narrow card vote majority. The only co-ordinating body that opened its doors to blacks and whites on equal terms was dissolved. What is important is that there was no legal bar, even in the Industrial Conciliation Bill, preventing blacks and whites joining a single co-ordinating body.

The formation of TUCSA in 1954, which barred African trade unions from affiliation, clearly demonstrated the readiness of white workers and some non-whites to sacrifice trade union principles at the altar of apartheid.

The Federation of Free African Trade Unions of South Africa (FOFATUSA), formed in 1960, was a co-ordinating body which embraced mainly those African trade unions which were branches of trade unions affiliated to TUCSA, e.g. the African Tobacco Workers' Union and the African Clothing Workers' Union. Most of these unions are tied hand and foot to the registered parent unions. They occupy the same offices and depend heavily on their parent unions. In a policy declaration FOFATUSA stated that it was interested only in the economic problems of the workers and would not 'meddle in politics'. When SACTU refused to accept 30 000 pounds offered by the International Confederation of Free Trade Unions (ICFTU) because too many strings were attached to the offer, these funds were channelled to TUCSA to organise African workers.

When FOFATUSA established a branch in Durban in 1960, SACTU met its leader, 'Dum-dum' Nyaose, who 'expressed regret that FOFATUSA was organising African textile workers whose union was an affiliate of SACTU'. There were also a number of other cases of 'overlapping' owing to Nyaose's deliberate attempt to 'organise' the already organised workers of SACTU. Serious conflict, which took on a racial character, arose among Indian and African workers in the textile industry. The problem was only solved by SACTU's intervention. Although Nyaose assured SACTU that he would refrain from any activities that may undermine SACTU, in practice he did the opposite.

SACTU at the time was at the height of its strength and all attempts to weaken it, whether these came from the employers, the police or disrupters, failed miserably. However, state action against SACTU and its affiliates, particularly through banning orders, imprisonment and police harassment, paved the way for the ascendancy of the right wing.

TUCSA AND FOFATUSA

In 1970 TUCSA, which had a liaison committee with FOFATUSA, decided to admit FOFATUSA unions to demonstrate its 'non-racial' character with the object of regaining admission for South Africa to the ILO. Earlier the ILO had kicked out the country because of its apartheid policies. Moreover, TUCSA credentials were challenged by SACTU delegates at the ILO on the basis that TUCSA was not representative of the workers of South Africa, as it excluded African workers.

The admission of African trade unions to TUCSA was no doubt a step forward and a victory for the progressive forces. But the TUCSA–FOFATUSA détente rankled with opportunism, because African trade unions were being admitted purely for the sake of expediency and would be sacrificed whenever it became expedient to do so.

TUCSA's adventure into 'non-racialism' ended in tragi-comedy. Instead of appreciating the true intentions of the TUCSA leadership, which was to get South Africa back into the ILO, 23 affiliated unions with about 86 000 members immediately disaffiliated from TUCSA as they wanted no association whatsoever with African unions. The irony was doubled when the ILO refused to accept the ruse and continued its ban on South Africa. The TUCSA leadership was embarrassed and, thinking not of the principles involved but of the affiliation fees lost, decided to sacrifice the African workers. A number of FOFATUSA unions disaffiliated from TUCSA even before the axe fell on them to 'save the TUCSA embarrassment'. However, a few of the unions refused to disaffiliate and preferred to be kicked out. African unions once again became a football in the apartheid game.

THE FORMATION OF SACTU

Although the Trades and Labour Council was non-racial, it did not enjoy the whole-hearted support of the African trade unions and the smaller trade unions of the Indian and Coloured workers. This was because these unions did not have the financial means to pay affiliation fees and other dues to the Trades and Labour Council. This raises an important question of the financial strength of black and white trade unions respectively.

Most of the white unions have established Industrial Councils with employers in their respective trades and industries. These permanent bodies deal with all workers' problems and negotiate agreements for wages and other conditions of work. Both employers and the unions pay equal amounts to maintain premises, full-time functionaries, inspectors, etc. of the Industrial Council. Workers' subscriptions are deducted from their pay packets through stop orders.

In many instances where the closed-shop principle operates (and even where it does not), the prospective employer insists on the trade union membership card before a worker can obtain work in an industry.

Union–employer relationships have to be good, otherwise the employer could easily conspire to smash the Industrial Council and thereby the closed-shop and stop order agreements.

Trade unions over the years have accumulated assets worth millions of rands. They own buildings, cars, and plush offices with furniture and equipment. Many full-time functionaries of the unions earn salaries that put them into the ranks of the upper-middle class. A few Coloured and Indian trade unions, especially those under white leadership, like the Garment Workers' Union, also own buildings and other assets. But many of the unions, while enjoying Industrial Council facilities, do not have large assets.

It is not a virtue to be a poor union with no assets. The workers are entitled to every facility that can be extracted from the employers to strengthen their collective bargaining position. Unfortunately some trade unionists regard accumulation of assets as an end in itself and not as a means to advance the cause of the workers to a better life. There are many trade unions with progressive leaderships that have waged militant struggles and yet were able to keep their assets, the Industrial Councils and other privileges intact through sheer strength and strict adherence to working-class principles. Most union leaders, but by no means all of them, are full-time functionaries with an eye to keeping their lucrative positions. They do not want to antagonise the employers and the state. They are afraid of 'politics' or strikes or anything extra-parliamentary. They therefore take the line of least resistance. Some become cynical in their attitude towards the smaller black unions and sacrifice trade union principles and workers' unity.

The majority of unions of the African, Indian and Coloured workers are small. The African unions in particular are not legally recognised and do not enjoy any trade union facilities. The state and employers do everything to undermine the already precarious position of these unions. Trade union subscriptions collected by hand by shop stewards are not regular. The result is that functionaries are poorly paid or sometimes not paid at all, or that rent is not paid, which means eviction. Police raids, confiscation of documents, bans and arrest of leaders, and deportations are the order amongst black workers.

Because African trade unions were unable to afford the high affiliation fees, they remained outside the Trades and Labour Council and formed the Council of Non-European Trade Unions (CNETU) in 1940. Because the unions paid a nominal affiliation fee the membership of CNETU grew to about 100 000 by 1946. The mineworkers' strike and, more particularly, the Nat government's onslaught reduced the membership of CNETU.

When the Trades and Labour Council was dissolved and the South African Congress of Trade Unions (SACTU) formed in March 1955, CNETU disbanded and its affiliated unions joined SACTU. While provision was made in SACTU's constitution for unions that could afford to pay full affiliation fees, those unions in financial difficulties were allowed to maintain their affiliation by paying a nominal fee. Financial considerations, while important to SACTU and its affiliates, were not the main criterion. SACTU set itself the task to organise and lead the workers to higher wages, a better life and to freedom. All other factors were subsidiary. At the inaugural conference of SACTU it was decided that SACTU would identify itself closely with the struggle for freedom. After all, the workers were oppressed as blacks and exploited as slave labour – these twin evils could only be resisted if the workers threw their full weight behind the political and economic battles.

Therefore SACTU became a member of the Congress Alliance, took part in the Congress of the People (COP) in 1955, and in various general strikes and other national campaigns of the Alliance. Reciprocally, the fellow Congresses actively helped to organise the unorganised workers into SACTU under the slogan 'Trade union and Congress membership are the spear and shield of the workers'.

WHY SACTU WAS FORMED

The struggle of workers for political rights is not unusual. In 1913 Mahatma Gandhi led a passive resistance campaign, which involved a nation-wide strike of sugar, mine, railway and other workers. The loss of the municipal franchise, the threat to freehold land and citizenship rights, discrimination in jobs, the constant threat of repatriation to India and, above all, the three pounds poll tax were the issues that galvanised the workers into action. Thousands were jailed and victimised. The three pounds poll tax was withdrawn and other concessions were made.

The International Socialist League, and later the CPSA, were the political arm of the workers. In the 1922 Rand Strike the workers had to resort to arms to press their demands. The Nat–Labour coalition of 1924 is an example of political pressure by workers to gain economic advantages. The influence the workers enjoyed at the ballot box assured them a sympathetic ear in Parliament.

It would be tedious to enunciate the innumerable hardships of the black workers that make political action inevitable. Yet there are trade unionists, some of them honest, who believe that trade union and political struggles should be kept apart. They blame SACTU for bringing the government down upon itself. As already shown, SACTU's policy was correct. If it adopted any other course it would have been no different to TUCSA or any social welfare institution.

To convince the protagonists of 'economic only' policy for the trade unions otherwise, here is a sample of the black workers' burden which makes political action a necessity:

- Urban Areas Act: 'No Bantu shall remain for more than 72 hours in a prescribed area unless he produces proof …' – tens of thousands of Africans are prosecuted for infringements of this edict. In 1970, 621 000 were charged for pass law offences.
- Bantu Labour Regulations: 'No African may leave his homeland unless he is registered at the Tribal Labour Office …' – this is the instrument that restricts freedom of movement.
- Native Building Workers Act: Africans may become builders only in their own areas.
- Native Labour (Settlement of Disputes) Act: ensures no right to collective bargaining by denying trade union rights to Africans. Only 'yellow' employer-chosen factory committees are allowed.
- Industrial Conciliation Act: prescribes job reservation which has potentially affected 208 000 blacks since the determinations were made. This law encourages splinter unions, makes trade union donations to political parties illegal and makes strikes difficult.

  Through governmental pressure and through the medium of white-led trade unions, mixed unions either formed separate branches or split on the basis of race. The furniture, building, distributive, laundry, textile, engineering, motor, liquor and catering, electrical, woodworkers and many other unions agreed to split.

  The result of the splitting was that while white members and mixed unions decreased by 91 per cent, Coloured and Indian unions registered an increase of 80 per cent. The racial compartmentalisation of workers, typical of the divide-and-rule policy, is proceeding unabated.
- Apprenticeship Law and Colour Bar: bars Africans from apprenticeship in skilled trades and occupations.
- Physical Planning Act: gives the government powers to allocate or restrict African labour to certain areas and to certain employers.
- Group Areas Act: all blacks are segregated into locations or townships, mostly built long distances away from workplaces. For about half the blacks no alternative accommodation was provided after removal.
- Social and cultural: schools and universities are segregated. The best and most advanced are reserved for the whites, while the blacks are allotted to institutions that are claimed to be commensurate with their 'state of civilisation'. Bantu Education envisages that Africans

'would not rise above certain forms of labour'. This sounds ludicrous after 325 years of white 'civilising mission'.

Notwithstanding the recent token of lifting the ban on blacks in certain public places, most of the areas of culture, learning, art, music, entertainment and leisure remain closed to blacks. In any event, even if they were open, only a few blacks would benefit. The existing system of class exploitation, segregation and attendant degradation of most of the blacks to the status of low-paid labourers make it well-nigh impossible for blacks to scale the heights that the majority of the whites have attained. Only the overthrow of the system, which denies the blacks basic human rights, will redress the wrongs and bring about a change in values.

The result of all these and other repressive measures is that the legal existence of SACTU has become virtually impossible. The trade union movement is not highly organised and is divided. Of the economically active population at the end of 1968 only 30,3 per cent of the whites, 16 per cent of the Coloureds, 21,2 per cent of the Indians and a mere 0,3 per cent of the Africans were organised into trade unions. Of the 582 927 organised workers 426 000 are whites, 108 000 Coloureds, 32 655 Indians and 16 040 Africans. One need not go far to seek reasons for the cheapness of black labour.

From the time of its formation SACTU realised that it was working against great odds. Because SACTU affiliates were largely the African unions, which were not recognised by law, the employers were encouraged by the Department of Labour and the police to ignore SACTU's demands and to dismiss its leading workers and in this way destroy the trade unions.

What was envisaged under the Native Labour (Settlement of Disputes) Act was a panoply of employer-chosen stooge workers' committees that would displace the trade unions, destroy collective bargaining and place the workers at the continued mercy of their employers. SACTU carried out one of the most well-organised and effective campaigns against these sham committees. The result was that from 1953 to 1970 only 24 such committees were formed and none of them ever functioned properly. The workers had no confidence in them.

Far from killing the African trade unions, SACTU membership grew from 16 000 in 1955 to 53 323 in 1961, and consisted of 498 whites, 12 384 Coloureds, 1 650 Indians and 38 791 Africans. In 1961 SACTU had 65 officials and functionaries. Its constituent bodies at all levels were non-racial and it remains the only non-racial trade union centre.

In the face of concerted employer and government hostility SACTU and its unions have had to resort to strikes and other weapons, but only after exhausting all attempts to bring employers to the negotiating table.

The food and canning and the textile workers in all major centres, the dock workers in Cape Town, Durban and Port Elizabeth, clothing workers in the border industrial areas, match, transport and municipal workers, nurses and hospital workers and many others engaged in numerous militant battles. The campaign for a minimum wage of one pound a day launched by SACTU in 1958 was met with a stock reply that the economy of the country would grind to a standstill if SACTU's 'preposterous demands' were met. Yet a number of workers are earning this today, and the economy has not collapsed.

Practically every strike brought together the police, the Department of Labour, the Industrial Council and even some trade unions into an unholy alliance. It was typical for the cause of a strike to be completely ignored. Instead, the workers were arrested, charged, fined or imprisoned, ejected from their homes or endorsed out of an area altogether. Often the police brutally assaulted the workers. The Durban dock workers and the Amato textile workers of Benoni were victims of such police brutality.

In the face of such concerted action SACTU, with the help of the Congress Alliance, had to resort to extra-trade union forms of struggle. One method was the economic boycott. Blacks, who constitute the biggest market and therefore command substantial purchasing power, were called upon to use this power in their economic and political battles.

COMBINING TRADE UNION AND OTHER FORMS OF ACTION

Langeberg Koöperasie Beperk (LKB)

One of the earliest boycotts launched in 1957 by SACTU and the Congresses was against the Langeberg Koöperasie Beperk, a food and canning co-operative in the Cape. The Congresses held that LKB was controlled by members of the NP and as such aided and abetted apartheid. They demanded that the firm recognise the Food and Canning Workers Union, grant the union all facilities that are accorded to trade unions and that workers' leaders employed in the factories should not be victimised. The people of South Africa were called upon to boycott the products of LKB until it met the union and settled the dispute with the workers. It was also demanded that the firm repudiate apartheid and earn the support of the blacks.

Within a short while there was a country-wide boycott. LKB was panic-stricken and negotiated an agreement with the Congresses. The company agreed to recognise African and registered unions and to accord them all trade union facilities. It agreed to reinstate workers who were dismissed after a strike in Port Elizabeth. The Congresses insisted that LKB negotiate directly with the union on all points agreed upon. It was only after such negotiations with the unions that the boycott was called off. The firm produced its share register to prove that, amongst others, it had Jewish and English shareholders and was therefore not a Nat-controlled body.

Beacon Sweet Workers

Perhaps the best example of Africa-wide trade union solidarity coming to the aid of South African workers was the case of workers employed at the Durban confectionery works of Beacon, which dismissed 500 Indian strikers and replaced them with African labour. The workers were striking for higher wages after attempts to negotiate a settlement had failed. The firm tried to play off African against Indian workers – a notorious trick to create racial strife and confusion among the workers. But Africa was not fooled.

SACTU contacted trade unions in Africa, which in turn contacted employers in their respective countries dealing with Beacon to boycott the firm's products. Beacon faced the united protest of the continental union movement and also the importers of its products. The trade unions of Ghana, Tanzania, Malawi, Congo, Kenya and other countries demanded the immediate reinstatement of the dismissed workers and that the company address the workers' grievances. South African retailers also joined the campaign. Beacon beat a hasty retreat, reinstated the workers and made several concessions.

King George V TB Hospital

Black nurses employed at the King George V TB Hospital were not registered as nurses but as nurse aides. As a result they did not qualify for membership to the South African Nursing Council and the higher wages earned by its members. The Nursing Council, at that time, maintained a rigid colour bar and acquiesced in discriminatory practices such as differential salary scales for black and white nurses. SACTU organised the nurses into the Hospital Workers' Union in 1957. Within a year the union membership grew to embrace the nurses and other workers at King Edward and McCords hospitals and many nursing homes.

Apart from the low wages at King George, the quality of food was poor. Nurses complained of unauthorised deductions from their wages for minor infringements of rules. Above all, they were made to do domestic work and gardening at the homes of the white senior staff. Their bitterest experience was the corporal punishment that some of the nurses received for infringement of arbitrary rules.

In 1959 the Hospital Workers' Union took up the nurses' grievances with Dr Dormer, the Hospital Superintendent, who refused to negotiate. Attempts to use the good offices of the Catholic Church also failed to produce results.

After careful consideration, the union decided that a strike would hit the patients – all tuberculosis sufferers – more than it would the authorities. In addition, the nurses might incur the wrath of the public at large. The nurses embarked on a simple and unique form of action: they would be able to remain at work to carry out their duties as usual. But they would refuse to accept their monthly wages. They would also boycott the hospital canteen.

SACTU and the union mounted one of the biggest campaigns to obtain public support. SACTU collected food daily and the nurses were roped in to prepare it. At the end of the first month a long procession of hundreds of nurses marched past the pay offices but refused to accept the wages proffered. The disciplined column of nurses marching like soldiers going into battle, proud and determined in their bearing, captured the hearts of the public throughout the world. The photographs were published in numerous countries.

The response was electric. The trade union and nursing bodies in England, France, the USA, Canada, the socialist countries, Asia, Africa and Australia inundated the hospital with telegrams and protests. For three months the nurses refused their pay and food. Dr Dormer, an international expert on TB, was refused a visa to Uganda to address a conference due to be held in Kampala.

World pressure forced the government to appoint a Commission of Inquiry to investigate the grievances of the nurses. Higher wages, and improvements in food and other working conditions followed.

King Edward VIII and McCords Hospitals

The militant struggle of the King George V nurses inspired nurses at King Edward VIII Hospital. There was a one hundred per cent boycott of the meals supplied to them. After three months the hospital superintendent settled the dispute by improving food and other working conditions.

The non-nursing hospital workers at McCords, the most poorly paid workers in the hospitals, were inspired to action. Mass pressure forced the superintendent to agree to improve the wages and working conditions.

Potato Boycott

On 26 June 1959 SACTU, together with the Congresses, launched a national Potato Boycott. Over 60 000 people attended the floodlit rally at Currie's Fountain in Durban for the launch. Open-air meetings were held in all the major centres.

The boycott was a protest against slave labour conditions on the farms. There was abundant evidence that pass law and other petty law offenders were hired to farmers in areas like Bethal, where they were treated inhumanly. The food was miserable and the workers slept on cold concrete floors covered by sacks. They wore sacks for clothing. Disease and death were common. Those who tried to escape were flogged, sometimes to death, to intimidate others. Those who died were buried in the potato fields. On the blood and bones of these bewildered prisoners and workers grew the potatoes on which the populace fed.

There were angry protests. Eyewitness accounts of atrocities were given wide publicity by Ruth First in *New Age*, Henry Nxumalo in *Drum* and in the *Rand Daily Mail*. The state persisted in hiring out prison labour to the farmers, who in turn were its supporters. This goes on to this day, albeit on a slightly reduced scale with perhaps greater finesse.

Through the mass boycott potatoes, a staple diet of the black masses, were rotting on the farms and in warehouses. The government appointed a Commission of Inquiry into farm labour conditions. Farmers themselves began to effect changes. The boycott was called off after three months.

United Tobacco Co. Ltd.

One of the first boycott campaigns launched by SACTU and the Congress movement was against the products of the United Tobacco Company (UTC) in 1957.

In the 1950s the Durban branch of the UTC employed only African staff, while its administration was wholly white. The Durban workers were paid the lowest wages in the industry. By virtue of the organisational strength of the white and Coloured workers in the registered unions in the rest of the country, they and the African workers in these areas commanded a relatively higher wage. (Agreements arrived at by the registered unions are automatically extended to cover African workers to prevent unfair competition.) But because the Durban workers were all Africans, their union was not recognised and wages remained low.

All attempts by the African Tobacco Workers' Union to obtain higher wages and recognition failed. The Department of Labour stood behind the UTC. The workers decided to remain at the workbenches but to cut production. After all, no law said that a worker had to produce a certain quantity of cigarettes.

The managing director dismissed all the workers and called the police, who promptly arrested them for striking illegally. In reality the firm should have been charged with locking out the workers. The workers were found guilty and sentenced to a fine or imprisonment. The case was taken on appeal, but this failed too.

During the protracted trial, the UTC shifted its production to its Cape Town and Johannesburg branches. Although some of the workers in these two cities refused overtime for a while, their action was insufficient to help the Durban workers. The registered union raised funds and paid the legal fees, but did not call upon its members for a solidarity strike.

The firm dismissed a large number of workers. These workers were hounded by the police and endorsed out of Durban. Many had their passes endorsed 'striker', so that could not get jobs elsewhere.

SACTU and the Congresses launched a nation-wide boycott of UTC's products. The strike, followed by the boycott, shook the firm's shares on the stock exchange. Because it was an auxiliary of an international combine with headquarters in London, this had repercussions overseas. London started investigations into the Durban branch. The Managing Director was fired. Improved wages and conditions of work followed. The UTC reinstated a number of workers whose skills it needed very much.

Although many of the workers were dismissed, the workers were at least happy that their class brothers benefited from their struggle.

Bakers Ltd.

Since its formation in 1957, the African Baking Workers Union was confronted with the problem of securing employer recognition for the union. The company dismissed leading trade unionists to intimidate the other workers and prevent them from joining the union.

Dismissed workers, especially those taking part in trade union activity or strikes and go-slows, are endorsed out of the urban areas and sent back to the Reserves. This may result in the loss of a home in the urban township and in becoming a 'marked man' in the eyes of the Labour Bureau. Collective action, executed consciously and with determination, is the only answer and guarantee for success.

After painstaking organising over two years the union succeeded in uniting the majority of the workers in Durban and Pietermaritzburg. It then served demands on the employer for recognition of the union, higher wages and other improvements. It also sought direct representation on the Industrial Council. The company resisted negotiating with the union and SACTU intervened.

Bakers Ltd. then agreed to meet SACTU and the unions. The background to this particular meeting is essential. The period from 1958, which culminated in the country-wide crises in 1960, was one of the most revolutionary in the country's history. These years also saw SACTU's growth into a dynamic and militant movement. SACTU membership in Durban alone increased by over 16 000 and Congress membership also grew by the same number, which showed that the workers joined both the trade unions and Congress. SACTU and its affiliated unions won increased wages throughout 1959. Pressure for national action for higher wages, trade union rights and a better life was mounting. The anti-pass campaign was hotting up. The Potato Boycott launched on 26 June 1959 spread over the country like wildfire. This was the atmosphere in which the meeting between SACTU, the union and Bakers Ltd. took place.

Bakers Ltd. agreed to the principal demands of the union and proposed that the union present its demand for higher wages directly to the Industrial Council.

It came as a surprise to the union when, instead of implementing the terms of the agreement, the firm blandly informed the union that it could not accord it recognition and that it would entertain no further correspondence with it.

Although the baking industry was a so-called 'essential industry' in which all strikes were prohibited, the workers were now clamouring for action. Finally it was decided that a boycott of the firm's products be launched.

The boycott was launched at a mass rally. Within the few days it spread rapidly. People refused to buy Bakers' bread, biscuits and cakes. Overnight the people switched their preferences. The white residents of Durban were compelled to join the boycott because their domestic servants refused to buy Bakers' products. The Domestic Workers' Union played an important part in spreading the boycott campaign in the white areas by switching products without their employers' knowledge or permission. The boycott was complete throughout Natal. Support came from the rest of the country.

Government stepped in. Initially it restricted the supply of yeast and wheat quotas allocated to companies the previous year. All the companies except Bakers exhausted their yeast and wheat supplies within weeks. With the new restrictions they had to cut back production or close down altogether for lack of supplies. Specific areas of delivery were prescribed for each bakery. No exceptions to the rule were permitted. It appears that the government control boards heavily subsidised Bakers for the losses it sustained through the boycott, so much so that it recorded normal profits in that particular financial year. However, Bakers' shares took a plunge. Without state help it would been in grave financial difficulties.

An ironic situation arose when those detained under the Emergency Regulations in 1960 had to eat Bakers' products throughout their five months of detention. No other products were available. The prisons, hospitals, police stations and other government institutions as well as welfare organisations bought Bakers' products to save the firm.

The boycott shook all the employers and the government and forced companies to recognise the importance of black purchasing power.

Although Bakers Ltd. did not recognise the union, the workers received higher wages and conditions of work improved. Fortunately for Bakers, the State of Emergency intervened and a large number of SACTU leaders were arrested. State repression of SACTU and its unions and the banning of the ANC weakened the trade union movement and the Congress movement. A period of reaction set in.

Hammarsdale and Charlestown

The Hammarsdale Clothing Manufacturers were situated in a 'border area'[4] and employed over 500 workers in 1958 when SACTU organised them into the African Clothing Workers' Union.

The workers earned wages that ranged from 50 cents per week to the princely sum of R3 per week. The company boasted that it gave the workers half a pint of milk with bread and jam for breakfast. It held that the workers were learners and their productivity was low compared with urban workers.

The company closed two of its factories in Durban to open a single factory in Hammarsdale. The factory enjoyed large government subsidies, and tax and railway concessions. It received loans at low interest rates from the Industrial Development Corporation (IDC). It had plans for expansion, which were entirely dependent on the rate of profitability of the existing enterprise.

The union submitted a memorandum to the employers showing that the low wages forced the workers into a perpetual state of starvation. When the company failed to respond to their demands and threatened reprisals against the 'agitators', the workers went on strike. The company, with the backing of the entire state machinery, decided against any negotiations with the union or SACTU.

The workers were arrested and charged with striking illegally. Two officers of SACTU, Moses Mabida and myself, were arrested and charged with inciting the workers to strike. The company threatened to move its factory back to Durban if the workers did not return to work unconditionally. To sow confusion, officials of the African Clothing Workers' Union in Johannesburg, who had nothing to do with the workers' strike, appeared on the scene and alleged that I was personally intent on ensuring that the factory in Hammarsdale closed and moved to Durban so that 'my brothers and sisters could get a job there'. These two disrupters from Johannesburg, Lucy Mvubelo and another woman, both members of FOFATUSA, did everything to incite people to racial strife and begged the workers to return to work. The workers were infuriated at the lies spread by these two women and threatened to assault them. The two hastily returned to Johannesburg.

Government was not going to allow its border industries scheme, which was still in the experimental stage and closely tied to its policy of separate development and decentralisation of industry, to collapse.

The company played tough for 12 days. During this time it railed some of its machinery and equipment to Durban. Workers were told that their cause was lost. The intimidation tactic did not work. The 12 scabs in the factory dwindled to 6. The workers remained steadfast. For rural workers with little trade union experience this was a remarkable achievement.

At the end of these 12 days the firm capitulated. During the negotiations, attended by the unions, SACTU and the Congresses, the company granted higher wages and improved conditions of work, as well as union recognition. It re-employed all the striking workers.

Veka Clothing Manufacturers

Veka Clothing Manufacturers, owned by Dr Albert Wessels, was originally established in Standerton, where it employed about 600 Afrikaner women. The firm closed the Standerton factory and dismissed the 600 women to establish itself in Charlestown – a border industrial area. In Charlestown it employed a small white administration staff and over 600 African workers. Its shift to the Charlestown border industrial area meant freedom from union rates of pay. It also meant longer working hours, less holidays and tougher working conditions. Above all, the firm did not have to bother with trade unions, as Africans could not be legally organised. The employers tried to justify harsher conditions with the 'lower productivity' of rural workers. Trainee workers undoubtedly produced less but they could not be expected to be trainees in perpetuity.

The dismissed Afrikaner women begged in the streets of Johannesburg in protest against their unemployment. The Garment Workers' Union campaigned to close border industry factories. But SACTU felt that the union movement should recognise border areas as an inevitable result of decentralisation. As such, workers had to be organised into trade unions and their skills improved to the level of urban workers. SACTU organised the clothing workers at Charlestown and improved their wages and working conditions. During the general strikes of 1958 and 1961 the Charlestown workers registered a one hundred per cent work stoppage.

Match Workers Union

Since its formation in 1957 the Match Workers Union struggled for recognition. Lion Match Co. refused. When the union submitted demands for higher wages in 1959, the employers rejected these.

Instead of striking, the union decided the workers should *en masse* seek an interview to press their demands with their management during lunch hour. While the workers and management were locked into a discussion, a factory siren summoned the workers back to work. The manager abruptly ended the interview and ordered his workers to go back to work. When workers sought to continue the discussions, the manager summoned the police. They came in huge trucks, scores of cars and vans, fully armed with guns and truncheons. The Special Branch and the Department of Labour added to the mighty show of force. The police and government officials ordered the workers back to work. They ignored the workers' demand that the discussions should be allowed to continue until a settlement was reached. The police gave the workers the usual three-minute warning. Even before the three minutes were over, the workers were arrested *en masse*. Some of the workers trickled back to work. Some did so when they saw their colleagues being arrested. This was a fatal error on the part of the workers.

The company offered sleeping accommodation on the factory premises for those who went back to work. This was a device to beat the pickets. Management worked day and night to get the new workers trained. The company's branches in Johannesburg and Cape Town made up lost production. Meanwhile, hundreds of workers were charged with striking, found guilty and fined.

Although a large number of workers were dismissed, the firm granted higher wages and improved conditions of work. This was a victory. Lion Match Co. was a subsidiary of a large listed company. As a result of the strike, its share price plunged. This induced a British firm to make a successful bid to buy a large chunk of the firm's shares. Management changes followed.

Municipal Workers' Union
A placard demonstration was conducted by the Municipal Workers' Union to back workers' demands for recognition and improvements. The Durban Municipality, reputed to be liberal towards its employees, flatly refused to recognise the African Municipal Workers' Union. In 1959 it was one of the lowest paying employers of black labour.

The union posted a copy of its memorandum to the City Council to welfare organisations, ratepayers' organisations and prominent individuals (in fact everyone who enjoyed the municipal vote) and urged them to pressure the Council. The campaign received wide publicity. The workers did not strike, as they were concerned about losing public support, but they did gear themselves for action should it become necessary.

Pressure mounted. The municipal authorities ultimately granted increases and improvements. At the instigation of the Special Branch of the police and the Department of Labour the municipality chose a works committee which would represent the workers. Along with 23 other employer-chosen works committees throughout South Africa this committee provided another dummy institution. The union continued to grow in strength until the mass arrests under the State of Emergency led to its officials being arrested and later banned.

Unemployed Workers
When unemployment became acute in 1960, SACTU organised the unemployed into a 'union of unemployed', which recruited members, and held mass rallies and demonstrations to expose the harsh conditions of the unemployed.

African workers earning below R10 did not receive any benefits, and farm labourers and domestic servants were excluded altogether. Unemployment pay for those who received it was unsatisfactory. The workers wanted jobs, social security or, alternatively, decent benefits, which would keep them and their families alive.

In accordance with these demands, the union sought an interview with the Minister of Labour, who promptly arranged by telegram for such a meeting to be held in Pretoria. The delegation left for Pretoria amid a blaze of publicity because it was unusual for a government minister to meet a delegation of blacks – unemployed blacks at that.

Never did the government get into such a diplomatic muddle. The delegation, led by SACTU

Chairman Steven Dlamini, was made up of four black men and one black woman. When the delegation was already on its way to Pretoria the Minister informed the union that he had another appointment and would therefore not be available. The delegates, who had met SACTU officials in Johannesburg first, got a police reception. The SACTU offices were raided and documents and the memorandum that the union had prepared for the Minister were confiscated. When the delegates arrived at the Laboria Buildings in Pretoria, the entire building and the surrounding area were teeming with policemen. As the press from abroad and foreign ambassadors were present, the police were prevented from arresting the delegates and creating an international scandal. No action was taken against the delegates when they used the 'Whites Only' entrance to the building, although they had been directed to use the side 'Black' entrance.

The delegates were told what the Minister had publicly announced: that he had another appointment. Nevertheless, the delegates presented a copy of the memorandum to the Secretary for Labour.

Shortly thereafter unemployed white workers in Johannesburg were organised into a similar union by SACTU. At the inaugural meeting held at the Trades Hall many Afrikaner workers tore up their NP membership cards. When they sought an interview, the Minister granted it. But the white delegates pressed home the same demands the black workers had made earlier. In their discussion with the Minister they raised the problem of the black unemployed as well, especially the plight of Africans, who enjoyed no unemployment benefits.

By their action these white unemployed workers did far more than the organised white workers had ever done in a lifetime of trade unionism. The unemployed demonstrated that unity between white and black workers was possible and necessary for saving the working class from exploitation. The unemployed received increased benefits and were paid for a longer period.

Dock Strike

When 2 000 dock workers went on strike for higher wages in 1959 the police retaliated by beating the workers with batons and truncheons. Workers were thrown out of their compounds and the government deported them out of the area. SACTU obtained photos of these police brutalities and had them published in many parts of the world.

In 1942, Johannes Phungula, a militant leader of the dock workers, was deported to a lonely area in northern Transvaal and never allowed to return to an urban area. The workers revere him to this day. Since then, the workers have gone on strike several times, but never did they reveal their leaders.

A constant problem was that scab labour from the rural areas filled workers' places during a strike. Unemployment and starvation in the reserves have made the poor unemployed an easy prey for the labour-recruiting agents and the government's Labour Bureau. The greater the reserve of labour, the lower the wage rates and the easier it became to replace unskilled labour.

International Appeal

In 1959 SACTU appealed to the World Federation of Trade Unions (WFTU), the International Confederation of Free Trade Unions (ICFTU), the British Trade Union Congress (TUC), the All India Federation and other federations for moral and financial help for the dock workers.

Messrs Millard and De Jonge, two representatives of the ICFTU, met SACTU in the presence of senior members of the Liberal Party, among them Alan Paton and Professor Leo Kuper. The ICFTU made any help it would render to SACTU or its affiliates conditional upon their not taking part in 'party politics'. It alleged that, by becoming a member of the Congress Alliance, SACTU was committing its membership to a particular political philosophy. It also alleged that Leslie Messina, the General Secretary of SACTU at the time, as a member of the WFTU Executive Committee, committed SACTU to supporting a communist-controlled body. It wanted SACTU to break from these bodies before it would render any help. An offer of 30 000 pounds sterling and other aid was made on these conditions.

SACTU made it clear that its membership of the Congress Alliance was based on the wishes of its affiliated unions and that only its affiliates were free to change the policies and the constitution of SACTU. Nobody from outside should dictate policy to SACTU affiliates and, in any event, the workers should be entitled to take part in political activities in the same way as the British TUC or the American AFL-CIO supported political parties and lobbied Members of Parliament. Why deny the unions of black workers the same rights? SACTU gave an outline of the political situation in South Africa that made it incumbent on black workers to fight just as hard for their freedom and liberation as for higher wages and trade union rights. SACTU also made it clear that it was honoured to serve on the WFTU Executive Committee. It would gladly accept a similar offer from the ICFTU. SACTU was prepared to co-operate with any trade union body and was prepared to accept any help, provided no strings were attached.

SACTU, a member of the African Trade Union Federation, drew attention to the continental trade unions and the activities of the ICFTU officials. A number of African federations protested and some disaffiliated from the ICFTU.

Recently strenuous efforts were made by TUCSA, represented by Mrs Lucy Mvubelo and Mr Edgar Deane, to get the ICFTU not to support sanctions against South Africa. Both Mvubelo (FOFATUSA) and Deane (TUCSA) are black and were deliberately chosen with government blessing to project a non-racial image abroad and to make the sanctions-busting appeal as effective as possible. These toadies lamented that the black worker would be hardest hit by sanctions. Black workers are in any event hard hit in every possible way without any sanctions. The ICFTU rejected their pleas and called upon members not to emigrate to South Africa or take up skilled work that they said should be given to the blacks.

It is to the credit of the ICFTU that it refused to entertain TUCSA, saying that it was 'neither proper nor productive' for its representative to visit the headquarters of the ICFTU. Obviously bodies like TUCSA have tainted themselves too much with the apartheid brush to be acceptable as the workers' spokesmen.

RESPONSES BY EMPLOYERS AND THE STATE

The various forms of struggle of the workers – strikes, go-slows, placard demonstrations, mass interviews with employers – were by no means the only ones workers used. However, the strike was the common method of struggle.

In the years from 1958 to 1961 the country was in the grip of a series of crises. The economy was in depression, unemployment was rife, inflation was surging, consumers were hit by rising prices and there was pressure for higher wages. During this period there were the general strikes in 1958 and 1961 and a huge number of factory strikes. Natal, Pondoland and Sekhukhuneland were in revolt in 1959. Dipping tanks were smashed, the rural areas were in revolt against the culling of cattle and the betterment schemes, beerhalls and buses were boycotted and Bantu Authorities came under fire. Women demonstrated against pass laws. Workers fearlessly downed tools. The ANC was preparing for a pass-burning campaign. A defiant fervour gripped the country.

It was in this revolutionary atmosphere that employers granted increased wages to avoid the outbreak of a general strike. Even a small firm employing as few as five to ten workers granted its workers between seven shillings and six pence to ten shillings to 'keep them quiet'.

Government intervention by means of the State of Emergency, the banning of the Congresses, the wholesale banning of trade unionists through house arrest and restrictions on their movement followed by wholesale prosecution for sabotage weakened the extra-parliamentary opposition and blunted extra-parliamentary forms of struggle. The state made boycotts or 'economic sabotage' a punishable offence.

A concomitant of the state's action is that it has placed workers at the continued mercy of employers without giving them any countervailing powers to fight exploitation. Employers who used to take notice of their workers' problems during strikes and boycotts have been given the freedom to exploit them. The workers, who have no redress, may be referred to the machinery of the Settlement of Disputes Act. But the workers want nothing to do with dummy institutions that are intended to 'bleed them to death'.

SOME LESSONS

This essay deals at length with boycotts and demonstrations as instruments of struggle to indicate to the workers and the masses at large the methods of struggle that SACTU, deprived of trade union rights and of recognition for its affiliates, had to resort to, to win improvements. The workers may draw some useful lessons from these struggles to advance their cause.

The workers must be cautioned that boycotts, which imply reliance on the public for support, should be used sparingly and called off when the campaign is at its height. Boycotts should be regarded as instruments and not ends in themselves.

The organising of workers is the urgent task that faces the movement. The recent strikes in Natal, Port Elizabeth and Namibia show clearly that given proper leadership the workers will respond. The building of trade unions is a painstaking job and should be undertaken by all those interested in alleviating the sufferings of the workers.

The workers must pressure the homeland governments to grant them trade union rights, which must be extended to cover workers not only in the homelands, but in the Republic as well. Labour is the chief export of the homelands and remittances earned by these workers keep the fires in the homelands burning. At present, labour is exported cheaply to swell the profits of those who employ it. The challenge for the homeland authorities is whether they will continue to connive at the exploitation of their citizens as slave labour.

THE TASK OF THE WORKERS

The key challenge facing us is the building of working class unity. The registered trade unions of white, Coloured and Indian workers is concentrated in TUCSA and the South African Federation of Trade Unions. Both these bodies have sacrificed the African workers to appease apartheid's masters. Yet thousands of Indian and Coloured workers are still affiliated to TUCSA, presumably to maintain trade union unity.

Apartheid in the trade union movement must be scrapped if the workers are to play any significant role in the shaping of a new South Africa. The white workers are intent on maintaining apartheid and white supremacy, while the black workers want it overthrown.

A weak African trade union movement may excuse the Indian and Coloured affiliates of bodies like TUCSA. But their task must not be to passively accept white *baasskap* and other monstrosities. They must challenge and lay bare every shade of discrimination and apartheid in these bodies. In this connection it is necessary for the black trade unions to organise the unorganised workers and to resuscitate SACTU and its affiliated union and inject new life into them so that SACTU may play once again the proper role as South Africa's premier non-racial trade union centre. This is the urgent task of all class-conscious workers. The political situation is rapidly changing and the workers must not be found napping, since their influence is absolutely necessary to reshape South Africa's destiny.

It is important for the black workers to remember that although white workers are aristocrats of labour and are privileged, they are basically workers. They do not own the means of production, nonetheless they identify themselves so closely with the ruling class that they have become almost indistinguishable from the ruling class itself. They will therefore have to be fought until they are brought to their senses. Only then is unity on a national scale possible with them. But the black workers must be prepared to work with any genuine white trade unionist on the basis of complete equality, not *baasskap*.

THE BLACK WORKERS' CONVENTION

The emergence of the Black Workers' Convention is a manifestation of the black–white confrontation that apartheid forges. Blacks must inevitably band themselves together in a united front. Ultimately the sheer might of unity of the black trade union movement could help to bring about black–white worker unity. A good example is that of the African Mine Workers Union in pre-independence Zambia – only after it grew into a powerful union was unity possible between black and white workers. Respect for the dignity of the black man can only be attained from strength, and not from weakness. Black workers must realise that workers the world over have always been confronted with ruling-class hostility. Anti-combination laws of England were used to transport workers to far-off lands for trivial offences. Although South African workers are not hanged for organising trade unions, they and their families are slowly tortured to death by low wages that result from the lack of a right to collective bargaining. The fate of the workers is tenuous as long as the system of exploitation of man by man is allowed to continue. To halt the exploitation the workers will have to organise themselves into powerful trade unions.

Arrests, court action, fines, imprisonment and victimisation are inevitable in any struggle. The workers must realise that they are many and the employers few, that without them the machines cannot run. Solidarity is their only route to a better life. Recently the workers in Natal, Namibia and Port Elizabeth showed their unwillingness to accept poverty wages.

Economic pressure has thrown open doors to skilled and semi-skilled jobs for Indian and Coloured workers. Many are employed in clerical and supervisory work. They are fortunate in that they can organise themselves into trade unions and thus bargain for higher wages. Separate development aims to inculcate in them a herd mentality, a race ego similar to that of the whites, but separate and therefore at a lower plane. But they must quickly disabuse themselves of false privileges and avoid becoming dupes in the race game.

The Indian workers have a militant and progressive past. From the time of Gandhi's leadership of the Natal Indian Congress they have consistently fought discrimination, exploitation and oppression. In 1945, 34 000 workers stood behind the Natal Indian Congress and overthrew the collaborationist Indian leaders. They participated overwhelmingly in the Passive Resistance Campaign of 1946 to 1948. After the worst race riots in the history of South Africa, fanned by anti-Indian propaganda and the Nat government, which was intent on repatriating the Indians to India, Indian and African workers in 1950 jointly participated in the national stoppage of work in protest against the Suppression of Communism Act and the shooting of workers on May Day 1950. In the Defiance Campaign of 1952, the Congress of the People in 1955, and in the general strikes of 1958 and 1961, the Indian, Coloured and African, as well as some white workers, combined into an even broader front against apartheid.

The Coloured workers, especially of the Western Cape, have had a militant past from the time of Dr Abdurahman and Jimmy La Guma. Their struggles to preserve their voting rights, the fight against dummy institutions and the militant struggles of the workers and their unions are indelibly written into history.

Workers must, of course, accept the skilled jobs and privileges that are available to them. After all, it is their due – the result of years of struggle. But these concessions must not lull the workers into a false sense of security. Job reservation particularly threatens over 108 000 workers who would be fired and replaced by white workers in any crisis situation. Wages between white workers and black workers employed in the same category differ widely. Residential segregation and other forms of discrimination exist. Blacks are condemned to develop separately, which means that they are never to enjoy the fruits of their own creation in a South Africa that they helped to build.

It is therefore incumbent on the Indian and Coloured workers to join hands with their African brothers to fight for a united trade union movement irrespective of race or colour, and for a truly free and democratic South Africa.

Consistent with the ruling class's divide-and-rule policy, each African tribal group is being compartmentalised into its own separate homeland with the promise of independence for each. In this context the various tribes working together in the mines, factories and farms are to divide themselves and think ethnically. One is to be a proud Zulu, Xhosa, etc., a proud Indian, a proud Coloured and a proud white. This race and group thinking is not only chauvinistic but also backward. It also conflicts with the demands of a modern economy such as ours.

Tribalism will tear asunder the various tribes, which capitalism has drawn together over the past one hundred years. The African people must not fall into the trap of tribal or group think-ing. While a tribal organisation may help to weld the people together it must be utilised as a means to forge greater unity among all workers. Zulus may band themselves together, but this is insufficient until they forge links with the African workers and until they join hands with Coloured, Indian and white workers. The workers have an excellent opportunity to transcend the tribal set-up by setting in motion trade union organisations in the homelands and urban areas and gradually building them on a national scale.

The white workers, the most highly organised of the working class, are lacking in class con-sciousness. Their vote is used to return reactionaries to power only because they preserve the white workers' privileges. The white workers are called upon to defend with their blood the sys-tem that relies for its sustenance on the exploitation of the black workers. Their selfishness *ipso facto* calls forth cruelty and inhumanity perpetrated against blacks.

If the white workers went into the townships and saw black children rummaging through dustbins for crumbs, if they saw children with bloated stomachs suffering from kwashiorkor, or if they knew of the illiteracy, hunger and constant harassment through efflux and influx con-trols, arrests, harsh and nightmarish laws, the lack of the most simple amenities, they would understand why the blacks are forging links to fight these hardships. If the whites could only join on a limited scale the throng demanding freedom and human rights for all irrespective of colour, there would be a change overnight in the entire set-up in South Africa. Are white work-ers prepared to accept the challenge? Posterity will judge them on their present actions.

From a narrow chauvinistic representative of the agricultural community the Nat govern-ment has evolved into the foremost spokesman of mining, industrial and financial capitalists. It has used its political power to coax the reluctant mining, banking, agricultural and industri-al sectors to toe the apartheid line. They have acquiesced in the balkanisation of South Africa, albeit reluctantly, since apartheid is against their best interests.

SEPARATE DEVELOPMENT

Separate development has many facets. Politically it is aimed at keeping the blacks satisfied with exercising political rights in their own areas. Economically it serves to decentralise industry, which hitherto has been concentrated in four major areas. It is envisaged that the homelands will be a reservoir of cheap but trained labour serving the border industries and the greater South Africa.

Over-arching separate development is the perpetuation of the colonial relationship that characterises black–white relationships in South Africa. The white metropolis, controlling as it does the wealthiest areas, rich in resources, worked by both black and white labour and commanding all the communications and strategic networks, places the homelands at the continued mercy of the mother country. In Mangope's Bophuthatswana, platinum, copper, fertilisers and other minerals are exploited by South African companies in return for a small tax allowance. Woe betide any homeland if oil or coal were to be found beneath its soil. It is not difficult to guess that two great enticements, mineral wealth and fisheries, are standing in the way of Namibian independence.

In terms of the Urban Areas and the Physical Planning Acts and in pursuit of separate development the government removed large numbers of Africans from the urban areas to the homelands. Consequently the pressure for labour was so great that in the Western Cape, especially after the Coloured labour was attracted to the urban areas by higher wages, farm jails were built to supply convict labour. By 1960 there were 23 such jails, 10 of which were in the Western Cape. Similarly in Bethal, African labour comes from the south-east Transvaal, buttressed by nine long-term jails. Besides this, a number of recruiting corporations such as the Philadelphia Boere Group (which recruits in the Transkei with government blessing and handles 1 000 to 1 500 contract labourers) were established to recruit labour. Although the Western Cape deported large numbers of Africans between 1967 and 1971, hostels were built to accommodate 56 000 immigrants. This figure is expected to double by 1980. The removals of the black residents from the Western Cape made migrant labour necessary.

Tens of thousands of Africans in the main urban areas are housed in hostels and compounds, e.g. 100 000 in Johannesburg and 15 000 in Durban. The number of people in registered employment in South Africa was 2 490 000 and of these, over 1,3 million were migrants.

People subjected to forced removals are settled in close-by rural areas. Poverty mounts as the population density increases. Fourteen municipalities in the Transversal, for instance, used all kinds of pressures to remove the Africans from their own townships to Isoteng (which is regarded as a 'rubbish dump') in Bophuthatswana. Similarly, Vendaland is poor and a farm labourer is regarded as fortunate if he earns 25 cents a day, without food or housing. Witsieshoek is crowded, the soil exhausted and so denuded that it cannot support its populace.

Natal, which is exempt from the restrictive provisions of the Physical Planning Act, may employ any number of African workers. To increase labour supply, the system of African labour tenants (on white farms) who worked without wages but held some land was abolished. About 300 000 to 400 000 had to give up their independence and work on contract on the farm or border industries. Labour is the watchword in separate development.

The Transkei, which is to become independent on 1 October 1976, depends heavily on migrant earnings. The total number of migrants working in South Africa was in the region of 200 000; the mines absorbed about 73 000 and agriculture 43 000.

The government is decentralising the location of industry along the periphery of the homelands in Hammarsdale, Charlestown, Rosslyn, Pietermaritzburg, Brits, Rustenburg, Pietersburg, King William's Town, East London, Newcastle and Richards Bay through massive subsidies and infrastructure such as water, railways, electricity, etc. Investment in border areas is lucrative simply because labour there is cheap. No wage determinations apply in the homelands. Firms may pay virtually what they like.

White trade unions have insisted that job reservation be applied in border areas, as they are part of the white areas. Moreover they have refused to train black labour to handle skilled jobs in the homelands, which means that white labour and know-how have to accompany white capital into the homelands.

That separate development is closely tied with black labour exploitation is not unprecedented in South African history. The Constitution of the Transvaal Republic describes, among other things, a 'kaffir chief's duty' as 'keeping his people in order and requiring them to furnish labour as and when required'.

The place of the African in the white man's world cannot be more clearly put than in the words of the Transvaal Local Government Commission of 1921: 'The native should only be allowed to enter the urban areas, which are essentially the white man's creation, to minister to the needs of the white man, and should depart therefrom when he ceases to so minister.'

It is claimed that the system of separate development with its inbuilt migratory labour system prevents urban slums. But it creates slums in the rural areas. Without doubt, the cheapness of labour helps capital accumulation and investment and reduces the cost of housing, sewerage, etc. But cheap labour breeds malnutrition and disease and it dehumanises man. It is also claimed that the migratory system makes labour control easier. Indeed it does! It is used to bludgeon labour into being cheap and menial, and to pressure and terrorise the workers with deportation if they went on strike.

Separate development is the antithesis of the panacea required to cure South Africa's ills. Capitalism has over the past century drummed in tribal, linguistic, political, social, racial and communal barriers. Since the discovery of gold and diamonds and the advent of mining and industrial capitalism, Englishmen and Afrikaners first came together, overcoming the enmity that existed between them since the pre-*trek* times. The various white minority groups joined them. Tribalism among the African people was shaken when the various tribes were brought together in the mines, the factory floor, in the shops, offices, etc. The Coloured and Malay people became a part of the skilled and semi-skilled labour force over decades. Gradually the Indians were forced to leave their farm and market gardens and move to the factories. The trickle became a torrent, especially after the economic take-off since the end of the Second World War.

About 1 400 000 whites and 5 700 000 blacks were economically active in 1969. But there was a shortage of over 70 000 artisans. Commerce had 35 000 vacancies. At the same time over 100 000 blacks were unemployed. Practically every sector of the economy wants the colour bar removed, but the white workers remain opposed to this.

CRACKS IN THE COLOUR BAR

The further development of capitalism is fettered by the lack of skilled manpower as a result of the colour bar. Competition among the various sectors of the economy for the limited supply of white skilled labour has pressured employers and government to throw overboard the colour bar and admit blacks into the sepulchre of skills acquisition. It is, of course, done at a price. A sufficiently large bounty is paid to the white workers for making concessions to their black brethren.

In 1964, the management and white employees of 12 mines agreed that black 'boss boys' may inspect the work area after blasting and that they need not wait for the white supervisor to certify clearance. Although this simple operation would have saved hundreds of man-hours and meant big pay increases for the whites for less work, rebel miners took strike action and swore to resist the 'kaffir onslaught'. Political pressure on the government, which had originally blessed the scheme, forced it to retreat.

But economic necessity forced subtle negotiations and ultimate agreement in 1967, that blacks could now handle explosives, drive locomotives and examine blasted areas. The lion's share of the increased wages was to go to the white worker, although it was really the black workers' productivity that increased. The white workers were not only to get higher wages, but also improved pensions, phthisis allowances and provident fund increments, which would raise wages by 11 per cent. Whites secured 80 per cent of the increased pay. The white workers were guaranteed permanent employment. A similar agreement for 'black advancement' was concluded for the coal mines.

A striking example of the desperate labour situation is Roberts Construction's attempt to employ African builders to do block laying at lower rates than artisans. The Department of Labour stopped the company from doing so. Soon thereafter, and with the knowledge of the Department, the firm re-employed the Africans. This time it overcame the job reservation restrictions by not issuing specialised tools. It issued garden trowels instead of bricklayer's trowels, axe handles instead of hammers, etc. to lay blocks.

Despite protests from white shoppers, OK Bazaars employed 35 black women as cashiers. The conditions of employment were that no white employees were to be dismissed, separate facilities were to be provided and no white workers were to work under black supervision.

Barclays Bank employed 31 Coloured women as receptionists. Other banks and building societies did the same.

Altogether 88 Coloureds, 101 Indians and 122 Africans were employed to do work previously done by white railway flagmen, stokers and trade hands. In addition, 1 371 Coloureds, 140 Indians and 12 698 Africans are performing work formerly done by upgraded white workers.

Apart from employing increasing numbers of black skilled workers, the employers are forced to dilute skilled work in another way – by employing labour-saving machines and have these operated by blacks. Labour is also fragmented through sub-division of work, e.g. there are now welders' assistants, shunters' assistants and mechanics' assistants. As this expedient becomes universal with the growth of the economy, white skilled workers will start feeling the pressure and develop a need to join hands with blacks to defend class instead of race interests.

When the Mine Workers Union in 1970 refused to train African mineworkers in the homelands, TUCSA, comprising Coloured, Indian and white workers, stood by the white Mine Workers Union. Although the white workers were assured of permanent employment, huge pay increases and other guarantees, they refused to yield. What common interests did Coloured and Indian workers in TUCSA have with the supporters of racism?

The ICFTU's ban of its 50 million members on emigration to South Africa, the pressure on the government by overseas investors to lift the ban on blacks, the demands of the economy and, above all, the pressure of blacks for freedom, equality and democratic rights have forced the government to close its eyes to unions negotiating with employers for black advancement.

The unions in the mines, in the building, iron and steel and the motor industries, as well as in the commercial, banking and civil service sectors have agreed to black advancement, but mainly with the aim of advancing themselves at the expense of blacks. Whites are upgraded to fill the positions of technicians, foremen, managers, charge hands and supervisors – captains of the black proletarian army.

All talk of 'rate for the job' without equality of opportunity for the blacks is a sham. It involves hypocrisy of the worst type when blacks are made to do skilled jobs at lesser rates of pay on condition that the difference is paid to the whites. This is open treachery and no amount of humbugging about black advancement will conceal it.

How could any policy that shuts out blacks from every position of privilege be in the interests of the blacks? How could the blacks who, together with whites, laboured and built the South African economy be told now that they have to develop along their own lines? Are they merely to continue to serve the mines, the farms, commerce and industry at sweated wages only to be told that they have no place in the body politic of South Africa?

Africans are expected to exercise citizenship rights in their homelands and to regard themselves as temporary sojourners in the white areas. Urban Africans, like the Indians and Coloureds, want to express their aims and aspirations and to exercise themselves on the issue of wages, housing, work, culture, education and other issues that confront them daily in the areas in which they live and work – not in some remote homeland. If the blacks are to develop along their own lines, white South Africa must be serious about it – it must not rely on black labour. The inevitable would follow: the economy would grind to a halt. It is clear that white South Africa wants it both ways. It wants black labour desperately but is not prepared to accord blacks the basic human rights that go with it.

Certain sections of the black population have opted for separate development, probably on the basis of 'half a loaf is better than none'. No doubt some may be genuinely motivated to alleviate the suffering of the people via separate development. But separation means discrimination and the acceptance of black inferiority. The question all lovers of a free and democratic life and fair play and justice need to answer is why the black man, who contributes so much to the economic well-being of the country, should not also enjoy political rights? The answer is perhaps that it will cause animosity and friction between the races. But the races work together. Recently they played soccer and rugby together; they took part in multi-racial gymnastics, tennis, athletics and cycling. Soccer and cricket are to become non-racial. A number of non-racial international seminars and conferences were held. Church mass is non-racial. The industrial colour bar is slowly cracking under the economic whip. Public places of entertainment are being thrown open, although the campaign is slow to develop into a flood.

International pressure and the recent liberation of Mozambique and Angola, the imminent collapse of Rhodesia and Namibia, and the constant threat of the outbreak of violence against South Africa have forced the government to grant independence to the Transkei. Similar promises have been made to the other homelands. Mixed sports and skilled labour for blacks are obviously intended to appease the world-wide anti-apartheid movement with which it is anxiously seeking détente.

But the foundations of apartheid remain intact. Territorial segregation, the colour bar, mass arrests and imprisonment, the suppression of freedom of speech, movement and assembly, the ban on black political organisations, the non-recognition of black trade unions, low wages for blacks, the high infant mortality rate, and the starvation of millions of men, women and children continue unabated.

Black and white can and should co-exist. No responsible black wants to drive the whites into the sea. As a matter of fact, the reverse is the truth. The Freedom Charter, unlike the present South African Constitution, envisages a South Africa in which black and white would live in brotherhood and harmony. It also envisages a South Africa in which the land, with its abundant wealth, would be shared by all. It prescribes work, comfort, security, education, political rights, the freedom of speech and assembly, music, art – all that mankind has been endowed with – for all its people, irrespective of colour, race or creed, and on the basis of complete equality.

But to attain the principles enshrined in the Freedom Charter there will have to be, unfortunately, a confrontation between the blacks who suffer so much under apartheid, and the whites, who gain so much by its perpetuation. The white edifice has to be blown sky-high before South Africa and its people are driven to sanity. Any patchwork is not going to suffice.

The backward feudal relations of serf and master the government is imposing is incongruous, especially in relation to the demands of the modern capitalist economy, in which increasing black and white cohesion is evident. Everything suggests therefore that the present system of apartheid and black exploitation should be scrapped and that black and white should undertake to build a South Africa free from the present evils. This must be done before it is too late.

JOHN POKELA

John Nyati Pokela was born on 21 September 1921 in Herschel, near the border of Lesotho. He attended Healdtown High School and graduated at Fort Hare University College in 1949. He obtained his Higher Education Diploma in 1950. After working as a teacher for a number of years he was expelled from teaching in 1961 because of his political activities. He went into exile in Lesotho, where he became a member of the Presidential Council of the Pan-Africanist Congress. He was kidnapped from Lesotho by the South African security forces and later sentenced to seven years' imprisonment. On his release he went into exile once more. He became Chairman of the PAC in 1982. He passed away in exile and was buried in Harare, Zimbabwe, on 13 July 1985.

JOHN POKELA
BY NKOSANA DOMINIC TSHABANGU

PROFILE

I am not sure I ever quite understood John Pokela as a personality.

A teacher by profession, Pokela was part of the group that broke away from the ANC in 1959 to form the PAC. He had taken refuge in Lesotho, where was lured into a trap, kidnapped, brought to trial and sentenced to seven years' imprisonment.

He arrived on Robben Island at a time when, despite our differences as rival liberation organisations, we felt an overriding need as political prisoners to stand together and confront the harsh physical and psychological regime imposed on us by the prison authorities. The stark reality was that this regime was designed to brutalise and destroy us as human beings.

Nelson Mandela, from his first day in prison in 1962, engaged with Robert Sobukwe in search of a common approach. On Robben Island he continued this search through discussions with Selby Ngendane and Clarence Makwethu. We had reached a point at which all organisations in the isolation section agreed to form a prisoners' committee. Although the ANC was the dominant force we agreed to allow the chair of the committee to rotate among the different organisations' representatives. We went so far as to allow the other organisations to occupy the chairmanship first.

John Pokela arrived at this point, and the process experienced an immediate setback. Was it a failure on his part to rise above party-political rivalry, to recognise that as prisoners we needed to stand together so that we could each not only survive but also endure prison with our ideal of freedom intact? Or was he driven by the internal leadership rivalries within the PAC?

The prisoners' committee survived, but not without hiccups. Despite the virulent anti-communism and anti-Indianism of the PAC, I served as ANC representative on the prisoners' committee with Pokela. It was around this time that Pokela met with Mandela to express his surprise at and appreciation for the role I was playing in the committee: it seemed as if he was having difficulty reconciling his experience with his preconceptions.

It was difficult to engage with him beyond dogma, to take discourse to the point where assumptions are clarified and tested.

I have always felt that deep within him there was a reservoir of resilience. He had a long background of political commitment, and was highly regarded in his organisation, which could have formed the platform for greater achievements.

I was cautious about approaching him to contribute to this collection of essays, but we were pleasantly surprised that he readily agreed. His contribution is therefore something of a rarity, affording us an opportunity to understand his views and the paths along which his thought moved.

TOWARDS FREEDOM

JOHN POKELA

One of the first observable stages in man's development and in his gaining a modicum of free-dom was man's movement away from animal characteristics towards assuming all the charac-teristics of a human being. Of further significance to our observation is that no culture or humanity is ever static. Thus, there is always in everything a perpetual state of transformation, motion and change. Where no change is permitted, atrophy and death set in. Likewise, noth-ing ever disappears without a trace in the sense that it gives rise to absolutely nothing that exists in later times. In the course of man's development we find that human beings have been col-lectively engaged in a perpetual struggle to master their environment and, in the process, they create a social environment that is the germ for and nucleus of what we term humanity. And it is indeed this that distinguishes man from other animals.

There has been significant growth in man's development. Hence a relatively high level of culture has been attained. We see a marked qualitative change in man's power of thinking and capacity to take action. This is accompanied by a progressive development of social organisa-tions possessing forms of communication endowed with speech.

Another thread in man's story is that, like all other animals, he initially depended entirely on nature. He collected ready food, along the banks of the Tigris and Euphrates or in the vast forests of tropical Africa, he sought shelter in the caves or in the branches of trees and he clothed himself with what nature provided. His whole life was one of adapting to nature. Man then, was at the mercy of nature, hemmed in, stupefied by his own ignorance and puzzled by the vastness and diversity of nature.

However, a decisive turning point was reached as man continued to falter, gaining experi-ence and skills, on the day man was able to reconcile his speech and the fruits of his collective labour. Both achievements constituted a collective contribution of a collective heritage. These two achievements are at the heart of society. As a result of this achievement, man's range of activities diversified and multiplied. He was able to leave behind that passive stage of mere adaptation to nature and to begin to move positively to conquer nature and tame it, such that it ministered to his own need. A positive social environment became a reality.

In this environment man acquired two attributes: that of being physically able to change nature and that of categoric conversion of things material and non-material. With these two weapons the sky was the limit to what man could achieve. Man proceeded on his tortuous way to transform himself and nature.

At this point we can look back into the distant past and say that the level human beings have reached is at a supreme stage in specific qualitative terms of man's evolution. It is a stage at which man is capable of achieving his freedom, which is the birthright of humanity as a unit, and as a whole. And we can now safely remark that language, work and humanity have no colour and no prejudices. Up to this point no man dominated another, no man colonised the country of another, no man treated another as a commodity, no man discriminated against another on the basis of colour, and none was dehumanised or cheated.

Some writers say that, as man became aware of himself not merely as a species but as an individual distinct from others and possessing a free will and his own personal destiny, man began to open up two divergent paths – the one distinctively individualistic, and the other positively collectivist. These constituted two linear times running concurrently at different speeds. Thus it is said that, as man left the cyclic period, he found himself torn between, on the one hand, his own rapid individual becoming and, on the other, the slow growth of society. Here, then, we discover for the first time two paths diverging fork-like. Indeed, two linear times running at different speeds of change, motion and transformation.

It does seem again that it is here where different wills and destinies of nationalities are initiated, governed in addition by different geographic patterns of the world surface and intercourse and of circumstances of each era.

We may now take Western man and African man as our points of departure. Levi-Strauss, the social anthropologist, simplifies an enormous argument in his indictment of European society: 'We Europeans have been taught from infancy to be self-centred and individualistic.'[1] On the other hand, before the arrival of colonialists, African man continued to so structure his society that it provided him with the security and harmony the vanishing mythical life no longer effectively provided. But he, too, like Western man, created a social environment and made history rooted in his way of life, his activities and his expectations. Thus history to him meant a living awareness of his essentially social personality identifiable in a community ethos.

Two basic principles emerge from the above. One is the individualistic principle, and inherent to it is an exploitative motive. Any society that emphasises this principle invariably must be led to the path of exploitation of man by man. Another is the collective principle, which invariably leads to sharing and distribution of the fruits of collective labour. Now, one of the tasks of man is that of freeing himself from the snares of individualism and all that is inherent to it.

If education and all the other machinery of coercion and cohesion emphasise one or the other of the two principles, the scales are tilted or tipped in favour of the emphasised, and then comes the sanction or otherwise of society. Basically then, the two principles are incompatible and contradictory.

We find that before the arrival of colonialists most of Africa had opted in favour of the collective principle. Thus Africa was at the height of communal life. And communal organisation in Africa is not just a matter of individuals clinging together to eke out an existence, nor is it comparable to rural communities in Europe. It is communal organisation that has evolved its own ethics, its own philosophical system, and its own forms of projecting and interpreting its realities and experiences. Nor does it relate this evolution to an urban centre. In brief, it is a communal structure that has affirmed its particularity.

Thus, even as late as 1962, after many years of colonial domination, it could still be said of Guinea, Ghana and Mali that capitalist relations are at a rudimentary stage, a national bourgeoisie is non-existent or almost non-existent, and at the same time there is no class of feudalists. Further we believe that when the colonialists arrived in Africa the tribal structure was already in a state of disintegration as a result of the evolution of the economy and historical events on the African scene.

When the colonialists arrived, two types of society existed. One had a centralised authority and an administrative set-up and well-defined institutions. Among the inhabitants of this society there existed marked divisions of wealth, privilege and status, and these always corresponded to the distribution of powers of authority. The second type of society had no centralised authority, but it also had an administrative machinery and judicial institutions. In this type of society there were no sharp divisions of rank, status and wealth.

The Yoruba of Nigeria and the Baganda of Uganda fell under the first type of society, where sharp divisions of status existed and where surplus from the farmers was squandered in high places. The Ibo of Nigeria and the Akiguyu of Kenya formed the second type of society. The Ibo and the Akiguyu political set-up did not carry with it economic privileges and it certainly did not confer on the holder power over the community's surplus or over the loot obtained from wars.

With the arrival of colonialism, Africa suffered devastating deprivation, plunder and dehumanisation. Africa was carved and parcelled to warring European powers. Africans suffered military defeat at the hands of superior arms. What was most appalling and devastating was the realisation that as a result of colonisation, land, which formed the material base, had been taken away, and further that the colonialists had demolished the political and economic institutions that were the life-blood of Africa. In the process of this rampant deprivation, political and economic power was denied them. This put a knife to the things that nourished our humanity, or as one writer put it, 'the electrode was put at their genitals'.

We now wish to present the legacies left behind by those patriots of Africa who were conquered by the colonialists. Since the emphasis of revolution is on southern Africa we arbitrarily draw more from this area, without forgetting about the rest of the continent.

As already pointed out, we believe that when the colonialists arrived in Africa the tribal structure was already in a state of disintegration owing to the evolution of the economy and historical events. Africans were already evolving greater groupings, which in turn were continually merging and consolidating into larger groupings. The move therefore was towards continental unity.

We know further that when the colonialists first came, African governments did not regard such people as constituting a threat to their survival. They sought to accommodate them and their presence positively by freely admitting them as equals, controlling them as one people, and assimilating them as they were accustomed to do with all foreigners. But alas, the white people kept aloof, sinking deeper into a group exclusiveness founded on discrimination and racism. Thus they imported to our continent a product of racism which remains a scourge and threat to world peace. Yet we cannot abandon the non-racist practices of our forebears. Consider the case of the survivors of the *Stavenisse*, a ship wrecked near the Transkei in 1686. When Simon van der Stel reported this incident to the Council of Seventeen, he extolled the finest practice amongst our people: 'It would be impossible to buy slaves [because] they would not part with their children or any of their connections for anything in the world, loving one another with a most remarkable affection.' This shows how our people resisted the insidious practice of slavery being imposed on them to mar social development. Again we find a foreign product – slave trade and slavery – being imposed on and equally rejected by our people.

About Moshesh[2] it is reported that Casalis, a French missionary, joined the Basotho and was building a house with the help of workers sent by Moshesh. The Basotho worked diligently and competed with each other in spite of the fact that the Frenchman had been strongly warned neither to reward them for services nor to spoil them with gifts. Moshesh had warned that 'if you do they will end by demanding that I also pay them to do anything for me'. Here it is clear that Moshesh was hitting at the root of that instrument of degradation and dehumanisation – wages or payments of the exploited.

In another context Casalis was extolling God's great wisdom in creating all men equal and 'of one blood', when one of Moshesh's followers challenged him: 'You are white, we are black, how could we come from the same father?' Moshesh, who was present, replied. 'Stupids,' he yelled, 'in my herds are white, red and spotted cattle. Are they not all cattle? Do they not come from the same stock? And belong to the same master? What of albinos? Were they not as worthy to be called Basotho as the blackest of the Basotho?' 'Black or white,' he continued, 'we laugh and cry in the same way or manner and from the same causes. What gives pleasure or pain to one race causes equally pleasure or pain to the other.' Thus again it is demonstrated that whilst Europe and its colonial system were planting their religious mission under the guise of one God, our people were showing that we were non-racists already.

In the military field we have to begin with the rare genius of our statesman Shaka. He was about 41 years old when he assumed power, and it is said he ruled only for a brief period of 11 years. In that time he forged one of the mightiest empires the African continent had ever known. Under his leadership his small insignificant clan rose from obscurity and gave its name to an all-powerful nation. During Shaka's lifetime the Zulu army was organised into a fearsome military machine, which transformed the age-old pattern of South African society. Thus his rule demonstrated positive nation-building.

One writer puts it this way: 'For generations oral tradition had hailed Shaka as the greatest of Zulu heroes. His name is frequently invoked in Zulu councils, his example is sighted as supreme authority ... He is the subject of eulogistic praise and chants and poems, the hero of more than one African novel.'

This story would not be complete and would not represent a true history if we confined ourselves only to Shaka in matters military. Other African patriots like Makana, that famous warrior and philosopher; Ndlambe, who virtually captured the Zuurveld; Tyhali, who inflicted one of the greatest war damages against colonialism; Moshesh, that great statesman and diplomat; and Sekhukhune, Mampuru and many others, are worthy of equal standing.

In the economic sphere we note that the historians concerned with development of the African nations tend to stress, as a cause of changes, the shortage of land, and that, by the eighteenth century, the population of southern Africa had so increased as to result in a shortage of land. I feel that this is an over-simplification and a mere parrot copy of arguments used elsewhere. I believe that land was not scarce. In a sense it only became scarce when colonialists arrived and paddocked Africans into reserves and locations.

We find that the middle of the eighteenth century became a watershed in the evolution and development of trade. Many nations from far and wide were attracted to trade with Africa and 'big business or extremely voluminous' trade became the order of the day.

On the African side, the most important commodity was ivory and, on the other side, the important goods were cloth, brass and beads. The African chiefs, as executive officers of state, monopolised the ivory trade. As a result they or most of them experienced internal growth and consolidation. We can thus say that trade influenced developments in the following ways:

- The wars that were fought over matters of trade increased militarism and consolidation of the people into larger aggregations and in turn led to further prosecution of trade.
- The accumulation of wealth derived mainly from trade helped the process of consolidation of states and in large measure, by distributing goods obtained from long-distance trade, a chief could command increased loyalty from within and without the normal lineage structure. But what is more significant to us is that a large proportion of what the chief obtained through trade was distributed free of charge amongst his people.

We find that amongst the Pedis and during the rule of Shaka export of ivory to Delagoa Bay formed an important part of trade and that during that period trade was highly organised. As suggested by Captain William Owen in 1823, a caravan of 1 000 porters transported between 300 and 400 elephant tusks and a large quantity of cattle.

As a fitting conclusion to the legacies of our forebears, it is proper to make a passing reference to the revolution they faced before being defeated by the colonialists, namely the *mfecane* (*lifaqane*). One notable feature of the *mfecane* is the quality of leadership that emerged from this crucible. According to one historian, 'many of them were men who demonstrated not only courage, powers of leadership and military skill but the capacity of original thought and action, the ability to devise or adapt new institutions and new techniques to solve new problems, the statesmanship to rise above a narrow tribal point of view. They demonstrated the capacity of Africans to respond to challenges and that the traditional tribal education had a far less cramping effect on the development of human personalities than some have supposed.'

The memory and traditions that derived from the *mfecane* have certainly played and do play, even in our own period, a vital inspirational role among freedom fighters. For that period, more than any other, represents an heroic period in terms of circumstances and of the leaders who emerged. Many defined their unity and sense of identity in terms of this period, and their determined psychological attitude to minority rule is the result of this period. In our times, the traditions born of the *mfecane* continue to possess a fascination and form a bulwark of self-respect around us.

Let us now turn to colonialism. In Azania[3] the year 1906 marks the end, or to be more correct, the suspension of armed resistance by the African people against the forces of colonialism with the end of the last of the Wars of Dispossession. It was immediately after this war that the Boers and the English combined to form the Union of South Africa and joined together in the political oppression, economic exploitation and social degradation of the African people.

This period also witnessed the birth of British neo-colonialism, which, though it allowed the Afrikaner to lord over the African people, subtly continued to exploit both black and white workers. Indeed, the period was marked by an ingenious policy of divide and rule. This period marked the erosion of the political rights of the African people as more and more draconian laws were passed, which ensured perpetual suppression and subjugation, and which reduced the black man to the status of a third-class citizen in the land of his birth.

Ironically, throughout the continent and even beyond the seas, the spirit of resistance persisted, but this time in another form. The year 1900 had seen the inauguration of the first Pan African Conference that aimed at making this century a century of the Coloured man. In 1912 in South Africa the African people established the African National Congress. Throughout Africa and beyond the seas a cultural movement continued to forge ahead. It began as a negritude movement. Its aim was to act as a conscience to the African to resist de-culturation by imperialism. Its leaders understood clearly that de-culturation was a process whereby Africans were being consciously and deliberately dominated, their culture was denied existence, was doubted and questioned as being uncivilised, and thus needed their determination to resist.

Let us return to our story about the Afrikaner and the English. The statement made about white workers must not lead us to an erroneous conclusion that in fact a white worker was on the same Poverty Datum Line as the African. That could never be the case since there was a white minority government that made laws aimed at making Africans perpetual hewers of wood and drawers of water.

Why did British imperialists appear to be succeeding? The British appeared to be succeeding in dividing the people of this country for the following reasons: they were the victors of the Anglo-Boer War and they had properly assessed the situation after this war and realised that the Afrikaner in particular possessed an almost inherent racist attitude or had acquired one; and the British convinced themselves that the chief enemy to imperialism was the African, who had proved himself to be a stubborn resister, as was seen in the nine destructive Wars of Dispossession. To put it in another way: we remember that in 1879 at Isandlwana the Zulus had executed one of the most devastating massacres to be recorded in the annals of British colonial warfare. British Prime Minister Benjamin Disraeli was reported to have remarked: 'A remarkable people, the Zulus, they defeat our generals, they convert our bishops, they have settled the fate of a great European dynasty.' The British therefore feared that the African people possessed the biggest effective and permanent weapon – superiority in numbers, which, when combined, could effectively and decisively be used against imperialism. It therefore dawned on the British imperialists that their salvation would lie only in their unity with the Afrikaners. They felt that if they harnessed and channelled the Afrikaner's inflexible racism, they could win the Afrikaner to their side as a junior partner and ally against the African majority.

By 1910 the Afrikaner was still a rural and feudalist man, who scarcely grasped the intricacies of a sophisticated industrial society which came in the wake of the mining revolution. The war against the British had left him a poor man. The British imperialists had discovered that they could not use the Afrikaner profitably in his raw state. As a consequence, British artisans were imported to come and tutor him. This action of the British imperialists marked the beginning of the consciousness of the Afrikaner as an industrial worker and this, combined with his racist and Calvinist religion, helped him to forge ahead.

In Europe there was an awakening of the downtrodden working classes. The imported British artisans carried in them the seeds of discontent and when later they were faced with the terrible and exploitative conditions in the mines of South Africa, they formed themselves into unions.

Sensing the potential danger of trade unionism the British capitalists decided to use this awakening of the white worker to achieve their own purposes. The backwardness of the Afrikaner formed the stumbling block. However, the imported artisans soon organised Afrikaners into trade unions too. But this was unity amongst the white workers. Realising this, both the British statesmen and workers decided to harness Afrikaner racism as well.

From that time on, the emphasis was placed on the protection of the rights of white workers as against the rights of African workers and against the capitalists. This racial approach suited British neo-colonialism and South African politics became nothing more than the politics of colour.

The Africans did not sit down and cry crocodile tears. Oh no! A new organisation came into existence, namely the Industrial and Commercial Workers Union (ICU) and joined the forces of those who fought to uplift the African and free him from destitution, humiliation and exploitation. The ICU suffered from the fact that it was a semi-industrial and semi-political organisation without a real, full grasp of its mission. Nonetheless it left its mark on the sands of history.

At the same time white supremacy was growing by leaps and bounds. This led to the formation of the Labour Party, which, together with an Afrikaner government in 1924, sealed the fate of the black man in industry and left him excommunicated and defenceless.

We have already said that the last attempt of the Africans to regain their land and freedom was in 1906 when a group of African patriots led by Bambata staged a revolt against the British colonialists. This last desperate attempt on the part of a section of the indigenous population using primitive weapons marked the beginning of a new page in the history of oppression of our people. True enough, a hybrid progress in African franchise had been made in the Cape, whereby a certain category of Africans enjoyed a qualified vote. But the number was so insignificant as to be meaningless; equally observable were half-attempts by Cape liberals to have the clauses entrenched.

In spite of this, the impression that remained dominant in the minds of the British imperialists was that they now had got the gold in the country and did not want to offend the Boers anymore. They decided to console him by allowing him to lord over his hated enemy, the African. The imperialists decided to let the African pay for all the offences the imperialists had committed against the Boers while they (the imperialists) went on to fill their bags with gold and diamonds. The British, in fact, continued to allow the Boers to run governments while they (the Britons) managed and ran industry, commerce and mining. We know that this strategy has been the cornerstone of British imperialism ever since. As a result, the English in South Africa have played an insignificant part in politics but a significant part in its economy.

The establishment of the Afrikaner authority in government began a new chapter in the history of this country. In the process, the Afrikaner discovered the sterility of British colonialism. Equally, the British imperialists discovered the potential danger of an estranged Afrikaner. And finding that they could not win him, they felt they had to join him.

A scapegoat had to be found for both parties. That scapegoat was the African, who was defenceless, politically disenfranchised, militarily disarmed and legally inhibited. Draconian laws were passed, none more pernicious than the Industrial Conciliation Act, which sought to exclude all Africans from registered trade unions. The frustrated Afrikaner did not confine himself to economic exploitation of the African. We also saw the intensification of anti-blackism. War was therefore declared on our people, men, women and children. They burdened and chained us with the pass laws. In the field of education the story was the same. The African was to be given an inferior type of education that prepared him to serve and minister the needs of the white communities.

The irony was that the English were benefiting more than the Afrikaner and were making exorbitant profits in the process. The Afrikaner, under the delusion of an empty political power, was being kept down too in the economic sphere. The situation has not improved much even today except for a few Ruperts, Marais's and Wessels.

However, human endurance has its limitations. And it has its limitations among the Africans too. A spirit of defiance has been rising among the Africans and deeper and wider knowledge was acquired. In 1943 came Mziwakhe Lembede, propagating African Nationalism as a unifying force. In 1945 we again saw the imagination of the African people come to fruition in the decisions of the Pan African Conference in Manchester where the leaders felt that pan-Africanism must be planted in the soil of Africa; further, they embraced socialism in their ideology. A dynamic movement was regenerated and it began to sow the seeds of freedom in the hearts and minds of Africans everywhere. Amongst the leaders that attended, a true will for independence and freedom could be seen. One observed among these nationalists, who were ready to impart a new ideology to their people, a revolutionary potential and the possibility then of national liberation by peaceful methods.

The early 1950s saw the emergence of Africanists in Azania who were propelled by the desire for positive action and were opposed to multi-racialism. The true spirit of these men was concretely and effectively translated by the Pan-Africanist Congress (PAC), which was launched as a ship of freedom on 6 April 1959. The PAC was launched at the time of the 'awakening of the peoples of Africa', which had begun and was given expression by the independence of Ghana in 1957.

Now, if we are to achieve our goals and fundamentally attain our major aims, namely the achievement of maximum satisfaction of the needs of our people, the achievement of political and economic overthrow of imperialism, colonialism and neo-colonialism, cultural enrichment of our people, and if we want to reconstruct the history of the continent, psychologically recreate a new ethos of a people zealous and dedicated to create and live in a new society, we must radically change the pattern of the present set-up and, in its place, establish a society which is non-racial, Africanist in origin, socialist in content and democratic in form. We must reject multi-racialism because to us multi-racialism is nothing else but apartheid multiplied.

The early Europeans succeeded in deceiving themselves and the world that they represented humanity in its most civilised form and by a twist of a trick elected themselves the leaders of humanity. They have heaped abuse on us, declaring us half-developed and without a history and without a worthwhile human contribution. That is why even outstanding scholars like Hegel could proclaim for all to hear that the African has contributed nothing to humanity but slavery.

For centuries unnatural suffering has existed among our people. There can be little doubt that this suffering is unprecedented in scale. Further, we are aware that our suffering is caused by economic, political and social factors. Look around us, and about us: we have been robbed left, right and centre. We have been exploited, deceived and bestially humiliated and condemned to poverty of the worst type, which is corrosive in its effects and stupefying in impact. We have been denied our humanity. This is neatly put by Levi-Strauss: 'Western man began to see that he would never understand himself as long as there was a single race or people on the surface of the earth, that he treated as an object.' Western man has taken a detour most of us know. A detour that took him through many statuses before he came back to humanity. He had passed through the stages of slave and slave owner, serf and feudal lord, worker and capitalist and was now entering the stage of socialism. Not so with African man, who had been moving along a helicoidal path to humanity and socialism.

We know that after centuries of unreality our people have awakened to the truth. Whilst exploitation and enslavement remain immeasurable and the suffering remains inhuman, and whilst the waste in manpower remains and wealth is being squandered, the spark of freedom has been lit. Knowledge of our strength and potential is equally increasing. And we now say that no one has a right to adopt a psychological indifference to the suffering and struggle of the people. If conditions are accepted passively it is clear that the sufferings will never improve or be eliminated, for we know from experience that the thirst of imperialism can never be quenched or subdued by mere words alone. We are strengthened by the knowledge that oppression and domination have no stamina.

We have reached the stage of purposeful direction. Nkrumah has given a sharp and graphic picture of colonialism and neo-colonialism. He concluded that existing colonies may linger on but no newer colony will be created; that neo-colonialism represents imperialism in its last and perhaps its most dangerous stage; that the essence of neo-colonialism is that the state that is subject to it is in theory independent and appears to have all the characteristics of a sovereign state. He goes further to add that the methods of neo-colonialism and colonialism are varied and variegated. For instance, troops of an imperialist power may be stationed in a neo-colonialist state. Not only that, the neo-colonialist state may supply raw materials, whilst goods from the imperial power are exported to such neo-colonialist state. Civil servants from the imperial power are often placed in positions where they control and dictate policy of a political, economic and cultural nature.

Further, we find in such instances that foreign capital in the colonies or dependent states is used for the exploitation rather than for the improvement of the social conditions of the indigenous people. Investments, too, lead to widening the gap between the rich and the poor countries, and for those who practise neo-colonialism this means exploitation without regress. In addition, neo-colonialism, like colonialism before it, postpones facing social issues that will have to be faced. Further, neo-colonialism, like colonialism, exports the social evils and conflicts of the capitalist countries. This, in my view, is the most serious and heinous phenomenon, for class interests are being introduced and nourished on a continent that has been predominantly egalitarian.

Whilst it is true that these things have happened and have helped to influence present trends, many of us still feel that it was not really directly from these developments that the truth was born. What seems indisputable is that the truth of the new resurgence was born first and foremost of the determination of the exploited Africans to fight not only for economic justice, but for their identity as human beings, to rid themselves of the eternal foreigner, the other who had invented and imposed for centuries upon them his wretched doctrine of other-ness, of hereditary excommunication. The last need of imperialism and its cognates is not for raw materials, exploited labour and controlled markets, but for mankind, which it counts for nothing.

To achieve our freedom we must re-examine our political, social and economic conditions. Julius Nyerere has correctly pointed the way in his famous speech: 'We have been oppressed a great deal, we have been exploited a great deal and we have been degraded a great deal. It is our weakness that has led to our being oppressed, exploited, disregarded. Now we want a revolution, a revolution which brings to an end our weakness so that we are never again exploited, oppressed and humiliated.' Fanon says: 'After centuries of unreality, after having wallowed in the most outlandish phantoms, at long last the nation gun in hand stands face to face with the only force contending for his life, the forces of colonialism.'

Nkrumah says: 'I see before my mind's eye a great monolithic party growing out of this process [of training freedom fighters] united and strong spreading its protective wings over the whole of Africa.'

If we are to achieve freedom and unity, Africa must be united. Nyerere says, 'African Nationalism differs from the nationalism of the past in that the African national state is an instrument of unity and not for dividing her.'

The whole people as an organised force must take their destiny into their hands. United and strong they must forge ahead. We must carry out an intensive and thorough education. And it is this realisation which made us launch a campaign in 1960 with the aim of freeing the mind of the African. This campaign will never succeed unless it is backed up by a thorough and systematic education that involves the entire population.

Last but not least we must succeed in reconciling mental and manual labour. When the African revolution has taken its full course and attained its purpose, and humanity is fully re-established on our continent, only then can we declare: we are free. Only then can history accurately reflect its true programme of a humanity rediscovered and rejuvenated. *Izwe Letu Ma-Afrika!*

EDDIE DANIELS

Edward John Daniels was born on 25 October 1928 in District Six, Cape Town. He went to work after primary school and joined the Liberal Party in 1959. He joined the National Committee for Liberation, which later became the African Resistance Movement, in 1961. The National Committee for Liberation launched its sabotage activities, in which he participated, on 26 September 1961. He was arrested in July 1964 and sentenced to 15 years' imprisonment.

He obtained his Matriculation certificate in prison and went on to graduate with a BA and a B. Com. degree. After his release he obtained a Teacher's Diploma and became a teacher.

His memoirs, under the title *There and Back: Robben Island 1964–1979*, were published by Mayibuye Books, University of the Western Cape, 1998.

EDDIE DANIELS
BY SAM NHLENGETHWA

SAM 2001
NHANGTHUD

PROFILE

If anything had to be done or needed to be done, whatever the risk involved, Eddie was ready and available. Doing what was a necessity in fighting against injustice was, for Eddie, freedom.

Eddie served a sentence of 15 years on Robben Island. He belonged to the Liberal Party and the African Resistance Movement (ARM). He was the only Coloured sentenced with a group of young white South Africans – the regime released the others before they had served their full sentences.

Eddie received several visits by Judge Jan Steyn. The judge was keen to secure an early release for Eddie. He offered to take up the matter on Eddie's behalf. He felt that there were good prospects if Eddie was prepared to give an undertaking that he would not resort to the use of violence again.

Politely and without hesitation, Eddie turned down the proposal. Even after the judge painted a picture of changes under apartheid, Eddie was unmoved. His argument was simple. He was implacably opposed to injustice. Indeed, if the changes were as depicted by the learned judge, it may well be that there may not be a need to use violence to bring an end to apartheid. And he would prefer that peaceful means be used. An undertaking, however, would bind him and if conditions had not changed he could not, in conscience, tie himself through such an undertaking.

After these visits by the judge, some of us would urge Eddie to reconsider his stance. After all, why place such weight on an undertaking given in prison? Besides, it may well be possible to formulate the undertaking in such a way that it may suffice to get him out of prison, without compromising his principles. In no way did any such arguments shake his resolve. He was bound by his word. His integrity was beyond compromise or purchase.

And so he served his full sentence, his integrity untarnished.

There is a deep and abiding sense of caring that embraces the core of Eddie's being. In his company one always felt secure.

LET US WORK TOGETHER FOR UNITY

EDDIE DANIELS

South Africa is a beautiful country. It is rich economically. But spiritually it is sick and ugly. Its spiritual sickness and ugliness is a result of the rabid racism that is both legal and traditional and dominates South African life.

South Africa is a country steeped in racism. Generation after generation has been so indoctrinated with it that it has seeped into their very bones. The people of South Africa may be divided into two major racial groups:

1. The whites, who are made up mainly of the Afrikaners and English, a large sprinkling of Jews and Germans and a few Italians, Portuguese, Japanese, Chinese and Greeks, etc.[1]
2. The blacks, who are made up of Africans, Coloureds and Indians.

When it is opportune, the racist regime refers to the whites as one group; otherwise the Afrikaner is referred to as the *volk* (the Afrikaner chosen people). The Africans, who constitute the largest racial group in South Africa and who were once considered one group have since, for the purposes of political expediency, been separated into tribal-ethnic groups such as Zulu, Xhosa, Sotho, etc. One of the arguments put forward by Nic Rhoodie in justifying white rule in South Africa is that the whites are numerically larger than any individual African tribe or the Coloured or the Indian group.[2] He glosses over the fact that 'white' here is used as a term that embraces different white 'tribes', any one of which is smaller than the Xhosa or Zulu tribes, and that the total number of whites is less than the African group itself and is still smaller when compared with the blacks as a whole.

DIFFERENT INTERPRETATIONS OF FREEDOM

All people in South Africa want freedom but in the main the ideal of freedom as envisaged by the whites contradicts the ideal of freedom as envisaged by the blacks. What does freedom mean to South African whites? To the Afrikaner it means absolute political domination – naked power and essentially dominance over the blacks. This, they claim, is based on divine teaching. To obtain this political dominance over the blacks the Afrikaner requires and obtains the co-operation of all whites in the country. But this forced co-operation with other white groups is frustrating to the Afrikaners, whose main desire is the domination of all groups in the country. They yearn to dominate the English because of their Boer War memories and the inferiority complex the English gave them. They would kick out of the country all the 'honorary whites', as well as the other minority groups such as the Italians and the Portuguese. They would only welcome into the country the Nazis who fled after the collapse of Hitler and whom many Afrikaners supported during the Second World War. The English and the Jews do not fear competing with blacks for economic positions. To them political freedom means getting rid of the prejudice-laden Afrikaner via the ballot box. This is because the moment is drawing near when the social advantages of apartheid are outweighed by its economic disadvantages and by its political repercussions.

What does freedom mean to the blacks, who are denied a meaningful say in the governance of their country and who are subjected to laws of extreme humiliation and brutal oppression? It means the destruction of all racist laws and practices based on racial discrimination, and their acceptance as full citizens of the country with all the democratic rights that go with it.

Because of the different aspirations of freedom by the different groups, freedom can only be obtained by one group at the expense of the other and therefore one has to choose which side one will support: the dominant white group, whose rule is based on racial oppression, or the oppressed group, whose rule will be a democratic one, and race, creed and religion will not be criteria for citizenship.

THE PROS AND CONS OF THE POLITICAL SITUATION

How then is it possible to attain the goal of freedom as envisaged by the democratic forces in South Africa? There are many forces opposed to the goal of freedom:

- The government's armed forces are well organised and highly trained in using the most modern weapons for war and security. Its political police, known as the Special Branch (SB) and its police force are highly trained. All whites undergo compulsory military training.
- The physical power of the white racist regime and its propaganda have succeeded in intimidating many blacks not only not to resist them, but even to support them in their racial oppression, as is the case with blacks serving in its police, army and navy. Government agents have resorted to terrorising, torturing, kidnapping and even murdering political opponents.
- Government's internal security is tight. Anti-government suspects are banned, placed under house arrest or banished; others are continually harassed and employers are often intimidated by the SB to dismiss any employee suspected of anti-government political activity. This makes it difficult to organise the people to resist the government.
- South Africa is the world's largest producer of gold and as an industrialised country it has strong trade links with powerful and influential countries. This directly or indirectly stabilises and strengthens the government.
- The whites fear losing their superior status *vis-à-vis* the blacks as well as their high standard of living, which is obtained at the expense of the blacks. They have developed a phobia of being swamped by a vengeful and relentless black tide.
- The government, through its Bantustan policy, the establishment of the Coloured Representative Council (CRC) for the Coloured group and the South African Indian Council

for the Indian group, hopes to thwart the national struggle as well as reduce international pressure on it. It spends millions on local and international propaganda and makes a great play of its Bantustan policy, government institutions, 'mixed' sport and social amenities.

- There is much disunity and suspicion among the anti-government forces. The methods and tactics employed by the different organisations often differ. Some are prepared only to work within the framework of the laws, others illegally but non-violently, whilst still others work legally and illegally, non-violently and violently, as it suits the moment.

- Whites in South Africa have relatively free access to firearms, whereas blacks may only obtain these legally under the most stringent conditions.

Against these we should note the following forces in favour of freedom:

- Because the whites are, relatively speaking, a small group and cannot trust the blacks so far as to give them military training *en masse* or put them into important security positions, the overall security arrangements fall on their own shoulders. They have an immense land border and a long coastline to guard, and all the countries bordering it are enemies of apartheid. In addition, they must maintain internal security as well as keep the wheel of the economy turning. This, in the long run, will prove to be an unbearable strain on the forces available to the government.

- Generations of blacks have been born into this racist environment. They have had to adjust their behaviour so as to minimise the impact of their humiliating social position and also, in some cases, to deceive themselves to believe that their dignity is not under perpetual assault. Thereby blacks have rationalised their non-opposition to, and, in some cases, even their collaboration with the government. The advent of organisations such as the South African Students Organisation (SASO) and the Black People's Convention (BPC) augurs well for the future. These organisations are largely made up of black youth – tomorrow's leaders – who refuse to passively accept the yoke of social inferiority. The students' strikes at the various universities in the face of physical attack and intimidatory measures have shown their determination and militancy.

- It has been argued in certain quarters that it is wrong to stage trade boycotts against South Africa because it is the poor (that is, the blacks) who will suffer the most. This is true; when a country becomes impoverished it is always the poor who bear the brunt of the suffering. But we are used to suffering. We suffer every day and we are prepared for additional hardships for the cause of democracy.

- Let South African whites look around at the rest of the independent countries bordering on our country. They will see that their fears of being swamped by the blacks are unfounded. In none of these countries have whites been 'kicked into the sea'. Of course, whites, like all other citizens, must obey the laws of the land, and failing to do so they must expect to be punished accordingly. In all these countries all citizens are needed to help build up the economy. This applies also to South African whites. Under a non-racial government their presence in helping to build South Africa into a leading nation in Africa and an influential nation in the world is important, because they hold the leading economic and skilled positions in the economy.

- There is a strong likelihood that the Bantustan policy will rebound on itself. South Africa's border area will have increased. These Bantustan governments are continually going to 'blackmail' the South African government for further concessions both in land and economic aid, and these rural areas will prove an ideal training ground or areas of transit for anti-government guerrilla forces. The Bantustans occupy only 13 per cent of South Africa. They comprise largely rural areas and can never hope to support their population adequately. Further, the majority of the blacks still live in poverty-stricken locations situated in the 'white areas' and no 'uhuru'[3] arrangements have been made for them. Therefore dissatisfaction and frustration can be expected to linger and grow.

- In spite of the Bantustans, the majority of Africans will still live and work in the 'white areas'. The government's policy of 'separate but equal' national groups is meaningless to Coloureds and Indians.

- The Bantustan governments and government institutions such as the CRC and the South African Indian Council may also be points of opposition and frustration to the government. Already an anti-government group, the Labour Party, has taken over power and commands more influence. This may well encourage it to take a more militant stand.

- The government's local and international propaganda mean nothing to the dedicated freedom fighter, as the government ignores the fundamentals. The fundamentals are the vote, equal opportunities based on merit for employment, equal pay for equal work, the right to belong to and form trade unions, equal educational facilities for all, the right to associate freely with others and free movement for all South Africans within its borders. Until the fundamentals are attained there will always be violent opposition to the government.

- The internal forces ranged against the racist policies cover a wide front. They include the Progressive Party, various religious groups, the Christian Institute, the Institute of Race Relations, the Civil Rights League, the Black Sash, NUSAS, SASO, BPC, SANROC, the Liberal Party, ARM, NEUM, PAC, SWAPO of Namibia, the Congress Alliance, the SACP and Umkhonto weSizwe (MK), among others. The aims and activities of some of these organisations differ widely but they are all contributing to the eventual destruction of apartheid.

- Increasingly militant organisations have come to accept that the only answer to apartheid is armed force. In the early 1960s the ARM and MK (the military wing of the ANC) launched the sabotage movement. The membership of ARM consists largely of liberals and MK is made up of members of the Congress Alliance and the SACP. Since then, MK and SWAPO have launched active guerrilla movements against the South African government.

- The democratic forces are receiving increasing international support. Organisations such as the United Nations (UN), the Organisation of African Unity (OAU), the International

Labour Organisation (ILO), the World Council of Churches, the International Defence and Aid and the Anti-Apartheid Movement (AAM) have consistently assisted us. So, too, have Western, African, Asian and socialist governments. The African and socialist governments have also made available training facilities (military and otherwise) as well as arms to help prepare us for the military struggle. Through international organisations such as the UN and the OAU, the ANC, the PAC and SWAPO are succeeding in whipping up resistance to apartheid.

- A small military victory against the oppressor will be small statistically but large politically. The whites have always beaten down the blacks when they dared to rise and tried to better their own living conditions. This was so because the whites had the arms and the military machine while the blacks had their labour power plus sticks and stones. Because the racist whites, based on their belief of racial superiority, consider it unthinkable that blacks can better the whites – and so do many blacks – a small military victory on the part of the blacks over the whites gives the blacks a tremendous morale boost and explodes the fallacy of racial superiority. The whites, in turn, suffer a morale decline and an increase in insecurity. They gaze at the blacks with whom they are forced to live and work and wonder how long these blacks will die for apartheid and how long they can still be trusted.

THE CONTRIBUTION OF THE ANTI-APARTHEID WHITES

In the South African situation the overall majority of whites support the discriminatory policies of the government, as both the National Party and the United Party are advocates of discrimination based on race. However, there is a courageous white group, albeit small, which has made a significant contribution to the anti-apartheid struggle. Members of this group are to be found in the arts, like Breyten Breytenbach; in the churches we find such men as Canon Collins, Reverend Michael Scott and Reverend Ffrench Beytagh; in the SACP people such as Abraham (Bram) Fischer, Lionel Foreman and Joe Slovo and his wife Ruth First; in the COD Helen Joseph; in the Liberal Party people such as Alan Paton, Peter Brown, Randolph Vigne and Dot Cleminshaw; and we also have the support of members of the Institute of Race Relations, the Civil Rights League, the Black Sash, the Christian Institute and NUSAS. In addition, there are the illegal and violent organisations, Umkhonto weSizwe and the African Resistance Movement. The former has a number of white members in prison. They include Dennis Goldberg, David Kitson and John Matthews, who are serving terms of life imprisonment, 20 and 15 years respectively. John Harris of the ARM paid with his life on the gallows for his opposition to apartheid, while a number of his fellow members such as Hugh Lewin, David Evans and Barauch Hirson were imprisoned.

Though South African whites and apartheid may be considered synonymous, this is not so. This small group of courageous South Africans makes the difference. The democratic forces are fighting all the forces that make possible and support apartheid, and not the white people of South Africa.

THE DEVELOPMENT OF THE MILITARY PHASE

Organisations opposed to apartheid have tried all possible methods to bring about a peaceful change. Such methods have ranged from prayer meetings to national strikes, but all to no avail. Instead, in the early 1960s the iron fist of the 'master race' became more brutal.

Because of the futility of legal methods, which had largely been made illegal through bannings and new laws, organisations resorted to illegal methods such as slogan painting, illegal broadcasts and sabotage. By 1964 the Nat government had destroyed the sabotage movements and the supreme courts of the land had imposed vicious sentences on those found guilty of sabotage so as to intimidate others into not adopting the same methods. The Nat government was riding high while the country cowered.

But far-sighted and responsible organisations had begun, since the early 1960s, to send their members for military training to countries that were prepared to offer this type of assistance, making arrangements with foreign governments for military and financial assistance, and for establishing offices in these countries. Large successes had been achieved in these efforts and a new phase of the struggle against racism was entered into – guerrilla warfare.

Since 1964, the dominant organisations in the field were the ANC with its military wing, MK, and SWAPO. These two organisations have consistently carried out political and military attacks against the racist regime. Both the ANC and SWAPO are members of an alliance, which includes Frelimo of Mozambique, the MPLA of Angola and the Zimbabwe African People's Union (ZAPU) of Rhodesia.

NAMIBIA AND RHODESIA

The situations in South Africa, Namibia and Rhodesia have many similarities. This is because we are all fighting minority racist governments. South African and Namibian freedom forces are fighting a common foe, the South African government. In Namibia, SWAPO is the dominant opposition force.

The Namibian situation differs from the South African situation in that the South African government has eventually recognised the right of Namibia to be an independent country, but one which it still desires to lead to 'responsible independence', that is, in which to establish a puppet government.

In Rhodesia the organisations in the field against the illegal Smith regime are ZAPU and the Zimbabwe African National Union (ZANU), both of which have come together under the African National Council and are waging a guerrilla war against the Smith regime.

THE FRUITS OF ORGANISED VIOLENCE

Throughout human history man has used violence against man and it is usually the group or class that uses violence most effectively that is most successful in a violent conflict. Man's motive for violence may be broadly divided into two streams:

- to enrich himself at the expense of his neighbour;
- to free himself from the chains of oppression imposed on him by his fellow men.

Seldom has an oppressor restored to independence a servile and unprotesting victim, but history is full of revolts and revolutions in which the oppressed have risen against the oppressor.

Many nations have grown rich and powerful through the use of violence. They have done so through colonisation and the exploitation of these colonies for their own benefit. If we look at the world map we will see that since the Second World War numerous countries have attained their independence through violence. In Africa we have Algeria, Guinea-Bissau, Mozambique and Angola. In Asia we may take as examples China, Korea and Vietnam. Cuba is a notable case in South America, where even at present guerrilla movements are operating in almost all the countries where the masses consider themselves oppressed. World-shaking violent revolutions have occurred in the United States of America (1776), France (1789), the Soviet Union (1917) and China (1949).

The white oppressors in South Africa, who use violence to maintain their doctrine of racial superiority and to improve themselves economically at the expense of their fellow black citizens, rationalise that South Africa is their country, that they are citizens of no other country and that therefore they will fight to death in defending their country, that is, their racist laws. The democratic forces in South Africa appreciate that South African whites are citizens of this country and embrace them as fellow and equal citizens – but not as superior citizens. If South African whites accept our standpoint then together we can build and defend our country if and when it is necessary.

When a successful revolution occurs, as, for example, in Cuba and Algeria, those who believe in the overthrown regime had to either leave the country or comply with the laws of the new government in power. The same will apply in South Africa.

In Africa, three countries – Rhodesia, Namibia and South Africa – are still fighting against oppressive governments. Some freedom movements in southern Africa have, after travelling the long and bitter road of non-violent struggle, turned to violence. History shows that organised violence, even though protracted, has been the key to freedom for many countries. It therefore seems that the freedom forces in southern Africa have at last firmly grasped the key that will make victory possible for them.

WE SHALL WIN!

Apartheid will be destroyed! But at what cost? In the first place it is the government that has the power to change the apartheid laws and bring about peace. It may do this simply by scrapping all discriminatory laws, or by calling a national convention of all the responsible leaders of the country to discuss a blueprint for a new South Africa.

Thus far the South African government has failed to use its power to bring about peace and therefore it must bear all the responsibility for past violence, suffering and death. In the future the violence will increase in intensity and scope. More and more of the government forces will be suffering and dying for a lost cause and all the more fear, horror and hatred will be unleashed within this country. For all this, the government must bear the full responsibility. Apartheid is a lost cause, as can clearly be seen by the retreat of the government from its stand in the early 1960s to the mid-1970s. In 1965 the defenders of apartheid were expected to die defending their country against 'mixed' sport and social amenities; in 1975 they are expected to die defending 'mixed' sport and social amenities. It can therefore be expected that the values the forces of apartheid are expected to die for in 1975 will be different to the values they will be expected to die for in 1985.

The most powerful force opposed to apartheid at present is the African National Congress. But it is relatively weak compared to the forces of the government. Therefore, looking at the situation solely from the view of the physical forces ranged against each other, the struggle will be a long, drawn-out one. But if we take into consideration the international pressures levelled at the apartheid government then the picture becomes much brighter.

There was a time when the South African government and its supporters spurned international opinion, but since the 1960s it has become more attentive. In the field of sport the South African Non-Racial Olympic Committee (SANROC) and the Anti-Apartheid Movement (AAM) have succeeded in preventing South Africa from participating in a number of international sporting events. Politically, South Africa has also experienced the 'winds of change', which are mounting in intensity. South Africa was forced to leave the British Commonwealth, the ILO and other international organisations and therefore suffered a loss of political influence and trade advantages that it enjoyed as a member of these international bodies. South Africa was forced to introduce the concept of Bantustans to try and justify its unjustifiable policy of racial discrimination to the world – the very Bantustans that will contribute to the downfall of the government. With the formation of the OAU, more political pressure was brought to bear on South Africa. Some countries tried to get South Africa to change from its racial laws through political pressures, others have adopted trade boycotts and hostile stances towards the South African government.

But what may, perhaps, be considered as the most significant development is that because of its intransigent attitude towards and oppressive pressure on the people of South Africa, the government has forced the organisations fighting for freedom to adopt organised violence against it. In this sphere, governments supportive of the freedom forces have generously come forward and offered money, military training and facilities, as well as arms to the freedom fighters, while also making their political channels available to these organisations.

This is a force that the South African government cannot stop indefinitely. Vietnam has shown the tremendous cost in money and manpower that is required to combat determined guerrillas. South Africa has neither that kind of money nor manpower. In addition, South Africa has a tremendously long land and sea border to guard. Almost four-fifths of the population are opposed to the government, and it has to keep the wheel of the economy turning. All this will place an insupportable strain on it, which will not only crack the 'granite' wall but will destroy it. The democratic forces of South Africa are fighting a moral and just war.

UNITY IS THE KEY TO VICTORY

The Liberal Party of South Africa has been willing to work with all anti-apartheid organisations and has done so consistently. Its membership, when compared with organisations such as the ANC and PAC, is small, but its political role is large. It is true that it has been made legally ineffective by the passing of the Mixed Membership Law: it has officially disbanded. But the passing of a law or the disbanding of an organisation does not destroy the principle of men and women of calibre and character working together. If it cannot live on in the light of day then it must live clandestinely, nurturing itself until the moment once again dawns that will enable it to take its rightful place in society again. The Liberal Party of South Africa is not the first organisation to be cast outside the legal framework of society. In almost all societies where people have struggled for democracy, the oppressor has used his power to destroy the organisations of the people. As a matter of fact, Christianity was built on the courage, resolution and idealism of those early Christians who lived clandestinely and who scurried from place to place for survival; those Christians who maintained their principles and beliefs irrespective of the legality or illegality of the matter. Therefore, although the Liberal Party has been destroyed by the law, our principles of universal adult suffrage, equality before the law, the full respect for human dignity, that is, full democracy to be accorded to all South African citizens irrespective of race, colour or creed, are indestructible and these principles and beliefs will still live on long after apartheid has disappeared into the mists of time.

The Liberal Party was founded in 1953. It came into being for two main reasons: first, South African whites who were opposed to apartheid needed a political home; and secondly, they wanted an organisation that would also be opposed to communism.

At the time such anti-apartheid whites felt that the Congress of Democrats (COD), which had also just come into existence earlier in 1953 and which was an all-white anti-apartheid body, was dominated by communists and hence the creation of the Liberal Party of South Africa with a qualified franchise. It may also be argued that the Congress structure, that is, the ANC, SAIC, CPC and COD constituting the Congress Alliance, did not meet the non-racial ideas of other anti-apartheid supporters. Be that as it may, by 1960 the Liberal Party had an unqualified franchise and was working in close harmony with the Congress Alliance.

The Liberal Party was one of the truly non-racial political organisations in South Africa. Its membership was based on calibre, character and merit and not on race as determined by the South African government.

The importance of the Liberal Party in the South African political context was that it provided one of few political homes for anti-apartheid whites. Within its ranks black and white were able to meet and discuss on a basis of equality; a unique occurrence within this racially compartmentalised land. And because of this non-racial policy it has been able to co-operate fully with the other anti-apartheid organisations. By 1959/1960 the Liberal Party began to engage in extra-parliamentary struggle while continuing its parliamentary struggle. It engaged in protest meetings, marches and placard demonstrations, which it conducted alone or in conjunction with other organisations opposed to the government. It officially participated in the 1961 stay-at-home called by the Congress Alliance. Its official organ, *Contact,* was the only South African newspaper that reported on the atrocities that occurred in Robben Island prison in the early 1960s, under the banner headline 'Devil's Island'. This report was based on affidavits sworn to largely by members of the PAC who had just been released. The government destroyed this organ of the Liberal Party by consistently banning every successive editor.

With the banning of the ANC and PAC, the Liberal Party stepped into the front line and came under direct attack by the government. Its members were increasingly harassed by the Security Branch and were systematically banned. In 1963, the Liberal Party launched its 'sit-in demonstrations' campaign. This campaign had its successes, but it came to an end because of the persistent arrests of volunteers who participated. But the members of the LPSA have made and are making important contributions in organisations such as Defence and Aid, the Institute of Race Relations, the Civil Rights League, the local UN Association, NUSAS, the Black Sash, and the now defunct Coloured Convention, as well as in anti-apartheid organisations abroad and in welfare organisations such as SHAWCO and KUPAGANI.

With the banning of the ANC and the PAC, the LPSA made available its public platforms to prominent members of these organisations, thus enabling these organisations to continue carrying their messages to the masses. It also did this for the Coloured Convention when the government banned its national meetings. Where necessary it also made its political and legal machinery available to members of these organisations.

Thus, as the struggle became more and more intense, the role of the LPSA became more and more militant and its co-operation with other anti-apartheid organisations deepened. There was a time when the LPSA was reluctant to work with the Congress Alliance because of the latter's communist membership and the willingness of the Congress Alliance to work with the SACP, but faced with the high calibre of the Congress Alliance and its members this reluctance eventually disappeared.

The aim of the Liberals is to destroy apartheid. They have the respect and trust of both the ANC and the PAC. They must therefore use their good offices to bring these two major national organisations as well as others under one roof or at least to a greater degree of political co-operation. It is important that these organisations concentrate on fighting the government rather than trying to score political kudos and vie for the same sources of membership, thus giving the enemy a longer lease on life. In Mozambique, Frelimo was born as a result of a number of freedom organisations merging. In Rhodesia, ZAPU and ZANU have merged. Therefore it is also possible that it may happen here. The name of the new political organisation is not important. What is important is that we get our priorities straight, which means that our most important task is to destroy apartheid. That is why our respective organisations have come into being in the first place. And we will achieve that task more easily and speedily if we fight hand in hand rather than against each other.

WHAT IS THE PRICE OF UNITY?

To speak of unity is one thing, but to actually achieve it is another. What, for example, can the Liberals concretely offer the new organisation? Will they, for example, embrace the principle of armed struggle? The actual participation or non-participation in violence is not necessarily an impediment to unity because a successful army is not only made up of its fighting soldiers, but also of its supporting forces made up of doctors, nurses, propaganda organs, cooks, transport drivers and factory workers. Thus, for those who do not desire to participate in violence there are many other important and necessary functions to fulfil in the struggle. What committees would Liberals expect to serve on in the new organisation? This would really depend on their positive contributions to the new organisation and the give and take and goodwill of the organisations that are prepared to merge their individual identities for the greater ideal.

The PAC has had a short and chequered legal career. It came into being in 1959, when it broke away from the ANC. It launched the 1960 anti-pass campaign that gave rise to the Sharpeville and Langa riots. This campaign resulted in many of its members being arrested, and shortly afterwards it was banned. Thus the organisation hardly had time to consolidate itself before it was driven underground. Some of its members are known to have participated in guerrilla activities up north but its total membership and its future potential to the struggle may be difficult to estimate because of its internal divisions. But when it has settled its internal divisions and consolidated itself then it can be an important force in the fight against racism.

The dominant organisation in the national struggle against apartheid at present is the ANC and its military wing, MK. The ANC was founded in 1912 and has used the whole gamut of political weapons in the struggle. These political actions ranged from active co-operation with the government in power with the hope of winning concessions to national strikes in which all the people were asked to observe a stay-at-home. Its political maturity stood it in good stead when it was banned. It soon consolidated itself and brought into action its underground machinery.

In December 1961 the ANC announced its military wing, MK, by launching a sabotage campaign, which the government succeeded in halting around 1964. But in the meantime, from the early 1960s, the ANC was already sending members for military training to other countries in Africa and the socialist bloc. This has resulted in the ANC launching its guerrilla movement.

The ANC has gone from strength to strength. It has repeatedly carried the struggle to the government inside and outside the country. It has political offices in many countries and it has militant members, some of whom are highly trained in military and non-military fields.

Thus anybody contemplating a common organisation made up of the serious anti-apartheid organisations will have to take into account these cold, sober and objective facts. Determined Liberals may be the political catalyst that can bring this about. This is a worthy challenge and task as it is in line with the goal of destroying apartheid. And if they should succeed, then they would have made a valuable contribution in bringing about a speedier destruction to this curse of racism, which blights our beautiful but unhappy country.

ANDIMBA TOIVO YA TOIVO

Andimba Toivo ya Toivo was born on 22 August 1924 at Omangudu village near Ondangwa in the Oshikoto region of Namibia. He attended the Ongwediva Industrial School for three years and graduated as a teacher at St Mary's School in 1950. He served as a teacher until 1951, when he left for Cape Town, South Africa.

In Cape Town he came into contact with members of various political organisations involved in the liberation struggle. He became a member, and later Deputy Chairman, of the Modern Youth Society, which was organised by progressive youth.

Together with Elias Tuhadeleni and other Namibians working in the Western Cape, he founded SWAPO. He was expelled from Cape Town and restricted to the north of Namibia, where he served as Organising Secretary of SWAPO. He was arrested and detained on several occasions. In 1966 he was arrested and taken to Pretoria, where he and other Namibians were tortured and interrogated. Altogether 37 of them were finally brought to trial under the Terrorism Act. Two were sentenced to five years' imprisonment, two were acquitted, and three were given suspended sentences. The others were sentenced to 20 years' and life imprisonment.

Andimba was released on 1 March 1984 and rejoined his colleagues in exile in September 1984. He became a member of the Politbureau and Central Committee and the Secretary General of SWAPO. After the first democratic election in Namibia he was appointed to the post of Minister of Mines and Energy in 1990. In 1999 he was appointed Minister of Labour.

ANDIMBA TOIVO YA TOIVO
BY KAGISO PAT MAUTLOA

PROFILE

Namibian political prisoners – all members of SWAPO – held a special position on Robben Island. South Africa, through the League of Nations mandates system, had virtually reduced Namibia to its colony.

Toivo and his comrades had been arrested in Namibia and then charged, sentenced and made to serve sentences in a foreign country for 'offences' perpetrated in their own country, Namibia. They had to determine a consistent approach to their imprisonment and therefore to the conditions under which they were incarcerated in South African prisons.

First, they held on to the principle that South Africa and its courts had no right to try them. It followed from this principle that South Africa had no right to hold them in South African prisons. The prison authorities tried their utmost to break down and erode this position of principle. When Namibian prisoners complained about conditions in prison, the authorities treated this as a *de facto* acknowledgement of South Africa's right to hold them in South African prisons. Led by Toivo, the Namibian prisoners therefore refused to raise any complaints. They stuck to their principles and demanded one thing: their immediate removal to Namibia.

At one stage Toivo was put into a cell across the quadrangle from us. He was kept almost entirely alone in that block of cells, consisting of about thirty single cells. Like all cells, it was about seven feet wide by seven-and-a-half feet long. The windows overlooking the corridor – a strip of four panes stacked vertically — were sealed and the two upper panes removed. There was also a two-pane window about seven feet above ground level, overlooking the communal section of the prison. For Toivo's incarceration in this cell, these two panes were painted black to prevent him having any view of the outside and the sky.

He was condemned to this cell for an indefinite period. His offence? During a late-night raid of our section a large number of warders had gone from cell to cell, forcing each prisoner to strip and stand naked while they searched his cell. From time to time the warders would assault the prisoner. Three warders led by a head warder, Carstens, entered Toivo's cell and the head warder descended on him, battering him with a series of vicious baton blows. Toivo retaliated – with a single blow he brought the head warder to the floor. Summoned before the prison authorities, he was charged with assaulting an officer. Toivo admitted throwing the punch, but demanded that they charge Carstens for the unprovoked assault on him instead.

Toivo remained in this cell, totally isolated. He was denied all reading material as well as the company of his fellow prisoners. We feared for his sanity. We smuggled news to him. And we urged him to lay a complaint against the conditions of his incarceration. Whenever a senior officer or the

National Commissioner of Prisons visited us, Mandela would take up the matter. On one occasion the National Commissioner went to Toivo and asked him whether he had any complaints. Toivo remained silent. The Commissioner then told Toivo that if he were to request his removal from the cell so that he could rejoin us he would facilitate this. Toivo had a simple response: 'You put me in this cell. You have the power to get me out of it. When you put me here you did not do so as a result of a request by me. I see no need for me to make a request for you to remove me from this cell.'

Eighteen months later, on the eve of a visit by the International Red Cross, the authorities took him out of the cell, removed all traces of the blackened windows, and brought Toivo over to rejoin us.

Then there was the time when Jimmy Kruger, then Minister of Justice and Prisons (the same Jimmy Kruger who in 1977 commented on the murder of Steve Biko in detention that '[his death] leaves me cold'), visited us on Robben Island. He had a long meeting with Mandela. In the course of this meeting Mandela urged him to see and hear Toivo.

Kruger called for Toivo and began aggressively with the statement, 'So you are from South West Africa.' Toivo interrupted and corrected him: 'Namibia'. Kruger insisted, 'South West Africa'. Toivo repeated: 'Namibia'. That was the sum total of their discussion. Toivo never got the chance to put his demand for their removal to Namibia, and Kruger never made the effort to hear Toivo.

In the course of the settlement process that led to elections and independence for Namibia, Toivo was released from prison in the mid-1980s. He was reunited with his SWAPO comrades and given a state reception in Lusaka by the President of Zambia, Dr Kenneth Kaunda. I was in the group of exiles who lined the walls of the reception hall. Toivo walked around shaking hands and hugging each one of us. Suddenly he spotted me and leapt across the room. The two of us hugged and embraced, and out of sheer joy set about play-fighting, punching and shoving and literally throwing each other around.

I woke the next morning with a fractured rib from one of his bear hugs. I suppose I can legitimately claim to have been tortured by the South African authorities and by my own comrade!

SWAPO LEADS NAMIBIA

ANDIMBA TOIVO YA TOIVO

The history of my country is shrouded in the distant past. The few published chronicles that do exist are either written by white men or are based on research conducted by white men. The young men and women of my people, who like young people in free societies should have undertaken the pioneering efforts of narrating the story of our past, have been denied the opportunity. They did not have the schools or the training to equip them. Those fortunate few, and they were only a fraction of a per cent, who did manage to acquire some education have been obliged to occupy themselves with the primary business of survival. Not for them is the luxury of the laboratory or the virgin fields of social research.

Much of what the white man has written is an echo of what has come down to us generation after generation by word of mouth. Close to a thousand years ago the Berg Damaras (a Negroid people whose language is Nama) were known to Namibians. In the twelfth century tribes of 'Bushmen' wandered freely across the lands, hunted the abundant game, imprinted their expectations and beliefs in marvellous rock paintings and made a niche for themselves in Namibian history. At about the same time the Khoi-khoi (or Hottentots) moved towards the coastal regions and made Namibia their home. Then from the northern lakes came the Ovambos, with their herds of cattle and their knowledge of agriculture and iron smelting, and settled in the northern parts. (Much later the whites arbitrarily cut a boundary line across the land occupied by the Ovambos, with the result that large numbers suddenly found themselves in a 'foreign' country, Angola.) The Ovambos were followed, according to white historians, by the Hereros who settled further south (though the indigenous story says that both the Ovambos and Hereros came together). The late venerable Chief Hosea Kutako, freedom fighter, patriot and elder statesman, told me that both the Ovambos and Hereros were grandchildren of Nangombi. Over the years Namibia came to be inhabited by an even richer variety of peoples, with unrelated backgrounds and differing tongues: Damaras, Basters, Okavangos, Caprivians, Kaokovelders, Coloureds and Tswanas. Although there was sporadic fighting and strife among some of these peoples, on the whole they had been living in harmony.

The first white man to set foot on Namibian soil was Bartholomeu Dias, who landed in 1487 in the bay he called Angra Pequena (now called Lüderitz, but which is known to our people as Okakovemia). At about the same time another Portuguese navigator, Diogo Cam, set up a cross at the place, which since came to be known as Cape Cross. But they were merely passing by. Then, 274 years later, in 1760, one Jacobus Coetzee came from the Cape, had a look around, and went back and reported on the large herds of cattle owned by the Nama and Herero people.

Henceforth white people began to cast their covetous eyes upon our country and its resources. Here can be traced the roots of South Africa's imperialist design. From here onwards there was constant pressure on the Cape and British government to annex Namibia. Hard on the heels of Coetzee came Hendrik Hop, who drew a map of the Orange River. In the early 1790s, Van Reenen and Brandt arrived at Okahandja, the Herero capital. They found copper in the Swakop River and thought it was gold. During this same decade Dutch and British navigators proclaimed Walvis Bay a possession of their respective governments. But neither government backed their claims.

In 1802 the London Missionary Society established a mission station at Warmbad. In 1840 the Rhenish Mission from Germany set up stations in Namaland and Damaraland. Whites from South Africa settled permanently in Namibia between 1875 and 1914.

In the mid-nineteenth century rich guano deposits were discovered on the islands off the Namibian coast and in 1861 they were annexed by the Cape government. In 1878 the British acquired Walvis Bay and about 400 miles of the territory adjoining it.

This was the period of the Scramble for Africa. White men in far-away Europe sat around conference tables, and divided, carved and distributed the African continent among themselves. They behaved with the nonchalance of banquet guests partaking of portions of tasty meats. The viewpoints of the indigenous people, their livelihood, their ways and customs, their very lives did not enter into their deliberations. Their eyes could only see the extension of their own countries to foreign continents and the amassing of riches. Thus it was that in 1884 a German warship arrived at Angra Pequena and proclaimed a protectorate over Namibia. The ostensible reason for this move was to secure the interests of Adolf Lüderitz, a German citizen who had set up a trading station at Angra Pequena two years previously. The Deutsche Kolonial Gesellschaft administered the territory until 1892, when it was formally taken over by the German government. During this period the 'protection' was extended over the whole of Namibia, including Walvis Bay.

The behaviour of the whites in Namibia followed the familiar pattern of colonisation – first there were journeys of exploration; then came the missionaries; these were followed by traders; and finally came the soldiers with guns, bringing with them permanent settlers.

From the beginning white encroachment was fiercely resisted by the people. In 1869 a party of whites from the Transvaal under Hendrik van Zyl explored the area around Ghanzi. The indigenous people immediately smelt danger and Hereros and Namas united to resist. Van Zyl was killed and the rest of the party forced to flee back to the Transvaal.

The 30 years of German rule witnessed the same determination of the indigenous people to resist white domination. The Witboois (Bondelswarts) were the first to revolt. They were only subjugated in 1894. The Hereros and Namas fought to preserve their system of communal land ownership against private ownership imposed by the Germans. This war lasted from 1904 to 1908. The Namas fought 295 battles, and the Hereros 88 battles against the Germans. Over 2 000 Germans lost their lives, but in the end their superior weapons triumphed. In the course of these battles the indigenous population was decimated. The Namas were reduced from 20 000 to 15 000, while of the 100 000 Hereros only 20 000 remained. The Ovambo Chief Nehale, hearing that the Germans had crossed the southern boundaries of Ovamboland, sent his army to go and push them back. He fought them at Namupuni. Later the brave Chief Mandumne, who resisted the Portuguese, fought the South African forces between 1916 and 1917.

Elsewhere on the continent other white men inflicted similar and often worse suffering upon the black people. And the world looked on, unconcerned.

It is the vastness of the land and the riches in its soil that brought the white man to Namibia. It is out of this greed that he obstinately refused to surrender the country to the people. The staggering 318 877 square miles that make up the surface of Namibia equal three-quarters of the area of South Africa. Namibia shares common boundaries with a number of countries. Its border with South Africa runs for 480 miles, with Botswana for 800 miles, with Zambia 150 miles, and with Angola 700 miles.

The soil of our country has yielded rich deposits of diamonds, lead, copper, zinc, tin, beryl, bismuth, manganese, phosphates, salt, marble and limestone. For years these have been mined and worked with the sweat of the labour of black people, but the product of our toil only helped to make the white man richer. Our people have continued to languish in poverty and illiteracy.

The First World War came and white men in distant Europe began to maim and kill one another. Our country, too, was dragged into this conflict. We had no say in the matter. Namibia was then German South West Africa. Germany was the principal belligerent power. So we, too, became involved in the war. Our nearest enemy country was South Africa and in 1915 soldiers from there marched in, fought and conquered our country. The war ended in 1918. The League of Nations was set up and in accordance with some complex calculations undertaken by the 'wise' statesmen who had gathered at Versailles we were declared a 'C Mandate' and handed over to South Africa, to 'promote to the utmost the material, moral and social well-being of the indigenous people'. We were not given away altogether as South Africa's property. German South West Africa disappeared and we were baptised South West Africa.

This only meant a change of masters, and we had to adapt ourselves to the ways and dictates of our new rulers. Save for the formality of receiving an annual report and the occasional investigation of a commission the League of Nations paid scant regard to our plight. In the course of one of these rare occasions when we were remembered, the Mandates Commission of the League questioned the policy of segregating Africans and confining them to reserves, and also remarked on the 'apparent assumption by the white population that Natives exist chiefly for the purpose of labouring for the whites'.

The new masters had arrived with new ways. Turning a blind eye to the poverty and suffering of human beings, one of the first things the new rulers sought to do was to teach us to give a new value to dogs. They imposed a dog tax. Our people could not quite grasp the import of this innovation. Besides, they were too poor to pay. But the masters would have their tax and they began to harass, coerce and force the people to pay. So the Bondelswarts, the very ones who were the first to rise against German oppression, once again led the path to resistance against the new persecutors. Mustering whatever weapons they could 600 warriors of the tribe, together with their women and children, rose in revolt. The South African forces reacted swiftly and viciously. Not satisfied with mowing down the people with machine guns, Prime Minister General Jan Smuts (world statesman and one of the founding fathers of the League of Nations) sent in aeroplanes to bomb the 'rebel' camp. Over one hundred warriors and several children were killed. The people's resistance was once again subdued. There were protests and voices of disapproval at this callous massacre. The League referred to it mildly as the 'Bondelswarts affair' but refused to condemn South Africa. Soon the plight of our people vanished into the recesses of the world's memory.

The years rolled by and we became a forgotten people, except by our 'guardians', who set out on a scheme to propagate 'civilised' values and ways among us. Thus, for instance, by 1938 they had succeeded in establishing a government school for the African people with an enrolment of 93 pupils. In addition the missionaries ran 75 schools with 4 512 pupils. The attitude of the South African government towards education was stated by the Administrator of South West Africa in 1926, who declared that the aim was 'to develop the Native on his own lines, that is in his own language, with his own habits and mode of living in so far as these are not in conflict with the great general principles on which civilisation rests. Any attempt to force him to abandon his native customs and to give him instead the aspirations and outlook of life of the Europeans is to be deprecated ... The method of achieving this aim is to help him develop step by step from his present raw Native state. Any desire to show early results by making him skip a number of rungs in the ladder of progress is unsound and bound to have disastrous results in the end.' During 1938 and 1939 the government spent £134 529 on the education of the children of 30 000 whites and the magnanimous sum of £17 000 on the children of 300 000 blacks!

Of the total land surface of over 82 million hectares, 17 499 577 hectares were given to the blacks and 25 614 210 hectares to white farmers. The remainder of the 82 million hectares also belonged to the whites in the form of urban areas, game reserves and unalienated Crown lands. This was the position in 1937. By 1962 the area of land occupied by blacks had increased to 21 964 178 hectares.

From the outset, blacks were excluded from government and administration. At first the country was ruled by an Administrator, assisted by an advisory council of six – all whites – one of whom had to be an expert on matters concerning the blacks. Then in 1926 a Legislative Assembly, Executive Committee and Advisory Council were established – again all were whites. The Legislative Assembly was, however, not empowered to legislate for the blacks. 'Native Affairs' were the concern of the Administrator, who ruled by proclamation. Naturally the most pernicious of South Africa's racial laws, including passes and influx control, were proclaimed.

In 1939 the Second World War broke out. The South African government appealed to the people of Namibia to join the war effort and to help crush the monster of Nazism. Lofty promises were made to us, including the return of the land to the indigenous people. In 1941 Chief

Hosea Kutako and his councillors undertook a tour of the reserves to mobilise the people on the side of the Allies. Many responded with enthusiasm. I, too, was carried away and decided to make my little contribution for the defence of 'democracy' and 'freedom'. After six years the war ended and we waited with great hopes for the fulfilment of the promises. But alas! It turned out to be just another one of the white man's promises. We who volunteered were rewarded with a measly £30 and subsequently with apartheid. Our country was almost surrendered to South Africa as a gift. Our dreams and hopes were crushed. Life remained much the same as before.

From the time the South African forces conquered German South West Africa in 1915 there have been persistent attempts to incorporate the territory into South Africa. At Versailles General Smuts made a bold attempt and almost succeeded. The British supported him, but President Woodrow Wilson of the USA thwarted the scheme. Through the years the clamour for incorporation grew apace, and moves were made to take over Namibia as the fifth province of South Africa.

In 1946 General Smuts went to the first session of the United Nations in New York. Again he was confident that the new world body would, in deference to his prestige as world states-man and his authorship of the preamble of the UN Charter, reward him with the long-coveted but elusive ties. Indeed, he as much as promised his countrymen that he would return from New York with South West Africa in his bag. But he had reckoned without the tremendous upsurge for freedom that had swept through the oppressed peoples of the world. Prime Minister Jawarlal Nehru's sister, Mrs Vijayalakshmi Pandit, represented newly independent India. She happily accepted the assistance and advice of the delegation of the South African Indian Congress (SAIC), who had travelled to New York to help secure world condemnation of South African racism.

The people of Namibia were prevented from sending their own delegates to New York. So Chief Hosea Kutako delegated the fighting clergyman to deputise for him. Reverend Michael Scott had recently been released after serving three months in prison for taking part in the Passive Resistance Campaign conducted by the SAIC in South Africa. The Indian Congress gave him invaluable assistance. In New York he left no stone unturned to lobby the delegates and acquaint them with the real feelings of the people of Namibia. Also present from South Africa was Dr Alfred Xuma, President of the African National Congress (ANC), who, together with the SAIC delegates, assisted Reverend Scott. Andrei Vyshinsky represented the Soviet Union. At that time there were only three independent states in Africa: Ethiopia, Liberia and Egypt.

When South Africa came up for discussion as an item on the agenda, Mrs Pandit and Mr Vyshinsky led the attack and exposed the brutality, injustice and racist practices of the South African government in Namibia. Thereafter all the pleadings of General Smuts and the assis-tance rendered to him by the imperialist powers were of no avail. The General Assembly reject-ed his attempts at incorporation and sent him home empty-handed.

The late Tshekedi Khama of what was then Bechuanaland also gave much valuable assis-tance to the cause of Namibian freedom. In particular, we recall with gratitude his advice and his moral and material support to Reverend Scott to facilitate the mission to the UN.

In 1948 the Nats came to power in South Africa. They had long pressed for unilateral action in the incorporation of Namibia. In 1949 they passed legislation that gave the whites of Namibia direct representation in the South African Parliament. In the same year they declared Reverend Scott a prohibited immigrant in South Africa. In 1954 the affairs of the black people of Namibia were placed under the direct control of the South African Bantu Administration Department. All the evils and inhumanity of apartheid were now to be extended to Namibia. Nat cabinet Minister Eric Louw had earlier informed the UN that South Africa would no longer submit annual reports on South West Africa. At the same time he told reporters in New York that his government was resolved to keep the control of his own country and the mandated territory of South West Africa in the hands of 'representatives of European culture' lest it falls into the hands of a 'black proletariat with strong communist backing'.

The attitude of the Nats towards the Namibian people was to be but an echo of what the South West African Administrator had said in 1926 with regard to education. The object was unmistakably to keep the black people in a state of perpetual subservience as hewers of wood and drawers of water. Meanwhile the future of Namibia became a perennial issue at the UN. Twice the International Court of Justice was solicited to rule on the technicalities of international law. But no relief was forthcoming from that direction.

In 1957 Ghana won her freedom, and Kwame Nkrumah became President. A wave of excitement, pride and encouragement swept across the continent. 1960 became Africa's year as almost 20 states gained independence. Others joined in quick succession, including some mandated territories. Prime Minister Harold Macmillan referred to this as the 'winds of change' when he addressed the South African Parliament.

After centuries of slavery and exploitation the African giant was standing up to take its rightful place alongside the free people of the world. The names of Kwame Nkrumah, Ben Bella, Patrice Lumumba, Gamal Abdel Nasser and Jomo Kenyatta became household words and they were hailed in the same way as Jawarlal Nehru, Ahmed Sukarno, Mao Tse Tung, Fidel Castro and Martin Luther King were hailed by the peoples of Asia and Latin America and by black Americans.

Within a short time the African states combined to form the Organisation of African Unity (OAU) and inevitably they joined together with the countries of Asia to form the Afro-Asian bloc at the UN and other world bodies. The whole character of the UN began to change. The cause of Namibia now assumed a new importance in world affairs. The Soviet Union and the socialist countries that President Samora Machel rightly referred to as the natural allies of the oppressed people invariably supported the Afro-Asian bloc. The General Assembly and the Security Council passed stronger resolutions on Namibia. In 1966 the Assembly revoked South Africa's mandate over Namibia. Calls were made to the Security Council for more drastic measures to force South Africa to quit Namibia. Because of the machinations and obstructive tactics of imperialist powers, little came of these resolutions.

In the wake of the winds of change the people of Namibia, too, began to feel the urgent need for a political organisation to lead their struggle for freedom. On 3 August 1957 the South West Africa People's Organisation (SWAPO) was formed in Cape Town. Elias Tuhadeleni and I were among its founding members. Soon its message and its organisation were carried into Namibia. Another organisation, the South West Africa National Union (SWANU) also came into being. Both SWAPO and SWANU were open to all the people of Namibia, but it is doubtful whether any whites joined them. The whites have yet to produce people of the calibre of Jack Simons, Bram Fischer, Brian Bunting, Joel Carlson, Alan Paton, Dennis Goldberg, Helen Joseph, Ray Alexander and many others who have without reservation thrown in their lot with the liberation struggle in South Africa. In Namibia young men organised themselves into student social groups, which were later converted to organs of political bodies.

SWAPO's policy is to weld the people of Namibia into one nation and to bring the struggle for freedom and independence to a victorious conclusion.

The Nat government, sensing that pressures from all sides were building up against South Africa, took measures in the hope of maintaining its stranglehold on Namibia. In 1962 the Odendaal Commission was appointed to inquire into various aspects of the lives of the Namibian people and to make recommendations for a five-year plan for the accelerated development of the black people in the reserves and urban areas. The Commission produced its report in 1964. As expected, it came forward with a diabolical plan for the imposition of Bantustans in Namibia. The policies of separate development were to be more rigidly and rapidly applied. It made no bones about the fact that the whites would remain masters over Namibia. It recommended the extension of the land area occupied by the blacks from 21 964 178 to 32 629 364 hectares. The remaining 50 million hectares were to be retained by the whites.

Hosea Kutako immediately expressed his disapproval of the report. Other black groups and political organisations in Namibia did likewise. The Special Committee on Apartheid of the UN declared that the 'interpretation given by the Odendaal Commission to the term self-determination made it meaningless.'

The South African authorities ignored the feelings and interests of the people of Namibia and in defiance of world opinion proceeded to create Bantustans. They relied on the support of discredited chiefs and other elements. The people of Namibia began to rally in greater numbers behind SWAPO and rejected the Bantustans. SWAPO intensified its activities for freedom and independence in one undivided country.

South Africa was bent on remaining in Namibia and continued to move towards a head-on collision with the people. In order to facilitate the work of their stooges and hirelings they unleashed a campaign of repression against all who opposed them. SWAPO was singled out for victimisation. Ever since it was established in 1957, SWAPO has been striving to conduct its activities in a non-violent manner. Under increasingly difficult conditions, and in spite of harassment and provocation, SWAPO continued the task of mobilising the people. The South African government increased its use of violence. We could no longer hold peaceful meetings;

our members were hounded and forced to lead miserable lives. Guns were issued to chiefs and headmen and were being freely used against us. Many of our members were forced to flee and take refuge in Botswana, Zambia and Tanzania. Wholesale persecution continued and at last our patience reached breaking point. Our honour and self-respect as a people demanded that we stand up against the oppressor. SWAPO was left with no alternative but to take up arms and meet the enemy on its own terms. Our responsibility to our members and our obligation to the people made it incumbent on us to train and equip our young men to meet the situation. We dared not allow them to be constantly mauled, batoned and shot without making an effort to defend them.

In a desperate effort to preserve white supremacy in southern Africa the Nat regime forged a close alliance with the Portuguese colonialists and the racist Rhodesian minority government. These reactionary forces combined their resources against the freedom struggle. SWAPO realised that the only way to beat this unholy alliance was by uniting and working in closest co-operation with other liberation movements in neighbouring countries. Therefore SWAPO formed a firm alliance with its sister organisations, the ANC of South Africa, the MPLA of Angola, Frelimo of Mozambique, ZAPU of Zimbabwe and PAIGC of Guinea-Bissau and the Cape Verde Islands. We know that this mighty united force is sure to triumph. Here again the states of free Africa and the socialist countries rendered every assistance. In 1965 the first trained soldiers of SWAPO began to infiltrate Namibia. Training camps, where local youth were given elementary training in guerrilla warfare, were set up under the leadership of Elias Tuhadeleni and J. Otto Nankudhu. On 26 August 1966 the South African police made a surprise attack on one such camp in Ovamboland. In the fighting that ensued, two freedom fighters were killed and one wounded. Eight men were taken into custody. Further arrests followed and eventually 37 of us were tried and sentenced in Pretoria. This was a further temporary setback for our movement.

Soon activities started again and the youth of Namibia continued to leave the country in ever larger numbers to undergo military training. Many also received political training while yet other young men and women were trained in various academic fields. SWAPO now has a considerable fighting force and guerrilla activity has begun with renewed vigour.

In the past two years, historic developments have taken place that fill us with pride and confidence, hope and determination. SWAPO's sister organisations have had resounding victories and as this is being written the PAIGC is occupying the seat of power in Guinea-Bissau, Frelimo in Mozambique and the MPLA in Angola. It is also gratifying to learn of intensified activities in Rhodesia and the mounting success of the Zimbabwe People's Liberation army. The racist regime of Smith will crumble under the victorious forces of the Zimbabwean people, and majority rule will be achieved.

At this late hour the South African racists are still desperately engaged in attempts to thwart the freedom forces. So-called 'constitutional talks' have been initiated with the aim of creating various Bantustans. In this way South Africa is hoping not only to perpetuate its racist policies but also to maintain indirect control over the lives of the Namibian people and their country.

But it is too late. Time has run out for apartheid and racism. As in Angola, Mozambique and Guinea-Bissau the freedom army of Namibia is sure to frustrate these evil designs, and lead the people to victory. SWAPO will be only too glad to participate in free elections or talks supervised by the OAU and the UN. South Africa must quit Namibia. Let the people of Namibia decide their own future. Even now we hope that the South African racists will come to their senses and quit Namibia, thereby preventing further unnecessary bloodshed and destruction, which will certainly yield a harvest of hate and bitterness.

The policy of SWAPO is clear. We believe in equality of opportunities for all men and women, irrespective of race, colour or creed. We believe the people of Namibia should have the right to full and unfettered franchise, and to live where they choose in our undivided country. Our country is big, its resources large, and our population small. We need the united effort of one Namibian nation to undertake the task of building our country for the future. The path of Bantustans is the path of disunity, division and discord. SWAPO's ideal in the building of one Namibian nation is to eliminate the conditions that give rise to and perpetuate group thinking. We realise that years of racist rule have succeeded to instil erroneous ideas in the minds of many people and a long process of re-education will be necessary to eradicate these false notions. SWAPO declares that the whites would have nothing to fear in the new Namibia. Full equality before the law is guaranteed for all people. It has never been in the past nor is it now the policy of SWAPO to drive the whites out of Namibia or to persecute them for the colour of their skin. All that is expected of them, as of all citizens, is the disavowal of racism in any form and the expression of loyalty to the new state. At the same time all will have to bear in mind that firm action will be taken against those who violate the laws of the country. Racial discrimination will be banned and will not be tolerated. Neither the whites nor any other group should expect to receive preferential treatment. The slightest indication of sabotage or obstruction to the policy of progress of the new state will be dealt with severely. In the new Namibia, the state will guarantee freedom of speech, assembly and worship. Great care, however, will have to be taken to ensure that this freedom is not abused.

As to what political form the new Namibia should take, this matter is obviously to be decided by the people of Namibia and their political organisation. However, in my view, in building the new state we should take the fullest advantage of the experiences of other emancipated people and apply the lessons learnt. We should take note of the difficulties and problems they have encountered as well as their approach towards finding solutions. We must take a close look at the independent countries of Africa and Asia, as well as the Soviet Union, China, Cuba and other socialist countries. Based on this wealth of experience we must endeavour to build a society that will ensure the complete elimination of the evils of colonialism, racism, class oppression, hunger, poverty, illiteracy and disease. We must strive to build a society where there will be complete fulfilment of our cherished dreams of universal education, full employment, planned production, proper health schemes and unending opportunity for the fullest development of a healthy cultural and recreational life.

A free Namibia will be honoured to join the OAU that binds all the people of Africa into one large brotherhood. In spite of the setbacks and difficulties, the years since its foundation have proved the great need for such a body. It has made a tremendous contribution to welding and maintaining the unity and solidarity of this continent. Above all, it has been a source of inspiration and invaluable assistance to the cause of the freedom forces. In world affairs, through its co-operation with the Asian and Latin American countries, the OAU has helped to make a significant contribution to maintaining world peace. Events such as the historic Lusaka Conference of Non Aligned States in 1969 have made it clear to imperialist warmongers that the people of these three continents will not be party to any war designs. Only in peace can there be a guarantee of progress.

A free Namibia will also join the UN and take its place in the world family of nations. Although in many ways the body has not lived up to expectations, particularly of the oppressed peoples, it has nevertheless made an undeniable contribution towards lessening world tensions.

In my opinion the greatest friends of a free Namibia will continue to be the people of the socialist countries, and in order to develop our country to its fullest potential we will have to enter into the closest economic, political and cultural relations with them. It will also be necessary to maintain normal, healthy diplomatic and economic relations with the countries of the West. It has been gratifying to learn that growing numbers of people in the Western countries have been prepared to accept SWAPO as the mouthpiece of the people of Namibia. In view of the history of close association with South Africa, the idea of establishing relations with it will have to be decided upon by the people of Namibia. This new relationship will have to be on terms of complete equality and in consonance with our dignity and self-respect.

As this is being written, young men and women of Namibia are bravely risking and sacrificing their lives in the battle against South African racism. It must be expected that the enemy will do everything to weaken and undermine our struggle. In addition to direct confrontation they will continue to utilise elements from among our people to achieve their nefarious designs. We have to be constantly on our guard. We must build up and maintain the strongest bonds of unity among our people. There is not the least doubt that victory is in sight. How soon we shall achieve it will to a large extent depend on how united we are. There is also a great need for unity among the political organisations. On examining the aims and programmes of SWAPO and SWANU in particular it is clear that their outlook on fundamental questions is in many ways the same. We should ask ourselves whether the time has not come for them to work in close co-operation with a view to merging. The continued disunity among the forces of freedom can only be of advantage to the enemy.

The cause of our freedom enjoys the wholehearted support of people throughout the whole world. It is up to us to strike the final blows against the forces of racism and reaction and to establish a free, independent, socialist Namibia.

ABOUT THE EDITOR

Sathyandranath Ragunanan ('Mac') Maharaj was born on 22 April 1935 at Newcastle in Natal. He became active in the political struggle in 1953 while attending the University of Natal, Non-European Section, Durban. He became a reporter for *New Age*, and took over as its manager for Natal when M.P. Naicker was among the accused in the Treason Trial. He went abroad in August 1957 and studied at the London School of Economics. In the United Kingdom he was a founding member of the South African Freedom Association and succeeded Solly Sachs as its secretary. He was also a founding member of the Anti-Apartheid Movement. He left the United Kingdom to undergo training in the German Democratic Republic in 1961 and returned to South Africa in May 1962 to serve underground. He was arrested in July 1964 and charged with Wilton Mkwayi and four others in what was known as the Little Rivonia Trial. He was sentenced to 12 years' imprisonment.

He was released in December 1976 and immediately served with a five-year house arrest order. He escaped into exile in July 1977 and was appointed Secretary of the Internal Political and Reconstruction Department of the ANC in December 1977. This department was mandated to create and maintain the underground ANC within South Africa and to supervise the mass mobilisation of the people within the country. He served on the Revolutionary Council and its successor, the Politico-Military Council of the ANC, since 1979. He was first elected to the National Executive Committee of the ANC in 1985 and re-elected in 1991, 1994 and 1997. He was a member of the South African Communist Party from 1958 to 1990, and served on the Central Committee (1963–1964, and 1978–1990) and the Politbureau. He retired from the SACP in 1990.

From 1988 to 1990 he was stationed underground within South Africa as the overall commander of 'Operation Vula'. He was arrested in July 1990 after he had received indemnity in May 1990. He and nine others were brought to trial in December 1990. The charges were dropped in March 1991. He became part of the ANC negotiating team in 1991, and was appointed joint secretary of the negotiating process. He was also joint secretary, with Fanie van der Merwe, of the Transitional Executive Council, which oversaw South Africa's transition to democracy.

After South Africa's first democratic election in April 1994 he was appointed Minister of Transport in the government led by President Nelson Mandela (1994–1999). He retired from Parliament in the 1999 election.

He obtained a BA from the University of Natal (1956) and a B. Admin. from the University of South Africa (1969).

Mac Maharaj is a member of the Board of Directors of FirstRand Holding Group, FirstRand Bank, Discovery Health and Softline Ltd, and is a trustee of the Nelson Mandela Foundation.

MAC MAHARAJ
BY KAGISO PAT MAUTLOA

ABOUT THE ARTISTS

BEN ARNOLD

Born 1942, Albertsville, Johannesburg

EDUCATION
1957–1959 Polly Street Art Centre (Skotnes)
1959–1961 Jubilee Art Centre (Khumalo)

SOLO EXHIBITIONS
1964 Guenther Gallery, Johannesburg
1966 Fielding Gallery, Johannesburg
1967 Avant Garde Gallery, Johannesburg
1968 USIS Auditorium, Johannnesburg
1969 Lidchi Art Gallery, Johannesburg
1970 Lidchi Art Gallery, Johannesburg
1971 Bosmont Recreational Centre, Johannesburg
1975 National Museum and Art Gallery, Botswana
1977 New Day, YWCA, Dube, Johannesburg
1979 Lidchi Art Gallery, Johannesburg

GROUP EXHIBITIONS
1968 CAP Festival, Cape Town; Argus Building, Cape Town; Lidchi Gallery, Johannesburg
1969 Polly Street Artists, Helen de Leeuw
1971 *Mother and Child*, Gallery 101
1972 Sculpture T.V.L., Gallery 101; 25 South African Artists, Gallery 21
1977 Festac, (Second World Black & African Festival of Arts & Culture), Nigeria
1978 National Museum and Art Gallery, Tuka Cultural Unit, Botswana
1979 *Renaissance II '79*. SAAA, Johannesburg and Pretoria
1981 *Black Art Today*, Jabulani Standard Bank, Soweto
1982 *Art Toward Social Development*, National Museum & Art Gallery, Botswana

1983 *SA Contemporary Art*, Milner Park, Johannesburg
1984 MAACA, Sunny Park, Pretoria
1985 *Tributaries*, Johannesburg
1986–1988 *Workshop Exhibitions*, DAMP Diepmeadow Town Council Cultural Organisation
1990 FUBA Gallery, Johannesburg
1993 *Land and Lives*, SAAA, Pretoria
1997 *Bag Factory Artists*, Sandton Civic Gallery, Johannesburg
1998 *Bag Factory Artists*, Bag Factory Gallery, Johannesburg
1999 *Urban Futures*, Bag Factory Gallery, Johannesburg
2000 *The Collection*, Bag Factory Gallery, Johannesburg
2000 *The Auction*, Goodman Gallery, Johannesburg
2001 *The Big Bag Show*, Goodman Gallery, Johannesburg

BONGI BENGU

Born 1970, Eshowe, KwaZulu-Natal

EDUCATION
1987 International School of Geneva, Switzerland
1987–1989 Waterford Kamhlaba, Mababane, Swaziland
1989–1993 BA (cum laude): Mount Vernon College, Washington, USA
1989–1994 M(FA): University of Cape Town, South Africa

AWARDS
1992 National Museum of African Art, Washington DC: Certificate of Recognition
1993 Mount Vernon College: Arts and Humanities; Fine Arts Award
1995–1997 University of Cape Town: AW Mellon Scholarship

1995–1998 University of Cape Town: CSD Scholarship

1996 Standard Bank Award: Trainee Curator at SA National Gallery, Cape Town

EXHIBITIONS

1996 *Cognisance: The Creative Cape*, Association of Visual Arts, Cape Town

1997 *La Bohème Noir*, Primart Gallery, Cape Town; *Survivors in Search of a Voice*, Johannesburg; *Art Salon*, Bay Hotel, Cape Town; *Solo Exhibition*, AVA, Cape Town; *South African Landscapes*, Primart Gallery, Cape Town

1998 *Solo Exhibition*, Spier, Cape Town; *Exhibition*, The A.R.T. Gallery, Cape Town

1998–1999 *Sicula Fixhentsa Xa Sisonke*, Travelling Exhibition, USA; *Family Ties*, Sandton Civic Gallery, Johannesburg; *Art Salon*, Bay Hotel, Cape Town

1999 *Group Exhibition*, AVA, Cape Town; *Bloodlines*, Karoo National Arts Festival, Oudtshoorn

2000 *Hourglass Project: A Woman's Vision*, Atlanta, Georgia

PROJECTS/WORKSHOPS

1999 Printmaking Workshop in London with master printer Jack Sheriff

COLLECTIONS

Sandton Civic Gallery, Johannesburg; Florida A&M University, Tallahasse, Florida, USA; Spier, Stellenbosch; MTN, Johannesburg Private Collections

DAVID KOLOANE

Born 1938, Johannesburg

EDUCATION

1986 Museum Studies Diploma, University of London, UK

SOLO EXHIBITIONS

1993 *Made in South Africa*, Goodman Gallery, Johannesburg

1994 *Made in South Africa*, Goodman Gallery, Johannesburg

SELECTED GROUP EXHIBITIONS

1993 45th Venice Biennale, Venice, Italy

1993 *Southern Cross*, Stedelik Museum, Amsterdam, Holland

1994 5th Havana Biennale, Havana, Cuba

1995 *Artiste Sud Africaine*, Galerie de Ballens, Switzerland

SELECTED AWARDS AND NOMINATIONS

1993 Finalist, V.O. Martell Award

1994 Quarterly Award Winner (second quarter), Vita Art Now

1998 Prince Claus Fund Award

KAGISO PAT MAUTLOA

Born 1952, Ventersdorp

EDUCATION

Leratong Primary School, Morris Isaacson Seconday and High School

1966–1973 Jubilee Art Centre, Johannesburg; Mofolo Art Centre, Soweto

1978–1979 Fine Art Diploma at ELC Art Centre, Rorke's Drift, Natal, South Africa

SOLO EXHIBITIONS

1995 *Unlocked*, Goodman Gallery, Johannesburg

1999 *Kagiso in Johannesburg*, Goodman Gallery, Johannesburg

TWO-PERSON SHOWS

1996 *If you Scratch*, with David Koloane, Gallery on the Round, Grahamstown and at Goodman Gallery, Johannesburg

GROUP SHOWS

1982 National Art Museum, Botswana

1983 *Schwarze Kunst aus Südafrika*, Germany

1984 FUBA/USSALEP, Thupelo Inauguration

1985 *Transitional Art*, Goodman Gallery, Johannesburg

1988 *Neglected Tradition*, touring show

1989 Third Cuban Biennale

1991 *Impressions of our World*, New York City; *Painted People, Painted Spaces*, Newtown Galleries, Johannesburg; *Made in August*, Newtown Galleries, Johannesburg

1992 *ICA – Inaugural Exhibition*, Newtown, Johannesburg; *Processed Image*, Newtown Galleries, Johannesburg; *Vita Art Now*, Johannesburg Art Gallery

1993 *Millenniums*, Newtown Galleries, Johannesburg, Everard Read Contemporary Gallery, Johannesburg; *Garfolies '93*, First Abidjan Biennale, Côte d'Ivoire

1994 *Bring the Ballot*, Rembrandt Van Rijn Gallery, Johannesburg; *Un Art Contemporain d'Afrique du Sud*, Association Francaise d'Action, the Grand Arche, Paris; *Deutsche Aerospace*, Munich, in collaboration with Mercedes-Benz SA; *Contemporary Art from South Africa*, Ottobrun, Munich, Germany; *Habitat Show*, Newtown Galleries, Johannesburg

1995 *Hassan, Koloane and Mautloa*, Newtown Galleries for Africus '95 first Johannesburg Biennale; *Vita Art Now*, Johannesburg Art Gallery; Venice Biennale, Italy; *On the Road – Africa '95*, Delfina Studio Trust, Bernie Jacobson Gallery, London, UK

1996 *Colours – Art from South Africa*, House of World Cultures, Berlin, Germany; *Hitch-hiker*, Generator Art Space, Newtown (AICA), Johannesburg

1997 *Lift Off*, Inaugural Exhibition of the Goodman Gallery, Johannesburg; Michel Luneau Gallery, Nantes, France; *Alternating Currents*, Second Johannesburg Biennale – *Trade Routes: History and Geography*, Johannesburg; *Vita Art Now*, collaboration with Kay Hassan, Sandton Civic Art Gallery, Johannesburg

1999 *AFRIQUES*, Group photography show at La Musee de la Photographie a Charleroi, Belgium

2000 Three-man Show, AVA, Cape Town

INTERNATIONAL ARTISTS' WORKSHOPS
Thupelo, Johannesburg/Cape Town, South Africa; Triangle, New York State; Thapong, Botswana; Robert Blackburn, New York City; Triangle, Cuba; Koj, Modinagar, India

PUBLIC COLLECTIONS
University of Fort Hare, University of Zululand, Johannesburg Art Museum, Tatham Art Gallery, Readers Digest, Several Private Collections, Meridian Biao Bank (South Africa), International Bank for Development and Reconstruction, The Sandton Town Council

SELECTED PUBLICATIONS AND CATALOGUES
Fotofest Catalogue, Colours Catalogue, Vita Art Now '92, Flash Art, Vita Art Now '97, Dakar Biennale '99

Havell, J. (ed.) (1995) *Seven Stories (Africa '95) – About Modern Art in Africa*: Catalogue, Whitechapel, London
Williamson, S. & Jamal, A. (1996) *Art in South Africa – The Future Present*. David Philip Publishers, Cape Town and Johannesburg
De Bord, M. (ed.) (1997) *Trade Routes: History and Geography – Second Johannesburg Biennale*, Greater Johannesburg Metropolitan Council, Johannesburg, and The Prince Claus Fund for Culture and Development, Hague

SAM NHLENGETHWA

Born 1955, Payneville, Springs

EDUCATION
1976 Art Foundation, Johannesburg
1977–1978 Fine Art Diploma, Rorke's Drift Centre

SOLO EXHIBITIONS
1993 NSA Gallery, Durban
1994 Grahamstown Arts Festival, Grahamstown
1995 Goodman Gallery, Johannesburg
1996 *Mine Trip*, Goodman Gallery, Johannesburg
1997 *Interiors*, Goodman Gallery, Johannesburg

SELECTED GROUP EXHIBITIONS

1985 Tributaries Exhibition, Johannesburg

1986 Academy Gallery, Paris, France

1987 Gallery 409, Baltimore, USA

1990 Goodman Gallery, Johannesburg; Fuba Gallery, Johannesburg; Cassirer Fine Art, Johannesburg

1996 Whitechapel Gallery, London

1997 Grafiska, Sällskapets Galleri, Stockholm, Sweden

SELECTED AWARDS AND NOMINATIONS

1991 Triangle International Workshop, New York, USA

1992 Delfina Studio Trust Summer award, London, UK

1993 Standard Bank Young Artist Award

1994 TENQ African Workshop, Senegal

1995 African Studies Association conference, Florida, USA

1996 First National Bank Vita Awards nominee, Johannesburg

NKOSANA DOMINIC TSHABANGU

Born 1965, Soweto, South Africa

EDUCATION

1982–1984 Open School, Johannesburg (under the guidance of Phillip Malumise and Vincent Baloyi)

1985–1989 African Institute of Art based at Funda Centre, Johannesburg

1990–1992 Certificate in Fine Arts. Studied under the guidance of Sokhaya Charles Nkosi

1993 Teachers' Certificate in Visual Art, Johannesburg Art Foundation

EXHIBITIONS

1986–1992 Student Annual Exhibitions at Funda Centre, Johannesburg

1987 Group Exhibition, Wits Gallery, Johannesburg

1990 Group show, Shareworld Art Gallery, Johannesburg

1992 Grahamstown Festival, Grahamstown; Cape Town Grop Show, Cape Town

1993 Development Bank Group Show; Pretoria Art Museum; Sandton Civic Centre Gallery.

1994 Berman Gallery, Johannesburg

1995 Everard Read Gallery, Johannesburg; African Johannesburg Biennale; Museo de Arte, Contmoraneo

1997 One-man show in Santiago, Chile; One-man show in Amsterdam, Holland; Group exhibition in Belgium

AWARDS

1993 Bertrams V.O. Most Promising Young Artist Award; Certificate of Merit Award

1994 Bertrams V.O. Art of Africa Finalists' Award

1997 Thami Mnyele Scholarship

WORKSHOPS

1991 Workshop at rural areas in Transkei, South Africa

1992 Participated in Plastic Painting with Luca Gasser from Lugano, Switzerland; Papier Mâché course with Michael-Bethe Sclassie from Ethiopia

1993–1994 Part-time art tutor at Open School, Johannesburg

1994 Participated in workshop in visual art teaching, Nelspruit, South Africa

1998 Mural Painting, Haarlem in Amsterdam, Holland

NOTES

MAC MAHARAJ: WHERE THOUGHT REMAINED UNPRISONED

1   Nelson Mandela's contribution titled 'Whither the Black Consciousness Movement? An Assessment' was written and smuggled out in 1978.

2   This section of the prison consisted of single cells. There were 86 cells split into three wings, which overlooked a quadrangle. Generally it housed between 30 and 40 prisoners, the core being the seven Rivonia trialists, led by Nelson Mandela. At the beginning it was called the 'isolation' section; then the 'segregation' section; later, the 'single cells'; and finally it became known as 'B' section.

3   After I left prison, the prison authorities accidentally found a substantial part of the autobiography buried in the prison yard. Mandela, Sisulu and Kathrada, whose handwriting appeared in these notes, were punished by having their study privileges withdrawn for the rest of their imprisonment. Their study privileges were restored three or four years later.

4   The notes were successfully smuggled out of prison when I was released. They were handed over to Mandela after he was released in 1990. He used them as the core of his autobiography published in 1994 under the title *Long Walk to Freedom* by Little, Brown & Co., London (United Kingdom).

5   Using the script of the Khoisan language of the /Xam people, and literally meaning 'Diverse people unite.'

NELSON MANDELA: CLEAR THE OBSTACLES AND CONFRONT THE ENEMY

1   Anthony Sampson, *Mandela*, London: Harper Collins, United Kingdom, 1999, p. 245.

2   Jan van Riebeeck was appointed Governor of the Cape by the Dutch East India Company in 1652, a date that marks the beginning of colonial rule in South Africa.

3   The National Party, also referred to as the NP, stood for white Afrikaner rule and apartheid. The abbreviation 'Nat' is also used to denote a member of the NP.

4   The Freedom Charter was adopted at a conference attended by over 3 000 delegates who came from all parts of South Africa. They met at Kliptown, outside Johannesburg, on 26 June 1955. The Charter was subsequently adopted by the ANC and all constituent members of the Congress Alliance as their blueprint for a future South Africa.

5   This dispute, which surfaced in the late 1950s and early 1960s between the Soviet Union and the People's Republic of China, split the countries that had proclaimed themselves socialist, as well as the communist movement throughout the world.

6   There were white political prisoners who belonged to other political formations (such as the National Liberation Committee (NLC)/African Resistance Movement (ARM)), but all of them had been released by 1976.

7   The ideology of apartheid prescribed the physical separation of the population in terms of race (white, African, Coloured and Asian/Indian) as well as into ethnic groups in the case of Africans. On the basis of ethnicity the African people were to be separated into 11 groups, each with its own geographic area called a 'homeland', and later edified by the term 'Bantustan', because all 11 ethnic groups were part of the Bantu-speaking people.

8   The Spear of the Nation.

9   Its membership was drawn mainly from the ranks of the Liberal Party and the National Union of South African Students (NUSAS). It later changed its name to the African Resistance Movement (ARM). It ceased to exist shortly after the arrests.

10 From the age of 16, Africans were required to carry a 'pass book' on their person at all times, which indicated the bearer's identity, whether the bearer had permission to be in an area and for how long, etc. Failure to produce this 'pass book' on demand was a criminal offence. It was the most hated symbol of oppression.

11 Balthazar Johannes Vorster was Prime Minister of South Africa from 1965 to 1978.

12 Felix Houphouet-Boigny was head of the Ivory Coast from the time it gained independence from French rule.

13 Violet and Eli Weinberg, with their daughter Sheila.

14 Oliver Tambo was Acting President of the ANC at the time.

15 Potlako Leballo, then Chairman of the PAC.

16 Dr Yusuf Dadoo, Chairman of the SACP and leader of the South African Indian Congress; Reginald September, leader of the South African Coloured People's Congress; Lionel 'Rusty' Bernstein, acquitted in the Rivonia Trial, leader of the Congress of Democrats and the SACP; I.B. Tabata, leader of the Non-European Unity Movement; Randolph Vigne, leading member of the ARM and Vice-President of the Liberal Party. All were living in exile.

NELSON MANDELA: WHITHER THE BLACK CONSCIOUSNESS MOVEMENT? AN ASSESSMENT

1   This essay was written in Robben Island prison in 1978 and smuggled out to Oliver Tambo, the Acting President of the ANC. From the end of 1976 large numbers of prisoners who were supporters of Black Consciousness began arriving on Robben Island. Mandela and his colleagues

engaged in intensive discussions with them. This essay is a product of those discussions.

2   The references are to John F. Kennedy, President of the USA from 1961 to 1963, and Martin Luther King, leader of the Civil Rights Movement in the USA, both of whom were assassinated.

3   In 1953 the Communist Party was re-established as an underground organisation as the South African Communist Party (SACP), to distinguish itself from the CPSA, which had been banned.

4   The Zambezi river is the boundary between Zimbabwe, South Africa's neighbour, and Zambia.

5   The *Star*, 26 January 1971.

6   Richard (Rick) Turner was assassinated in Durban on 8 January 1978. It was widely believed and is now accepted that he was murdered by the apartheid security forces.

7   Abraham Onkgopotse Ramothibi Tiro was assassinated in Botswana in February 1974 by the apartheid security forces.

8   Currie's Fountain soccer stadium in Durban.

9   Mthuli Shezi is remembered as the first Black Consciousness martyr. He died from injuries after being pushed in front of a train by a white railway worker at Germiston station in December 1972.

WALTER SISULU: WE SHALL OVERCOME!

1   The regime of Ian Smith, Prime Minister of Rhodesia, made a unilateral declaration of independence (UDI) against British rule in order to frustrate attempts to bring about a democratic order based on 'one person, one vote'.

AHMED KATHRADA: INDIAN SOUTH AFRICANS – A FUTURE BOUND WITH THE CAUSE OF THE AFRICAN MAJORITY

1   Swanepoel's colleagues boastfully nicknamed him 'Rooi Rus' (Red Russian).

2   The term *'baas'* is demanded as recognition of the superiority of white males.

3   In the 1970s *'verligte'* and *'verkrampte'* gained currency in the Afrikaans language to describe those

who stood for 'enlightened' views and those who were 'hard-liners' respectively. The terms must be understood strictly within the parameters of debate within Afrikanerdom and the National Party in particular.

4 The terms 'kaffir' and 'coolie' are derogatory and used to refer to Africans and Indians respectively.

5 The South African Indian Council was established by the Nat government in 1964 as an appointed body to represent the views of the Indian community. It should not be confused with the ANC-aligned South African Indian Congress (SAIC), established in 1927.

6 Father of F.W. de Klerk who, in his capacity as State President, announced on 2 February 1990 wide-ranging measures that formally opened the path to a negotiated resolution of the South African conflict.

7 Ideology based on the concept of a 'master race'.

8 The size of the Republic is over 470 000 square miles.

9 All surveys concentrated on Natal, especially Durban. This is because the majority of Indians live there. The 1970 Census showed the Indian population in South Africa to be 620 436. Of these 514 810 lived in Natal, mostly in Durban, 80 563 in the Transvaal and 21 617 in the Cape.

10 If we follow Gerdner's categories of 'industrialists', the embryo of this class also exists among the Coloured and African people.

GOVAN MBEKI: THE ANATOMY OF THE PROBLEMS OF THE NATIONAL LIBERATION STRUGGLE IN SOUTH AFRICA

1 C.W. de Kiewiet, *A History of South Africa*. Oxford: Oxford University Press, 1964, p. 91.

2 Indentured labour from India was first introduced in 1860.

3 The White mineworkers on the gold mines went on strike and an armed clash between them and the army occurred.

4 M. Wilson and L. Thompson, *The Oxford History of South Africa*. Oxford: Oxford University Press, 1969, vol. 2, p. 307.

5 *Research and Marketing*, vol. 11, no. 3, September 1971 – the 1970 Census.

6 Wilson and Thompson, *ibid.*, vol. 3.

7 *Ibid.*, vol. 2.

8 H.L.M. Joubert (ed.), *Ciskei: A Bantu Homeland*, University of Fort Hare Press, 1971, p. 191. J.H. Smith, Head of the Department of Economics and a member of SABRA – the National Party brains trust – contrary to press reports, denies that job reservation in fact has been marked to any extent worthwhile. See also *Financial Mail*, 7/68, p. 205.

9 Francis Wilson, *Labour in the South African Gold Mines, 1911–1969*. Oxford: Oxford University Press, 1972, p. 111.

10 *South African Journal of Economics*, vol. 43, no. 2, January 1975.

11 The Freedom Charter was adopted at the Congress of the People, which assembled at Kliptown, outside Johannesburg, in June 1955, to hammer out a common policy for the people of South Africa. Thereafter it became a basic policy document for the Congresses that formed the Congress Alliance.

12 As per the 1970 Census.

13 *Fiat Lux*, July 1974. This monthly journal was published by the government's Department of Indian Affairs to provide information about Indian affairs in South Africa.

14 *Fiat Lux*, February 1974.

15 *Fiat Lux*, February 1974.

16 *Fiat Lux*, July 1974.

17 Edgar H. Brookes and Colin de B. Webb, *The History of Natal*, Durban: University of Natal Press, 1965, p. 300.

18 *Farmer's Weekly*, 15 October 1975, p. 77.

19 Statement made by J.G. Strydom when he became premier after the death of D.F. Malan.

20 Gillian P. Hart, *African Entrepreneurship*, Institute of Social and Economic Research, Rhodes University, Grahamstown, 1972, p. 122.

21 *Ibid.*, p. 155.

22 Wilson and Thompson, vol. 2, p. 219.

23 Sir Harry Smith was Governor of the Cape Colony from 1847 to 1852.

24 Brookes and Webb, p. 155.

25 See Dr Vilakazi's doctoral thesis on the Amaxadi, the Zulu tribe living in the Valley of a Thousand Hills.

26 Tomlinson Commission Report, 1965, p. 145.

27 *Ibid.*, p. 118.

28 About two-and-a-quarter acres.

29 W. Backer (ed.), *The Economic Development of the Transkei*. Lovedale Press, 1970, p. 10.

30 Backer, *op cit.*, p. 61. Kramer is one of the contributors to this publication.

31 Backer, *op cit.*, p. 10.

32 Tomlinson Commission Report, p. 211, para. 23.

33 Wilson and Thompson, p. 411.

34 G. Carter, *South Africa's Transkei*, London: Heinemann, 1967, p. 110.

35 *Ibid.*, p. 110.

36 *Ibid.*, p. 110.

37 C.M. Tatz, *Shadow and Substance in South Africa*, Durban: University of Natal Press, 1962, p. 156.

38 *Ibid.*, p. 156.

39 Wilson and Thompson, *op cit.*, p. 191.

40 Carter, *op cit.*, p. 69.

41 Carter, *op cit.*, p. 157.

42 Quoted in Carter, *op cit.*

43 Tatz, *op cit.*, p. 179.

44 Tatz, *op cit.*, p. 179.

45 Wilson and Thompson, *op cit.*, p. 500.

46 *Hansard*, 23.1. 1962.

47 Brookes and Webb, p. 246. Campbell was addressing the Natal Legislative Assembly in 1909.

BILLY NAIR: THROUGH THE EYES OF THE WORKERS

1 The closed-shop policy meant that a worker first had to obtain a trade union membership card before trying to obtain employment in an industry. Through the simple expedient of refusing membership to black workers, they were kept out of an industry or trade.

2 Phthisis is a wasting disease of the lungs that afflicted most miners. The allowance can be seen as a form of 'danger' money or the forerunner of a form of medical aid.

3 The international socialist movement was divided in its approach to and assessment of the First World War. In South Africa those who saw it as a war generated by imperialist rivalry opposed it and formed the 'War-on-War' movement.

4 See pp. 182–4 for an account of the economics of separate development and the creation of 'border areas' (short for border industrial areas) where black labourers deported from the urban areas to the 'homelands' are employed in the border industries at slave rates of pay.

JOHN POKELA: TOWARDS FREEDOM

1 Books and other publications used as reference material by the contributors fell into two categories: some were obtained legitimately as part of the prisoners' study materials; others were obtained clandestinely. It has therefore not been possible to trace all the references a particular writer may have used. This has been the case especially with John Pokela's essay.

2 The Basotho chief Moshoeshoe, who founded the Kingdom of Lesotho. Also spelt as Moshweshwe.

3 Also see Nelson Mandela's discussion of the name 'Azania' on pp. 50–51 in 'Whither the Black Consciousness Movement? An Assessment'.

EDDIE DANIELS: LET US WORK TOGETHER FOR UNITY

1 The Japanese and Chinese are considered honorary whites in South Africa, that is, in terms of the law they are considered to be white. This is because Japan and Taiwan are important trading partners of the Republic of South Africa.

2 N.J. Rhoodie, *Apartheid and Racial Partnership in Southern Africa*, Pretoria/Cape Town: Academia, 1959.

3 The Swahili word for 'freedom'.

ABBREVIATIONS

AAC	All African Convention
AAM	Anti-Apartheid Movement of Great Britain
AFL–CIO	American Federation of Labour – Congress of Industrial Organisations
AIF	All India Federation
AMWU	African Mine Workers Union
ANC	African National Congress, South Africa's premier national liberation organisation, founded in 1912. Ruling party since the first democratic elections in 1994.
Anti-CAD	Anti-Coloured Affairs Department
APDUSA	African People's Democratic Union of South Africa, an offshoot/breakaway of the Non-European Unity Movement. Now defunct.
APO	African People's Organisation (see CPC)
ARM	African Resistance Movement, successor to the National Liberation Committee, established in 1961. Became defunct by 1964.
ASA	African Students Association
ASB	Afrikaanse Studente Bond (organisation of Afrikaner students)
ASUSA	African Students Union of South Africa
AZAPO	Azanian People's Organisation
AZASM	Azanian Student Movement
BAWU	Black Allied Workers Union
BCM	Black Consciousness Movement
BIC	Bantu Investment Corporation
BPA	Black Parents' Association
BPC	Black People's Convention
CIA	Central Intelligence Agency of the United States of America
CNETU	Council of Non-European Trade Unions, founded in 1940 and dissolved in 1955 when SACTU was founded
COD	Congress of Democrats (also known as SACOD), founded in 1953. A constituent member of the Congress Alliance headed by the ANC. Now defunct.
COP	Congress of the People, held in June 1955 at Kliptown near Johannesburg, where the Freedom Charter was adopted
CP	Communist Party of South Africa (CPSA), founded in 1921, banned in 1950. Reconstituted in 1953 as the South African Communist Party (SACP).
CPC	Coloured People's Congress (also known as the SACPC), successor to the South African Coloured People's Organisation and the African People's Organisation (APO). Member of the Congress Alliance. Now defunct.
CPSU	Communist Party of the Soviet Union

CRC	Coloured Representative Council. Part of the tricameral parliamentary structure created by apartheid.
DRC	Dutch Reformed Church
FLEC	Front for the Liberation of the Enclave of Cabinda
FNLA	Front for the National Liberation of Angola
FOFATUSA	Federation of Free African Trade Unions of South Africa, founded in 1960
Frelimo	Front for the Liberation of Mozambique
ICFTU	International Confederation of Free Trade Unions
ICU	Industrial and Commercial Workers Union, founded in 1917
IDC	Industrial Development Corporation
ILO	International Labour Organisation
ISL	International Socialist League
LP	Labour Party
LPSA	Liberal Party of South Africa
Mdali	Music, Drama and Literature Association
MK	Umkhonto weSizwe, the military wing of the ANC
MPLA	Popular Movement for the Liberation of Angola
Nat	Member/supporter of the National Party, an all-white, Afrikaner-based party espousing the policy of apartheid
NAYO	National Youth Organisation
NEC	National Executive Committee of the ANC
NEUM	Non-European Unity Movement
NFL	National Front for the Liberation of Vietnam
NIC	Natal Indian Congress, founded by Mahatma Gandhi in 1894
NIYC	Natal Indian Youth Congress
NLC	National Liberation Committee (see ARM)
NP	National Party – all-white, Afrikaner-based party that fashioned the policy of apartheid. The ruling party from 1948 to 1994.
NUSAS	National Union of South African Students
OAU	Organisation of African Unity, founded in 1963
PAC	Pan-Africanist Congress, founded in 1959
PAIGC	African Party for the Independence of Guinea-Bissau and the Cape Verde Islands
PRP	Progressive Reform Party
SACOD	South African Congress of Democrats, also known as the Congress of Democrats (COD). Member of the Congress Alliance led by the ANC.
SACP	South African Communist Party
SACPC	South African Coloured People's Congress (also known as the CPC). Member of the Congress Alliance led by the ANC.
SACPO	South African Coloured People's Organisation (also see SACPC)
SACTU	South African Congress of Trade Unions, founded in March 1955
SADC	South African Development Community
SAIC	South African Indian Congress, the umbrella body combining the Natal Indian Congress and the Transvaal Indian Congress. Member of the Congress Alliance led by the ANC.
SANROC	South African Non-Racial Olympic Committee

SASCON	South African Students Congress
SASM	South African Students Movement
SASO	South African Students Organisation
SB	Security Branch of the South African Police (also known as the Special Branch)
SHAWCO	Students Health and Welfare Centres Organisation
SSRC	Soweto Students' Representative Council
SWANU	South West Africa National Union
SWAPO	South West Africa People's Organisation, founded in August 1957
TEC	Transitional Executive Council of South Africa
TIC	Transvaal Indian Congress
TIYC	Transvaal Indian Youth Congress
TUC	British Trade Union Congress
TUCSA	Trade Union Council of South Africa. Founded in 1954 after the dissolution of the SAT&LC.
UCM	University Christian Movement
UDENAMO	National Democratic Union of Mozambique
UN	United Nations
UNITA	National Union for the Total Independence of Angola
UP	United Party, once the ruling party of South Africa, and the official opposition party when the NP came to power in 1948 in the all-white Parliament of SA. Now defunct.
WFTU	World Federation of Trade Unions
Wits	University of the Witwatersrand, Johannesburg
YCL	Young Communist League. Now defunct.
ZANU	Zimbabwe African National Union
ZAPU	Zimbabwe African People's Union